KU-135-221

Original copyright
© 1976 Editions Denoël, 19, rue de l'Université, 75007 Paris.
Le Vélo
Jean Durry

© Copyright English language edition 1977
Guinness Superlatives Limited

Published in Great Britain by
Guinness Superlatives Limited, 2 Cecil Court,
London Road, Enfield, Middlesex, England.

ISBN 0 900424 62 1

Guinness is a registered trade mark of Arthur Guinness Son & Co Ltd.

Typeset by Moorgate Typesetting Co Ltd, London SE5 7TR.

Printed in France by Offset Aubin, Poitiers. (P 7257).

# THE **GUINNESS** GUIDE TO
# BICYCLING

Written by J Durry
Edited by J B Wadley

GUINNESS SUPERLATIVES LTD.

# Contents

# Editor's Foreword

A French cycling book translated into English! First time it's been done. Just what we've been waiting for. Marvellous!

This book will be welcomed by British cycling enthusiasts who look on France as the promised land. Every month, and every week during the summer Tour de France, they pore over French glossy magazines carrying big action pictures of star riders pedalling through sunshine and rain, moving slowly up high mountain passes and tearing fearlessly down the other side; sprinting on roads as smooth as a billiard table, clattering over back-breaking cobbled lanes.

Photographs are cut out, framed even, hung in bedroom and workshop and studied for hours. Eddy Merckx is sitting higher this year! Out comes the tool box and the saddle is raised an eighth of an inch. Poulidor used shorter toe-clips in that time-trial stage he won; down to the bike shop to buy a pair. Felice Gimondi has a new kind of handlebar bend . . . Barry Hoban a different derailleur gear . . .

Anybody with the money can have a bicycle as good as a world champion's, and by studying those side-on photographs find a riding position that cannot be faulted. Yet a great number of these enthusiasts – and some are grandfathers! – are frustrated because they do not understand the accompanying text. The younger of them are not content with having the same kind of bike, jersey and 'position' as Eddy Merckx, they want to ride like him too. Perhaps in all those captions and columns of type is the answer. If only they could read French!

When literally millions of French people say 'my sport is cycling', 95% mean that they follow it by press, radio and television and turn out to watch any big road race that passes through their district. The odd 5% are active touring or racing cyclists. Cycling stories in the media are therefore of human rather than technical interest. When Raymond Poulidor finishes third in the Tour de France at 40 years of age there are, for every one intrigued by the length of his toe-clips, 20 eager to read about 'Pou-Pou's' peasant days in Limousin. Nor are the big action shots published in the specialised press always chosen by the picture editor for mechanical or 'positional' reasons. One Sunday evening I was in the busy Paris office of a sports weekly a few hours after the finish of the Bordeaux-Paris race which I had followed. Lay-out men and artists were sorting out pictures and scheming their presentation. There was one superb shot of the winner, Bernard Gauthier, cleverly sheltering behind his Derny (motorised bicycle) pacemaker, side-on, sharp as a needle and showing his Mercier in marvellous detail. One for the boys at home! Two days later I bought the magazine at a kiosk. They'd used 'my' picture all right, but . . . all that gleaming bicycle and Derny had been cut and thrown away, leaving just the human side of the story – a huge blow-up of Gauthier's agony-riven face as he suffered the final stretch of the 350 miles 'Derby of the Road'.

Cycling is covered in the lay French Press much as motor-racing is reported in the British nationals. Thrills, spills, changing fortunes during the long battle, anxious wives waiting at home or in the pits, and only mention of technical matters when something goes wrong with the tyres, gears or brakes. In the specialised motoring magazines, however, treatment is different; technical details of various *marques* are discussed at length. It is 50 years since anything comparable appeared in the cycling press. There are no secret weapons in cycling warfare. Those who sigh 'If only I could read French' would be disappointed if complete issues of *Miroir du Cyclisme* were translated for them because there would be little mechanical and perhaps nothing at all 'physical'. The French – and other continentals – have long accepted that if a rider is not endowed with 'a little something' he will never make a star however hard his training, however expensive his bicycle.

British cyclists are coming round to that point of view, but in America where serious road cycling is in its infancy (her track riders were superb from the earliest days) there is widespread faith in the laboratory and drawing board. Those USA enthusiasts could eventually be right, of course, but in the meantime the position is as I found it a few years ago when talking to Italo Zilioli at the start of a Tour de France stage and noting (for an American cycling magazine!) what equipment he was using. 'Tell those readers this,' said the excellent Italian rider, 'Merckx could win the Tour on my bicycle, but I couldn't win it on his.'

I make these points because although translated and slightly Anglicised to clarify certain points, this book is essentially a French enthusiast's look at the sport and pastime of cycling. The balance is different from that of original British publications in which the beginner is taken slowly and thoroughly through the rudiments of cycling before learning of the two main aspects, racing and touring. The British side of the sport and pastime is treated separately from the continental which is run on very different lines. Why should this be, when other sports are played under the same basic conditions and rules? A few paragraphs of cycling history provide the answer.

In the 1880s Britain was far ahead of France and the rest of the continent in road and track cycling. When the first Bordeaux-Paris was run in 1891 British riders took the first four places, with the fifth man, a Frenchman, nearly six hours behind. G P Mills and his friends would probably also have cleaned up the first Paris-Brest-Paris (750 miles) a few months later had not the organisers decided to confine entries to Frenchmen! But whereas continental countries were welcoming and encouraging cycle racing on the open road and providing police and military forces to control crowds in the busy towns *en route*, British authority was firmly against such sport. Although organised by clubs on quiet country roads and keeping well away from big centres of population, races were constantly harassed by the zealous local constabulary acting under orders from county chiefs. Horse-mounted police literally charged among cycle racers and threw sticks in their wheels. Those not taken to hospital were charged at the local police station with 'dangerous conduct'. At length they were forced off the road in the mid-1890s and classic races – such as the Bath Road 100-miles and North Road 24-hours – transferred to closed tracks at Herne Hill and Wood Green. A few years later the time-trial was introduced and road sport revived on entirely different lines. These events were held quietly very early in the morning 'miles from anywhere'; competitors started at one-minute intervals and were dressed 'inconspicuously from head to foot' in black. The police did not interfere and time-trialing became the only form of British road sport for more than 40 years until, in 1942, 'mass start' racing was reintroduced on open roads. It has progressed remarkably well, but compared with the continent, is a participant rather than a spectator sport.

While British amateur riders were pedalling their secret trials – no prior publicity was allowed – a continental professional road class had grown up. Cycle manufacturers formed racing teams to advertise their machines, newspapers found that promoting big races was a marvellous boost to circulation. It was while searching for something bigger and better than Bordeaux-Paris and Paris-Brest-Paris

that Henri Desgrange in 1903 stumbled across the idea of a Tour de France that was to become one of the greatest sporting shows on earth. Today, just as an Englishman may hate cricket but cannot completely get away from ball-by-ball commentaries during test matches, everybody living in France is treated to a surfeit of Tour de France and dozens of other shorter races.

It is for readers with such a background that John Durry has written his book. I have edited the translation but not 'editionised' it; that is to say no substantial cuts of very French material have been made and something British substituted. That treatment would have caused a mid-Channel collision of interests and the total wreck of the project.

Details and illustrations of *cyclotourisme* in these pages are of particular interest. Because of the influence of road racing, French touring has developed on competitive lines, whereas the British participant is not in the least concerned with miles per hour, or miles per day. There are such 'potterers' in France, too, but they are far outnumbered by the Randonneurs and Cyclosportifs who might be likened to drivers in car club rallies who, without being Grand Prix 'aces', are much more sporty in their approach than the week-end motorist. Until quite recently this hard-riding type of touring was only practised in Britain at the beginning of the season with a series of '100 in 8' rides, contestants gaining certificates for covering 100 miles in under eight hours, using touring bicycles and non-racing dress. Now, following the participation of several British riders in the famous Paris-Brest-Paris trial, there is a growing interest in faster 'touring'.

Although France is the promised land in so many ways, British cyclists are far from pedalling in the wilderness. For generations Paris was not only the capital of road racing, but of the track game as well. Now following the demolition in 1959 of the Vélodrome d'Hiver and the Parc des Princes outdoor stadium in 1967, France has become something of a track backwater, despite the brilliance of Daniel Morelon. It is nearly 20 years since Paris staged a six-day race, while during that time in London we have had ten brilliant, thrilling spectaculars contested by the world's greatest indoor-trackmen. Moreover a kind of six-day supporters' club has grown up, with enthusiasts going by charter flight to other 'sixes' in Belgium, Holland, Germany and Switzerland.

Many of these excursionists have splendid private collections of action photographs, the most striking being those of high-speed sessions behind Derny pacing machines which are the highlights of most modern six-day races. Because of the disappearance of regular top-class track meetings in Paris I was not really surprised to find that not one

Derny-paced track racing photograph appears in these pages. (Also, professional racing being held in such high regard in France, male amateur road racing is scantily illustrated, but there are several photographs of the girls.)

A different way of cycling has produced a different kind of book, and here I must insert a familiar phrase: the editor does not necessarily agree with the author on certain points. British vintage cycle experts will also query historical references. This does not mean that we are right and John Durry is wrong; it could well be the other way round. As a government sports historian he has access to documents that have only recently come to light.

For my part I thought the author wrong in including the paragraph on page 70 about the 'legendary cylinder of hardwood that has to be inserted in the steering column'. Now, being something of a vintage model myself I remembered this had been a continental practice up to the Second World War, but had not heard of it since. In 1939 Richard Kemps came over to attack road records for a British firm. I met the Belgian professional at Victoria station and took him to the training camp at Kingston-on-Thames where two new bicycles were ready for him. Richard immediately got a spanner, took out the front forks and uttered a Flemish expression of disgust. He marched me off to a big store where he chose, and I paid for, a broom stick. Back at the garage he sawed off a four-inch length and tapped it down to the bottom of the fork column. I later learned that no Belgian would dream of riding without that wood insert, so often did front forks snap on cobbled roads.

So, on a Hercules bicycle and twopennyworth of Woolworth's broom stick, Richard Kemps in 1939 broke the London-Bath-London and Liverpool-London records. On reading John Durry's paragraph I asked a dozen experienced British mechanics and frame builders about the practice. Nine had never heard of it; the other three had but thought it completely unnecessary on modern bicycles. I raised the matter with the author when I met him in Paris. He was surprised that I was surprised and produced several books – including one by Jacques Anquetil – giving the same advice. Still dubious I went round to the Lejeune factory to see my friend Jacques Houssot who for 12 years was chief mechanic in the Tour de France. Did *he* shove bits of wood in front forks? Of course he did. Jacques opened a big chest containing thousands of the things and gave me a handful to bring home as evidence. The sequel to this story of the doubting editor is that I decided to examine my own Lejeune bicycle on which I have ridden about 25 000 miles during the last four years. Sure enough, after removing the front wheel, mudguard and brake bolt and poking a finger up the space, I found a piece of the hardwood whose utility and existence I had questioned.

No doubt those enthusiasts who do everything like the continentals will now add a few ounces to their machines, but I must remind them that they don't make broom sticks like they did in 1939, and that a really hard wood should be used.

Having gone into Europe before the establishment of the Common Market, British cyclists are familar with the mixed weights and measures situation brought about by metrication. A dealer sells a bicycle with a 24 in frame, 170 mm cranks, 250 g tyres, and says it weighs 22 lb. Newspapers report that Steve Heffernan is national 4000 m pursuit champion, that Martyn Roach wins the Bath Road 100 mile time-trial, that Eddy Merckx covers 49.431 km in one hour on the track, and that Phil Griffiths' winning average speed in the British Best All-Rounder competition is 25.969 mph. It is impossible to be consistent in this area, and difficult to decide when conversion to or from the metric system is necessary. To give equivalent figures every time a speed, length or weight is mentioned in this book would be to irritate rather than help the reader who, I believe, would prefer to do an occasional calculation with the aid of the conversion tables on page 217, where a continental-style gear table is also given.

In general the English equivalent of French words or phrases is used, but some remain untranslatable. A *rouleur* for instance, is a kind of pedalling Brendan Foster, capable of leading powerfully for miles at a stretch and burning off lesser mortals, but still unable to 'drop' men of real class who are in top form and determined to hang on. Nobody calls a bicycle 'the little queen' in Britain, so the original *la Petite Reine* is retained. Finally I must admit that after 40 years of refusing to use the word I have succumbed and agreed to accept 'echelon' to describe the device used by groups of road riders to combat awkward cross-winds. I must warn students of French cycling literature that they will never find the word used in that context. The staggered formation is known as *un éventail* which means a fan, the kind that keeps you cool, not the fan who is mad about cycling and who will get much enjoyment and instruction from this book.

J B WADLEY

# Preface

His name was Dodds. The few lists of champions that go back far enough mention no first names at all, only the initials F.L. When he prepared for action on the racing track at the Cambridge University Ground on 25 March 1876, he was perched on the saddle of a bicycle with solid tyres and the diameter of his front wheel must have been about 140 cm (55 in). Coupled with Dodd's name are the figures 25·508 km or 15·84 miles.

Apparently, this was not a lone attempt to establish a record as was the practice in later years, but the distance calculated to have been covered in the first hour of a race – the final result of which is unknown.

So, even if the feat is well and truly forgotten today, it was a British rider who, exactly a century ago, had the distinction of writing the first page in the history of the most famous of all cycling records, The Hour, or at least of being the first racer to be credited with a distance at the end of 3600 seconds' pedalling. It is perhaps not surprising that the 'record' idea came to us from England where, as Walter Umminger's attractive book* emphasises, stop-watches were being used as early as 1731 to verify performances down to the split second, starting of course with horse-racing.

A hundred years later, Dodds' descendant is Edward Merckx, world-famous as 'Eddy'. The Belgian set the seal on his great career by becoming 'Man of the Hour' on 29 October 1972 when he covered 49·431 km (30·75 miles) at the Velodromo Olimpico in Mexico City in the fateful 60 minutes. A few riders have since attacked Merckx's record but without success. For the time being at any rate, it represents the ceiling of human capacity.

So that means a difference of 23·923 km – just under 15 miles – in a century. It is not that large a gap, is it?

Now here we are about to set off on a new journey on two wheels, thanks to that magic vehicle that someone once called la Petite Reine. We are going to try to encompass the whole universe of cycling – from competition to holidays on two wheels; to piece together the essential facts about the machines themselves and the basic accessories that go with them; to nose out the main protagonists – known and unknown, enthusiastic beginners or veteran cyclists whose enthusiasm grows from year to year

Today, when we have just embarked on the last quarter of the 20th century, the bicycle, or should we say the 'bike', has taken on a new lease of life and is once again a feature of modern living. At one stage it seemed as if it was being gradually but inexorably overtaken by the motorised rabble, engulfed in a tide of cars. But now, we read, 'there are bikes all over the place' and 'enlightened bicycle-lovers' are being swamped in an avalanche of books about their sport – many of them excellent and delightful volumes. A sure sign that there has been a revival of interest among the general public.

Not only does this humble two-wheeled contraption, in its brilliant simplicity, offer endless opportunities for getting from A to B and for enjoyment – not to mention happiness, but I believe that it is also, and always will be, a subject that stimulates new ideas and new thoughts about life in general. There's so much more to say about it.

This book is not going to enter into any great detail about the subject – that is not the point of the series. After all, it is quite clear that any one of the individual chapters could be the basis for a detailed study in itself. On the other hand, although intended for the converted, for those who have already been bitten by the cycling 'bug' – this book is not intended to be restricted to the experts. I want to introduce the art of cycling to those who are still feeling a bit doubtful, who feel tempted to try it, but . . . I also want to make those who systematically turn up their noses at any form of physical exercise, who (though they do not realise it) are living as it were in slow motion, whose lives are incomplete – I want them to understand how you can get obsessed by bicycles.

Nowadays publishers have one decisive argument up their sleeve – illustrations. Illustrations can support any text – broaden its scope, throw more light on it – that does not appeal directly to the reader's imagination, to his ability to conjure up images for himself. The picture researchers who worked on this book did so with enthusiasm, patience and a desire for accuracy, but at the same time they were looking for beauty and poetry. I should like to think that both the cycling expert and the uninitiated will be stirred by them.

*Walter Umminger: *Des hommes et des records*. La Table Ronde, 1964.

# I

# FREEDOM
# ON TWO
# WHEELS

# LE VÉLOCIPÈDE ILLUSTRÉ

*Front page heading of No. 1 issue, dated 1 April 1869, of* Le Vélocipède Illustré, *the world's first successful cycling publication. Although symbolising a progressive journal, the lady pedaller of the Michaux-type velocipede seems more interested in the road already travelled than in that which lies ahead!*

*6 April 1890. After 18 years* Vélocipède Illustré *is published again. The original lady on her Michaux has moved aside to give pride of place to Miss Modern on a Safety Bicycle with all the latest equipment, including lightweight mudguards.*

# A hundred years ago . . .

An editorial in the first issue of the French journal *Vélocipède Illustré*, published on 1 April 1869, voices all the hopes that were being placed in the 'horse on wheels', whose design was becoming increasingly clear in the second half of the 19th century. The editorial was written by a man known as 'le Grand Jacques' – his real name was Richard Lesclide – and the first 40 lines, which sum up the reason for the magazine's existence, are reproduced here in their entirety by kind permission of the Library of the Touring Club de France, which has a large number of magazines and books about cycling:

> The Velocipede is rapidly entering our lives – and that is the only justification we need for starting this new magazine.
> And yet never has the famous phrase: 'People began to feel a need for a special organ devoted to a fashionable conveyance' been so appropriate.
> Indeed the Velocipede is gaining ground at amazing speed, spreading from France to the rest of Europe, from Europe to Asia and Africa. Not to mention America, which has outstripped us and now has the advantage of us in the race for further improvements.
> The Velocipede is a more serious plaything than people realise. As well as the great fun it offers, it is indisputably a functional article.
> It is one of the signs of the times; it is a personal affirmation of human strength, translated into speed by means of ingenious agents.
> The Velocipede is a step forward along the road traversed by the genius of man. It replaces collective, brutish, unintelligent speed with individual speed, rational speed, avoiding obstacles, adapting itself to the circumstances – and obeying man's will.
> This horse in wood and steel fills a gap in modern living; it does not merely answer a need, it fulfils people's aspirations.
> The Velocipede is not a mere flash in the pan – here today and gone tomorrow. As you can see from the fact that as it obtains a footing in the fashionable world, the government and the major public services are using it for special duties.
> It has now won complete acceptance in France, and we are founding a magazine under its patronage in order to bring together, in the same fellowship, its adherents and believers.

*Le Vélocipède Illustré* was not, in fact, the very first magazine of its kind. A newsheet called simply *Le Vélocipède* had appeared in Grenoble on 1 March 1869, but it folded after only a few issues, whereas Richard Lesclide was such a good writer and so full of dynamism that his publication kept going for three fairly successful years. In November 1869 the magazine had taken part in the cycle show at the Pré-Catalan in Paris and helped with the organisation of the very first 'city-to-city' race, Paris—Rouen.

In those days when the sport was still in its infancy it seems that it was practised in only a few countries in Europe, so its geographical distribution was limited. Yet from the moment in March 1861 when Pierre Michaux invented the pedal (thanks to a remark made by one of his sons, Ernest), this form of recreation had become remarkably popular. We have only to look at the surprisingly dense network of correspondents listed in *Le Vélocipède Illustré* in May 1872. It ran to an amazing total of 34 countries and free cities, several of which have changed their name or their frontiers since those days. Lesclide was clearly bluffing to a certain extent – he wanted to impress his readers by making the magazine seem ultra-serious. It is clear that in some of the places he mentioned there must have been only a handful of eccentrics capable of riding their bicycles. But all the same the list does help us to rough out the first map of the cycling world in those far-off days. It runs as follows: Austria, Bohemia, Hungary, Illyria, Silesia, Belgium, Denmark, Spain, Italy, Baden, Bavaria, Germany, England, Scotland, Ireland, Greece, The Netherlands, Portugal, Russia, Poland, Sweden, Norway, Switzerland, Bremen and Hamburg, Turkey, Egypt, the U.S.A., Havana, Mexico, Bolivia, Brazil, Chile, Peru, Uruguay.

However, the Franco-Prussian War very nearly killed the French cycling industry, which was enjoying a boom when the conflict broke out in 1870. The few remaining practitioners of the sport were soon being greeted with catcalls and sarcastic remarks. On 24 October 1872 Richard Lesclide was forced to do a moonlight flit. He had managed to add a concluding note to his 162nd issue. It was couched in terms of great sadness:

> For our part, we have great faith in the future [of cycling]. It is so deeply rooted both in our country and abroad that we need have no fear that it will wither away. But it may go through a bad patch and have to lie dormant for a while before we see a revival of its early triumphs. We'll be there cheering it on when the time comes for it to be resurrected.

It is unusual for this type of editorial – the editor signing off to the readers of a dying paper in a farewell disguised as a mere 'au revoir' – to anticipate a

The Dandy Charger

*London Published 15 Feb.y 1819 by John Hudson, 85 Cheapside*

*An engraving dated February 1819, only two months after Dennis Johnson had taken out his patent, shows how quickly the* draisienne *had become fashionable.*

resurrection. But Lesclide, whose farewell speech really was a premonition, went on to enjoy the boom in the 1890s. On 6 April 1890 *Le Vélocipède Illustré* was revived, selling for the same price as in 1869 – ten centimes. Among many other new colleagues Lesclide was to describe the first golden age of *la Petite Reine*.

Yes, there is no doubt that a century ago cycling – or rather the art of getting about under one's own steam on a machine with two wheels joined by a wooden or steel bar – already had a past to look back on. This seems a good moment to run briefly through the main events in that past.

## Sivrac or not Sivrac?

First, let us be cynical: the main lines of this 'prehistoric' era, with its celeripedes, draisiennes, boneshakers and velocipedes, have been told so often that readers even slightly familiar with the literature on the subject sometimes have the feeling that they are rereading the same thing all over again, in a slightly different form. Some versions are more lively than others: others show a greater understanding of the various episodes, but the basic plot is always the same. The reason is of course that all the various authors relied on the same source, which went under the name of Baudry de Saunier. His *Histoire générale de la vélocipédie* ('General History of Cycling') published in 1891, had a preface written in July of that year by the poet Jean Richepin and offered a very rich assortment of information. The number of researchers who have been brave enough to try to bring new facts to light is small indeed. Two who deserve mention here are Herbert Osbaldeston Duncan, whose huge book *The World on Wheels* was published in about 1926, and Louis Bonneville. Bonneville's *Le Vélo, fils de France* ('The Bike, a son of France'), published in Nice in 1938, charts the period 1868 to 1900 with a degree of accuracy that has never been equalled. The dates and facts these two authors gave were basically the same as those already catalogued elsewhere, but they threw new light on specific aspects of the 'romance' of cycling and entered into greater detail about them. Raymond Huttier, a fine French journalist, offered a more modern version in 1951.

On the other hand, if you really think about it, you realise that a large number of events that have been considered to be gospel and have been stated again and again with the absolute conviction that is the hallmark of a 'creed', ought really to be taken with a pinch of salt. For instance we are always being told that the '*célérifère*', or 'celeripede', as it was known in English, was invented in 1790 by a man called de Sivrac. Now the celeripede was a rudimentary wooden bar supported on two wheels and the rider sat astride and then strode forwards, thrusting his feet alternately against the ground. The smart young men of the Directoire period in France made this plaything relatively successful. This version of the story may be accurate. I would even go so far as to say that it probably is accurate. But who was Monsieur de Sivrac? When did he first ride his *célérifère* in public? What became of him? Was he really an 'inventor'? What documentary evidence can his supporters produce to show that he really was the first in the field? No one has ever asked these questions in a coherent way, let alone answered them.

Let us have a look at an amazingly abstruse pamphlet called *Le Livre d'Or du Cyclisme Girondin* ('The Golden Book of Cycling in the Gironde'). It was published in Bordeaux in 1934 under the auspices of the Departmental Committee for the Gironde, and edited by the worthy Gabriel Belliard, who was for many years the official archivist of the International Cycling Union and the 'sporting delegate' of the French Union Vélocipédique. In this pamphlet we read: 'The balloonist Blanchard invented the *vélocifère*, a machine that was described by the *Journal de Paris* on 27 July 1779'. Now doesn't that open up a new line of research?

In fact when a dogged researcher – his name was Serge Laget – held in his hands issue 208 of the daily *Journal de Paris*, which bears the date 27 July 1779, he found nothing but a detailed description of an experiment in 'mechanics', which involved demonstrating a machine that seems to be only very distantly related to a *vélocifère*. And, incidentally, the term itself is not mentioned. Yet this type of carriage travelled 'without the aid of horses'. Instead of shafts we hear of 'an eagle with outstretched wings'. And in particular of 'a man who transmits to the machine a motion of varying speed, by thrusting alternately with his feet . . . He is either seated or remains standing, with his legs partly hidden in a sort of trunk or chest in which the springs seem to be fixed'. So the mystery remains unsolved.

Let us give Monsieur de Sivrac the benefit of the doubt – after all, as we have seen, any doubt is refuted by this deeply rooted tradition – and agree that in 1790 he really did launch the *célérifère* or celeripede, which is as it were the dinosaur of moving machines propelled by human strength alone.

I was thinking along these lines when I read a remarkable article, written by Jacques Seray, in the

April 1976 issue of the monthly *Cyclisme Magazine*. Drawing from a thesis for a University doctorate obtained in Paris in 1950 by Mr Walter Jones of Toronto, the text showed that in fact M de Sievrac (and not Sivrac) born in Toulouse and living in Paris had, in June 1817, taken out an importation patent for a 'public carriage, known as a *célérifère*', imported from England.

This important contribution by Jacques Seray therefore brings forward the usually accepted starting date by more than a quarter of a century. According to him, Baron von Drais invented it all – the machine itself and the manoeuvrable front wheel. The man who has always been considered No 2 in the evolution of the bicycle, becomes No 1!

## From the draisienne to the velocipede

Until this revelation, Baron Karl Friedrich Drais von Sauerbronn (1785–1851) had only been credited with one discovery – an important one nevertheless – a method of steering the front wheel. This meant that there was no longer any need to strike the lion's head or horse's head on your *vélocifère* – only the name had changed slightly over a 25-year period – when you wanted to turn right or left. But it was still what was called in German a *Laufmaschine* – a machine you ran with. In fact rather than running you strode along and constantly had to renew contact with the ground to propel the machine.

In 1818 the baron patented his invention in France, and at the end of the same year he filed a patent application in Britain, where a coachmaker called Denis Johnson acted for him. The British promptly put their industrial genius to work on it. The 'hobby horse' became a fashionable sight and soon several hundred models were being made of it, 'entirely in iron'. Some were even spotted in New York, but they were soon out of fashion.

A few inventors stuck to their guns. In about 1839 a Scots blacksmith called Kirkpatrick Macmillan perfected a system involving a rear driving wheel and treadle cranks, which meant that the rider did not need to thrust his feet against the ground. But there was no immediate follow-up to his discovery.

Inventing something is no use if luck is not on your side. At about the same date – 1845 in Britain and 1846 in France – R W Thomson took out a patent in a completely different field – for a 'hollow rubber tube inflated with air' which was designed to improve vehicle wheels, as well as wheels on 'other moving bodies'. However, his invention completely failed to catch on and Dunlop knew nothing of this precedent when he 're-invented' the pneumatic tyre 43 years later.

The ingenious idea that saw the light in March 1861 had quite a different lineage. A coachmaker and wheelwright called Pierre Michaux had just released the giant Antaeus from a thousand years of servitude by taking the front wheel of a *vélocifère* that had been brought to him to be repaired and fixing first a 'leg-rest' to it, 'then, like the crank-handle of a grindstone, a crankshaft and pedals'. There was no point now in the 'rider' maintaining direct contact with the ground. Once the machine was in motion he could keep it moving for an unlimited period. This time the invention was a success. Pierre Lallement, who had worked for Michaux, went to America and there in 1866 took out the first known patent for a *vélocipède à pédale*.

By 1869 there were no fewer than 60 'velocipede-builders' in Paris and a good 15 or so in the provinces. The largest firm was called the 'Compagnie Parisienne' and was run by two brothers called René and Aimé Olivier. They claimed that their factory in the rue Bugeaud 'delivers 200 velocipedes a day!'. To borrow the words of the British author H O Duncan, in his *World on Wheels*, 'The tremendous progress made in France had no doubt put that country several years ahead of all the others'.

## From Saint-Cloud to Coventry

Duncan's comment was entirely justified – before, that is, the Franco-Prussian War broke out in 1870.

On 31 May 1868 a field of seven starters had lined up in the Parc de Saint-Cloud for the start of what was, so far as we know today, the first official cycling race in history. Over the next few weeks a whole calendar of sporting events was drawn up. Now in February 1869 there were still only a very small number of velocipedes in Britain, and they had all come from Paris. When John Mayall Junior managed to cover the 83 km (51·5 miles) between London and Brighton 'in about 12 hours' the press hailed it as 'an extraordinary event'. Yet in France a large number of cycling competitions were already taking place, a range of specialised journals and newspapers had sprung up, and technological research at a high level was being carried out.

When, on 7 November 1869, James Moore rode out of the night at 6.10 p.m. and crossed the finishing post that the local cycling club had set up at the gates of Rouen he carried off the prize for the Paris-Rouen race. What is more, his brilliant sporting achievement is shown by the fact that he had covered the sizeable distance of 123 km (76 miles) at an average speed of 11·808 km/h (7·50 mph), including stops. And all this in spite of the fine rain which had been falling steadily over the last few days and which did not let up during the race itself, consequently soaking the roads and making the appalling road conditions of the period even worse than usual. Another 32 contestants, including one woman ('Miss America', who was placed 29th), managed to complete the course in the 24 hour period allowed by the rules.

The Paris-Rouen race had been organised by the Olivier brothers and their Compagnie

Parisienne, with the backing of the *Vélocipède Illustré*, which devoted a large number of column inches to the cycling show that was held at the Pré-Catalan on 1–5 November before the actual race. Although many authors have claimed that it was the very first show of its kind in France, in fact it had been preceded a few months earlier by exhibitions held in Carcassonne on 18–20 July and Carpentras on 6–8 August.

Nowadays we can see that, as the long history of the sport has shown, competition cycling represented the perfect testing-bench for all types of equipment, as well as stimulating a never-ending series of technical improvements. The reason is, of course, that the participants were always looking for an exceptional performance from their machines and struggling with the tricky problem of devising the sort of safety factors that would allow them to take 'controlled' risks at higher and higher speeds.

There is no doubt that men like James Moore and his rivals played the same part as is played in 1976 by the Formula I test drivers, the motorcycling aces of the 'Continental Circus' or the downhill skiers hurtling along at breakneck speed. Some of their 'improvements' – for instance a drop in the weight of the vehicle from 30 to 28 kg (66 to 61·5 lb) – may make us smile today, but it must be clearly understood that the inventors of a hundred years and more ago had dreamed up from scratch – using whatever materials they had to hand – an amazing number of the accessories that are standard equipment on modern bicycles. No one will ever appreciate enough the improvements that were made in those early days. The 'pedal *draisienne*' of 1861 – if I may venture to call it that – with wheels of almost equal size and about 80 cm (31·5 in) in diameter was no more than a memory.

Or was it?

The machine ridden by the winner of the Paris-Rouen race was a real competition prototype. Like all the models of the period, it had a 'body and forks in wrought steel'. But its wheels were tyred in rubber, according to a system patented in November 1868 by Clement Ader, who was later to be one of the pioneers of aviation. The excellence of his system had been demonstrated in Lille on 7 June 1869, when a 'regional' cyclist called Dorrety, who came from Pont-Audemer, defeated some acknowledged champions who had made the journey specially from Paris. What is more, the hubs of the wheels had been equipped with steel ball-bearings. These were still fairly rudimentary and about 9 mm ($\frac{3}{8}$ in) in diameter – but they were a distinct improvement on simple friction. The ball-bearings were polished by the inmates of Sainte-Pélagie prison – the prison-governor built Moore's cycles. And finally, whereas the tyre and spokes of the normal wheel of the period were made of wood, some authorities state that Moore's had metal wheels

and that his front wheel, which was the driving wheel, had a diameter of 1·2 m (47 in), while the diameter of the 'very low' rear wheel was less than 0·4 m (18 in). His model therefore heralded the 'ordinary' or 'penny-farthing' of the future. It weighed about 25 kg (55 lb).

One of the models on show at the Pré-Catalan had four-speed gears controlled by a small lever. Another had mudguards. Yet another had a freewheel. Meanwhile the Parisian engineer Meyer was now in a position to construct a machine designed by a watchmaker called Guilmet. There is no doubt at all that their model was the ancestor of the modern bicycle, with its chain-driven all-metal frame. However, it was so far ahead of its time that it did not lead to any further developments for the time being.

In 1869, however, the Coventry Sewing Machine Company turned itself into the Coventry Machinists Company Ltd – the new trade name allowing them to make a cautious start on producing velocipedes. The next year the Franco-Prussian War broke out, paralysing the whole of French trade. The Coventry company seized the opportunity with both hands and their new sideline was promptly expanded. From now on the British led the field. Capital flowed into the business, which meant that when an inventive genius called Jules Truffault managed to reduce the weight of racing machines to 15 kg (33 lb) and then to 10 kg (22 lb), by using a consignment of sabre sheaths he had managed to come by cheaply to make hollow forks and wheel rims, the British bought the rights in his invention, paying him fairly low royalties. A convincing demonstration of Truffault's invention had been offered in 1876, over the 220 km (137 miles) distance Angers-Tours-Angers. The winner, by 50 minutes over his nearest rival, Thuillet, was Tissier, although his 'only method of overcoming friction was with primitive bronze bearings'.

By buying Truffault's patent the British gained the added advantage of being a step ahead of their rivals both in the organisation of cycling races and in the technical field.

## The age of the wondrous cinder track

Britain had become the promised land, the El Dorado of racing cyclists – thanks to her bold gesture in setting up permanent cycle-racing tracks. On 6 April 1874, for instance, a mile-long race, billed as the 'World Championship', was run in Wolverhampton, on a track that was 'the most wondrous track of the age, all in cinders'. The champion would win a cash prize, plus a valuable silver cup, although he would have to win it twice before he was entitled to keep it. There was a field of 75 starters and the betting was going well. James Moore beat the famous John Keen into second place by 1·5 m (5 ft) and the third prize went to Shelton, who was 30 m (33 yd) behind the winner. Moore's time was 3 min 2 s, breaking by 7 seconds the record set up in 1873.

This is a good opportunity to praise Moore, who was 25 by now and a British veterinary surgeon living in the Paris area. He was the first great name in world cycling history, having been champion in Saint-Cloud on 31 May 1868 and winning the Paris-Rouen race in 1869. He did not retire from the sport until 1878, shortly after suffering one of his very rare defeats, at the hands of Charles Terront, at Joinville-le-Pont.

The first cycling race between Oxford and Cambridge universities was advertised to take place on 16 June 1874, and then on 12 September the Paris champion, Camille Thuillet, who had gone to Sheffield with what he called a 'vélo' (so the modern colloquial term for a French bike was already being used at that date), was roundly beaten by his British rivals. Their machines were up to 1·5 m (5 ft) in height while his was only 1·25 m (4 ft 1 in).

So the penny-farthing was flourishing. Its development had been perfectly logical, because for the moment each turn of the pedal corresponded to one turn of the driving wheel – the front wheel – and therefore the higher the wheel the faster you could go – once you had got started, that is. Logic was also behind the urge, always dear to a sportsman's heart, to battle against time as well as against rival cyclists. This was what led to the popularity of the Hour Record after Dodds had shown the way.

So now we are back in 1876 – the year when H J Lawson patented the term 'Safety bicycle', which brought the rider back nearer the ground. Then in 1877 the famous James Starley applied the differential principle to the tricycle, which was subsequently to be the height of fashion in its turn. The city of Coventry set up a monument to Starley after his death.

So one way and another a hundred years ago British cycling was leading the field from a whole bunch of runners, who did not restrict their efforts to both sides of the Channel. In 1869 an American 'velocipedist' called Jenkins repeated tight-rope walker Blondin's feat by crossing the Niagara Falls, and the next year the Italians organised their own cycling race, from Florence to Pistoia.

The powers of organisation and hard work displayed by the British were always being held up as an example to others. In 1878 at the Atheneum in London the Stanley Bicycle Club organised a cycle show, which became known as 'The Stanley'. A model of its kind, this exhibition went from strength to strength until 1890, presenting over 1400 machines to the public.

The French press was always holding up the British as an example. French journalists envied their neighbours, admired them – and complained

*Two great rivals of 'Penny Farthing' days. H P Whiting on the right had comparatively short legs and could only straddle a 54 in wheel, whereas his tall rival the Hon. Ion Keith Falconer of Cambridge University rode a 60 in model. Even so the little man beat the giant in a 25 miles race at Lillie Bridge track, London in 1875. Whiting won by 100 metres in 1 hr 41 min 16·5 s – time-keeping at its best!*

about them. They claimed that virtually all the great inventions were made by Frenchmen. The period of confusion that had followed France's defeat by the Prussians in 1871 was receding into the past by now. Admittedly, the flamboyance of the prewar years was over, but there were a few signs of things to come.

In 1876 a boy of 19, who had started racing only the previous August at the Saint-Ouen festival and had made a pathetic showing, won the Paris-Pontoise race. Although he was more or less a novice, he easily beat Camille Thuillet into second place, covering the 62 km (38·5 miles) in 2 hr 53 min. He now started training for the tough contests that were to follow. He was to race on the other side of the Channel, even on the other side of the Atlantic, for 15 splendid years, taking on the greatest racing cyclists of his day over a wide variety of distances. On the day he carried off his first victory he was wearing 'a spotted shirt, coloured breeches, black and white stockings and a magnificent red scarf flung over the top'. His name was Charles Terront. In September 1891 he found everlasting fame in the greatest race there had ever been and which caused tremendous excitement – Paris to Brest and back.

An era that could not easily be foreseen was about to open – the age of the all-conquering *Petite Reine!*

Extraordinary machines were seen on the road around 1880, but they all played a part in the evolution of the bicycle. This is a 'parallelogram' tricycle with three different wheel sizes made by the Renard brothers of Paris.

Safety Bicycle by the Birmingham Small Arms Co., soon to become famous as BSA. This 1884 model had a 32 in rear wheel, and through the chain and sprockets could be 'geared up' to the equivalent of a 64 in diameter Penny Farthing front wheel.

A sporty-looking model 'Le Sphinx' made by Jules Truffaut, a Frenchman who later worked in collaboration with British manufacturers.

Véritable machine de sûreté

Another machine from a famous British manufacturer, Hillman, Herbert & Cooper of Coventry, and called the 'Premier Safety'. 'Ball bearings everywhere except the pedals', said the specification, 'it runs sweetly and is beautifully finished.' But the tyres were still solid.

Nothing to touch the Rover! The machine that was the true ancestor of the modern bicycle outclasses (in an advertisement!) a variety of other machines including a Penny Farthing, a Kangaroo, and an American Star with a small front wheel and large rear 'driver'.

Clément & Co called this a Safety Bicycle although it maintained the big front and small back wheel principle, with front wheel geared-up drive. Clément of Paris was moderately successful as a cycle maker, but his business really flourished when he later imported the new Dunlop pneumatic tyres.

# Freedom

Skimming over the ground, fleeing far from spiteful glances, I remember as if it were yesterday the timid beginners going off to lonely lanes and deserted roads to have the four or five lessons they needed before they could keep their balance. They were like the early Christians celebrating the mysteries of their religion in the catacombs in Rome. If an uninitiated pedestrian happened to pass by – perhaps a man on his way to work or one of the local women searching the country-side for herbs – they'd stop, hesitate, feeling all shy, afraid they might suffer the humiliation of falling off.

The journalist Pierre Giffard paints this picture in an illustrated study by Robida called *La fin du cheval* ('The End of the Horse') and published at the turn of the 19th century. With his usual kindly humour and vivid style he tells us of the not-so-distant era – ten years ago at the most, when he was writing – when to embark on learning to ride a bicycle seemed so eccentric that people tended to keep it dark. The talented Giffard, a 'populariser' in the best sense of the word, had entered the lists himself with a delightful chronicle. It had appeared on Thursday, 6 March 1890, in the *Petit Journal*, which had a large circulation and exerted a con-siderable influence, particularly among 'ordinary people' at a time when – and we must not forget this – cycling was an extremely expensive pastime. Giffard somehow managed to foresee the brilliant future that lay ahead for 'the moving machine' and to communicate it clearly to his readers. But he also had the knack of getting across to high society. On 4 October 1890 he managed to persuade *Le Figaro* to publish a four-page 'literary supplement' on cycling, illustrated with 22 witty engravings by Mars. This long article heralded the new era, whose bard and prophet was Giffard.

## Racing for a piano

The 'bicycle', as it was now called, is a wondrous thing, but the tricky question of who invented it has been the subject of endless arguments. Pioneers like Meyer had probably found the key and several patents opened up new areas of research. But, in fact, the permanent implementation of a system involving a chain-driven rear-driving machine was implemented on a permanent basis only as a direct reaction to the excesses of the 'penny-farthing'. The fact that early models were called 'Safety Bicycles'

shows that the manufacturers were well aware that the general public were afraid of falling off and wanted comfortable machines. Before you could get into the saddle of the 1878 'Renard' model, you had to clamber up no fewer than six rungs fixed at intervals along the frame – which meant you needed to be something of an acrobat! How on earth did you get back on if you happened to fall off somewhere in the country miles from anywhere?

Notable progress was made by the resourceful Jules Truffault who perfected his 'Sphinx' in 1876 with a front wheel of 0·75 m (30 in) in diameter – having taken the idea from the other side of the Channel, where it became all the rage a few years later under the name of 'Crypto', with champion cyclist Frank Shorland demonstrating its merits; the Marseilles cyclist Rousseau produced his 'Safety model' in 1877, with a front wheel of 0·9 m (35·5 in) in diameter and two-speed gears (the same principles were later followed in the British 'Kangaroo' model); a Bordeaux mechanic called Georges Juzan covered the 100 km (62·25 miles) between Bordeaux and Libourne in the Dordogne and back in 4 hr 40 min on a chain-driven cycle with both wheels the same size; plus a whole series of improvements made to tricycles along the same lines, in spite of the inherent disadvantages of their clumsy shape and considerable weight.

There is no doubt that Britain deserves the credit for moving beyond the stage of individual experiments. Enterprising manufacturers organised gruelling long-distance competitions – 24 hour trials among them – and produced new models on a large scale in a short space of time. In 1882 the manufacturers of the 'Facile' bicycle had alerted the general public to the advantages of 'small' bicycles by racing some of them between London and Bath and back. Then on 27 September 1884 George Smith won the 100 mile race organised by the firm of Hillman, Herbert & Cooper for their 'Kangaroo' cycle. He covered the distance in the sensational time of 7 hr 11 min 10 s, well and truly breaking the record of 7 hr 18 min 55 s set up in 1878 on an Ordinary. The following year, again in September, Smith won his second victory, breaking his own record by 5 min 54 s. On this occasion he was riding a 'Rover' model with a rear-wheel drive – that was the key factor – made by Starley & Sutton of Coventry. As we have seen, the manufacture of bicycles and tricycles had brought great wealth to Coventry. Then finally, on 20 October 1885, 'Teddy' Hale demonstrated the superiority of the 'Kangaroo' by knocking almost half an hour off the record at a stroke, with a time of 6 hr 39 min 5 s, and maintaining an absolutely even pace – there was only 53 seconds' difference between the times for the outward and the return journeys. The first prize consisted of 'a gold medal and a fine piano worth £66 sterling'.

From 1886 onwards the 'Bicyclette', a model made by the firm of Rudge, emerged as the foremost model of the day. Its success, which was slow at first but soon gathered momentum, was due mainly to an Englishman called H O Duncan. He had settled in France, where he battled valiantly with cyclists such as Terront, de Civry and Medinger.

## 'La Petite Reine' reigns supreme

What is . . .

> . . . the ultra-powerful moving body that over the last few years has been crisscrossing the roadways of the old and new worlds with thousands and thousands of biking enthusiasts aboard? Men, women, children and old people are all passionate, even fanatical, enthusiasts and their battalions are growing in strength every day. All the various social classes are represented in their army – the idle rich contemplating the possibility of setting up some sensational record rub shoulders with the workers, and with the clerk travelling to work every day on 'an engine' contemptuously referred to as a 'boneshaker' by the lucky owners of thoroughbred models.

This question is posed in a delightful book by Frederic Regamey called *Vélocipédie et Automobilisme* ('Cycling and Motoring', 1898) – note that the motorcar had already made its appearance by this time.

Nowadays, well into the 20th century and not so far off the magic year 2000, we are witnessing the great ecological movement among urban inhabitants, with everyone cracking up the idea of a return to 'healthy exercise'. As a result the second golden age of the bicycle is upon us, and it's interesting to draw a parallel with what was happening at the end of the 19th century.

By the beginning of 1890 there were still few velocipedists. However, two years later it could be said and proclaimed that: 'Cycling is today a new means of locomotion for everybody, one of the most reliable and economical means of transport; it will soon be a means of promoting a social revolution analogous to the railways and atlantic liners'.

First of all there was smart society, showing off their prowess in the avenues of the Bois de Boulogne in Paris after learning to ride a bicycle in one of the glittering riding-schools in the capital. They would go to the Châlet du Cycle to 'be seen'. If we study the names under the heading 'Cycling' in the 1897 edition of the *Annuaire des Sportsmen (Sportsmen's Annual)* we are bound to be struck by the list of foreign honorary members of the Touring-Club de France, which includes: Their Majesties Leopold II, King of the Belgians; Don Carlos I of Portugal; Alexander I of Serbia; Their Royal Highnesses the Prince of Wales and Prince Nicholas of Greece; Their Imperial Highnesses Grand-Duke Sergei Michailovich and Grand-Duke Boris Uladimirovich and many more. The 'Rallye-Vélo' (Bike Rally) committee included marquises, counts and princes, under the chairmanship of a duke. And the committee of the 'Omnium' was no less distinguished.

Then the Prince de Sagan was chairman of the Supporters' Committee of the first cycle show organised in the Salle Wagram in Paris in January 1894 and in which nearly 300 bicycle and accessory firms took part. But the Prince failed to turn up for the opening ceremony, and so did the Minister of Trade and Industry, who was later given a rocket by the cycling press for scratching from the ceremony at the last minute. The exhibition was nevertheless such a success that a second cycle show took place in December of the same year. An attractive poster by Forain advertised the show all over Paris. This time a visitor who had gone to the Champs-Elysées and wanted to inspect every single one of the 'velocipedes of all kinds, pneumatic tyres, wooden tyres and so on', plus a vast assortment of inventions and equipment – including class V, 'vehicles and motors' (a sort of motor show in embryo) – such an enthusiast would have to tramp up and down the Palace of Industry until he eventually came to the end at stand 464!

The bicycle had come to stay. It was still expensive – though getting gradually cheaper – but it was not merely a 'with-it' alternative to the stables owned by fashionable society. For instance in 1892 Messrs Alfred and Maurice Chérié published a splendid 'general illustrated directory of cyclists' for the Universal Cycling Bookshop. The directory ran to

ABOVE: *By 1892 traffic in Paris was beginning to change. Three years later la Place de l'Opéra was packed with bicycles, and horses drawing the buses were getting used to them – but cab drivers hated cyclists!*

BELOW: *A bicycle made for six . . . They were even made for ten or a dozen, but 'quints' (five pedallers) was the maximum size for pacing purposes in track competition.*

no less than 468 pages and listed clubs or individual cyclists all over France, plus another ten or so foreign countries – excluding the English-speaking countries. No less than 34 French specialist papers and magazines were listed, 23 of them in the provinces, along with 9 in Britain, 8 in Austria, 7 in Germany, 4 in Italy, 3 each in Belgium and Spain and 2 each in the United States and Holland – and most probably the list was by no means complete. That gives some idea of how widespread the cycling phenomenon had become.

It is difficult to envisage the important part played by this novel form of entertainment at the turn of the century. Roadside inns, empty until recently, found themselves with a new clientele with voracious appetites. A merry string of lights would dance their way back towards the towns as the evenings drew in. It is also only too easy to forget that the bicycle undoubtedly played an important part in emancipating women. For the first time ladies, young and old, could take part in an outdoor pastime with the members of the stronger sex, outside the traditional rigid framework of their lives. This transformation was soon to make itself felt in clothing – just think of the controversy that blew up over the sight of a 'female in breeches' riding past, or even in a 'divided skirt'!

For some people, who would otherwise scarcely ever have left their native village, cycling revealed new dimensions of space and speed, offering a radius of action much larger than walking. If you wanted to travel you didn't need a carriage or a stable any more. Your bicycle would eat up the miles instead.

The vast new fields opened up by the bicycle are summed up with touching emphasis by one of the characters in a book by the French novelist Rosny the Elder, who wrote *La Guerre du feu* ('The Fire War'). The book is called *Un autre monde* ('Another World') and it recalls the genuine amazement his contemporaries felt at this new means of creating a peaceful revolution.

> The advent of the bicycle is infinitely more than a social novelty – it's one of the great human events that has occurred since the beginning of mankind. I don't know if the arts of fire, writing and printing are more important – but I can see quite clearly that the slow beast that was man, because he had sacrificed his front paws so that he could 'explore the universe', once again became a fast-moving creature – one of the fastest-moving of all. The significance of this is immeasurable and I have no space here to develop the thesis that the bicycle represents the first stage of aviation . . .

This was a prophetic vision, for if we stick to the verifiable facts we find that a large number of racing cyclists moved on from bicycles to cars, then to aeroplanes – as pilots or as designers. One good example is Henri Farman, who was destined to be the first man officially to travel a closed circuit of 10 km (1090 yd) through the air. He did this clinging to the controls of a Voisin biplane on 13 January 1908, at Issy-les-Moulineaux near Paris. But at 20 he had won the French cycling championship over 100 km (62.25 miles) at the Buffalo stadium and two years later had won the Paris to Clermont Ferrand race organised by the Michelin company – with compulsory punctures! In Britain we find that many great figures of the automobile industry had also been prominent in the cycling world, such as C S Rolls and William Morris (who became Lord Nuffield).

Although the design of the bicycle of this period seems positively antediluvian in 1976, it had in fact been constantly improved over the years and had now taken on its classic form. If we study them carefully we can see that today's straight-handlebar models are the direct descendants of the contraptions recorded by the earliest photographers.

It is important to remember that the great popular interest created by cycling competitions had played a vital part in making the velocipede, and its progeny the bicycle, universally popular.

## 1200 km (750 miles) at a stretch

In September 1975 the Belgian cyclist Freddy Maertens won the Paris to Brussels race (about 291 km (181 miles)) in less than 6·25 hours, which meant a record average speed of 47 km/h (29 mph). However, the British cyclist Mills and his French colleague Terront had managed to make an indelible impression on the minds of their contemporaries in the year of grace 1891 by winning the races from Bordeaux to Paris and Paris to Brest and back respectively at 21·5 and 16·8 km/h (13·5 and 10·5 mph). The uninitiated could never have dreamt that man could pedal a distance of 572 km (356 miles) in 26 hr 34 min 57 s, let alone 1200 km (750 miles) in 71 hr 22 min. In a mere month or two this dual demonstration – both of the trained sportsman's prowess at pushing back generally accepted frontiers and of the extraordinary opportunities offered by the bicycle for getting from A to B under one's own steam and at speed – helped considerably to further the cause of cycling.

*Arthur Augustus Zimmermann, the 'Flying Yankee', gained fame on both sides of the Atlantic. On his first visit to Europe in 1892 he won the 1, 5 and 50 mile British championships, and the following year became the first official world champion by winning the 1 and 10 mile titles in Chicago. In that year, 1903, he won 101 races from 111 starts! 'Zimmy' turned pro, won hundreds of races, but no world title. Riding a gear of 68 in Zimmermann was perhaps the fastest pedaller of all time.*

### 3ᵉ COURSE (9 h. 1/2). — GRANDE INTERNATIONALE (Bicycles). — Course d'une heure.

5 Prix : **750 fr.** — Plus une prime de **40 fr.** par kil. et fraction de 1/2 kil., au-dessus d'un parcours de 28 kil.

Dans la dernière minute de l'heure et au moment du passage au poteau du Coureur de tête, la cloche sonnera. — L'arrivée aura lieu au passage suivant des coureurs devant le poteau.

| NOMS | FLOTS | COSTUMES | ORIGINES | CLUBS | POIDS | HAUTEUR | FABRICANTS |
|---|---|---|---|---|---|---|---|
| 1. F. de Civry | Cerise | Noir et cerise | Paris | V.-C. B. et S.V.M. | 10 kil. | 1ᵐ 41 | Rudge. |
| 2. Médinger | Marron et blanc | Noir et blanc | Paris | S. V. M | 11 » | 1 38 | Clément. |
| 3. Ch. Terront | Vert et rose | Noir | Bayonne | V.-C. B. B. | 10 » | 1 32 | — |
| 4. Laulan | Bleu et vieil or | Noir | Bordeaux | V.-C. B | 11 » | 1 35 | Garrard. |
| 5. Hommey | Blanc et mauve | Blanc | Paris | S. V. P. | 11 » | 1 40 | Hommey. |
| 6. J. Vidal | Blanc | Noir | Bordeaux | V.-C. B. | 9 » | 1 37 | Surrey. |
| 7. Bob | Rose | Noir | Pau | V.-C. B. et V.-C.B. | 12 » | 1 40 | Lavignasse. |
| 8. Racheller | Rose et bleu foncé | Noir | Bergerac. | V.-C. B. et S. V.B. | 11 » | 1 38 | Juzan. |
| 9. H.-O. Duncan | Vieil or et grenat | | Angleterre | V.-C. B. et V.-C.M. | 10 kil. | 1 42 | Rudge. |
| 0. Knowles | Bleu clair | | — | V.-C. B. et V.-C.B. | 9 » | 1 37 | — |
| 11. Ch. Garrard | Noir | Noir | — | S. V. G. | 10 » | 1 38 | Garrard. |
| 12. Noé Boyer | Jaune | Noir | Bayonne. | V.-C. B.-B. | 12 kil. | 1 32 | Clément. |
| 13. Dufresne | Vieil or | Noir | Paris | S.-V. P. | 12 k. 500 | 1 42 | Rudge. |
| 14. Jicey | Vieil or et mauve | Bleu | Bordeaux | V.-C. B. | 11 » | 1 38 | — |
| 15. Dubois | Noir et vieil or | Bleu marine | Paris | S.-V. M. | 10 » | 1 40 | Surrey. |
| 16. Henri Loste | Rose et vert foncé | Vert | Bordeaux | V.-C. B. | 10 » | 1 32 | Rudge. |
| 17. Louis Loste | Rose et vert clair | Marron | — | V.-C. B. | 10 » | 1 34 | Juzan. |
| 18. Lamballe aîné | Vieil or et cerise | Noir | Tours | V.-C. T. | 12 » | 1 35 | Clément. |
| 19. Jiel | Noir et jaune | Noir et jaune | Bordeaux | V.-C. B. | 11 » | 1 37 | Surrey. |
| 20. Poulard I. | Vert foncé | Noir et bleu | Dax | V.-C. B. | 11 » | 1 37 | Lavignasse. |
| 21. Émile Eole | Cerise et marron | Bleu | Paris | S.-V. P. | 12 » | 1 39 | Renard. |
| 22. Woman | Noir et rose | Rouge et jaune | Bordeaux | S.-V. G. | 10 » | 1 37 | Rudge. |
| 23. E. Dumolard | Vieil or et vert. | Bleu marine | Grenoble. | V.-C. B. et V.-C. G. | 17 » | 1 35 | Clément. |
| 24. Bill | Violet | Noir et bleu mar. | Pau | V.-C. B. | 10 » | 1 38 | Rudge. |
| 25. Juzan | Noir et vert | Noir | Bordeaux | V.-C. B. | 10 k. 500 | 1 34 | Juzan. |
| 26. Saint-Savin | Noir et cerise | Noir et rouge | Montpellier | V.-C. M. | 19 » | 1 52 | Rudge. |
| 27. L. Chauvin | Cerise et violet | Bleu marine | Narbonne | V.-C. B. | 11 » | 1 38 | Clément. |
| 28. G. Fourré | Rose et vieil or | Bleu | Cognac | Indépendant. | 18 » | 1 35 | — |
| 29. Lacabane | Blanc et violet | Blanc | Bordeaux | V.-C. B. | 10 » | 1 35 | Garrard. |
| 30. Theo | Blanc et vieil or | Noir | — | V.-C. B. | 12 » | 1 30 | Juzan. |
| 31. M. Pelletier | Grenat | Rouge | Cires-sur-Sergue. | V.-C. B. | 15 » | 1 35 | Garrard. |
| 32. R. Ollivier | Rose et violet | Noir et orange | Villeneuve-s.-Lot. | C. C. V. | 11 » | 1 32 | — |
| 33. Daniel | Rose et marron | Bleu | Bordeaux | V.-C. B. | 14 » | 1 37 | Rudge. |
| 34. Metché fils | Rose et jaune | Noir | Toulouse. | V.-C. T. | 10 » | 1 35 | — |
| 35. Gazave | Blanc et jaune | Noir | Bordeaux | V.-C. B. | 13 k. 500 | 1 38 | — |
| 36. Milano | Mauve | Rouge et bleu | — | V.-C. B. | 15 » | 1 32 | — |
| 37. Typou | Noir et bleu | Noir | — | V.-C. B. | 14 » | 1 32 | — |
| 38. Joey | Vert et jaune | Noir | — | V.-C. B. | 13 » | 1 42 | Garrard. |
| 39. Baby | Cerise et blanc | Noir et or | Pau | Indépendant | 19 » | 0 95 | Clément. |
| 40. Arza | Noir et violet | Bleu | Bordeaux | V.-C. B. | 16 » | 1 30 | Rudge. |
| 41. Tricoche | Vert clair | Noir | — | V.-C. B. | 13 » | 1 32 | — |
| 42. Ercey | Blanc et noir | Noir | — | V.-C. B. | 12 » | 1 32 | — |
| 43. F. Zolki | Marron | Noir et blanc | Port-Sainte-Marie | Indépendant | 13 » | 1 33 | Lassonjade. |
| 44. Colon | Bleu foncé | Bleu | La Tresne | V.-C. B. | 19 » | 1 32 | Colon. |
| 45. Dghems | Bleu et vieil or | Noir | Bordeaux | V.-C. B. | 13 » | 1 32 | Rudge. |
| 46. Pale-Ale | Blanc et vert | Bleu marine | — | V.-C. B. | 14 » | 1 32 | — |

This extract from a Bordeaux race programme of 1885 includes all the top French cyclists – de Civry, Medinger, Terront, Dubois, the Loste Brothers, Jiel – and also three brilliant visitors from Britain : Duncan, Garrard and Knowles. Details are given of the colours and costume worn by the riders, plus technical information on the machines they used.

## IMMENSE SUCCÈS DES MACHINES HUMBER

FABRICATION LA PLUS RENOMMÉE ET LA PLUS PERFECTIONNÉE

### Les plus hautes Récompenses à toutes les Expositions
### 22 MÉDAILLES D'OR

**1888** Tous les CHAMPIONNATS DE FRANCE ont été gagnés sur les HUMBER
Les Records établis sur les machines HUMBER vitesse et fond n'ont pu être battus.

**1889**
Le CHAMPIONNAT ANNUEL DES JUNIORS (Bicycles), couru le 23 juin, à Versailles a été gagné par M. ÉCHALIE sur une bicyclette HUMBER; M. BUGARD, second, sur une bicyclette HUMBER.
Le CHAMPIONNAT DE FRANCE (Tricycles), couru le 11 août, à Grenoble, a été gagné par COTTEREAU sur un Cripper HUMBER; BÉCONNAIS, second, sur un Cripper HUMBER, battant LAULAN et MÉDINGER.
Le CHAMPIONNAT ANNUEL DES JUNIORS (Tricycles), couru le 11 août, à Grenoble, a été gagné par M. NICODEMI sur un Cripper HUMBER (demi-course); M. FOURTANIER, second, sur un Cripper HUMBER.

**ANGLETERRE** Tous les Championnats (amateurs) organisés par la *National Cyclists Union* ont été gagnés sur les machines HUMBER.

5 MILLES. — *Championnat amateurs* (bicycles): 1ᵉʳ H. Synyer, sur un bicycle HUMBER; 2ᵉ F. J. OSMOND, sur un bicycle HUMBER.
25 MILLES. — *Championnat amateurs* (bicycles): 1ᵉʳ F. J. Osmond, sur un bicycle HUMBER; 2ᵉ F. P. Wood sur un bicycle HUMBER.
1 MILLE. — *Championnat amateurs* (Tricycles): 1ᵉʳ H. H. Sansom, sur un Cripper HUMBER; 2ᵉ W. H. Bramson sur un Cripper HUMBER; 3ᵉ A. du Cross, sur un Cripper HUMBER.
5 MILLES — *Championnat amateurs* (tricycles): 1ᵉʳ H. H. Sansom, sur un Cripper HUMBER; 2ᵉ E. B. Turner, sur un Cripper HUMBER.
25 MILLES. — *Championnat amateurs* (tricycles): 1ᵉʳ W. H. Bramson, sur un Cripper HUMBER; 2ᵉ S. Lee, sur un Cripper HUMBER.
1 MILLE. — *Championnat amateurs* (bicyclettes): a été gagné par F. T. Fletcher sur une bicyclette HUMBER.
25 MILLES. — *Championnat amateurs* (bicyclettes): a été gagné par F. T. Fletcher, sur une bicyclette HUMBER, battant le record de 25 milles (40 kilomètres) en 1 heure 16 minutes 31 secondes 2 5.

## HUMBER & Cⁱᵉ, LIMITED
### 19, RUE DU QUATRE-SEPTEMBRE, 19
(entre l'Opéra et la Bourse) **PARIS** (entre l'Opéra et la Bourse)

The programme for the 1889 French championships at Longchamp, Paris, included a full-page advertisement for the Humber company. It gives an idea of the number of races organised, the variety of machines still in circulation, and the excellent performances.

Once again competition cycling, by calling for and exploiting sophisticated techniques, had helped to develop the machine ridden by the man in the street, though utility models lagged behind the 'racing jobs' from the technical point of view. For instance the Paris-Brest-Paris race, which Pierre Giffard devised and organised, represented a triumph both for Terront, who outdistanced the plucky Jiel-Laval by almost eight hours, and for Michelin's removable tyres, still at the experimental stage, over Dunlop's 'glued tyres'.

Meanwhile the weight of racing cycles, even in the period of the 'penny-farthing', was much lower than is generally supposed – they were amazingly light in fact. One entry in the 'Cycles for Sale' column published in the Bordeaux cycling weekly *Le Véloce Sport* ('The Sporting Bicycle') on 28 January 1886 runs: 'Monsieur de Civry is selling his RUDGE racing Bicycle. Weight: 10.5 kg (33 lb). Height: 1·4 m (55 in). Can be used for outings'. Eight years later, by which time the Ordinary had been completely overtaken by the bicycle, a large number of cycle-builders at the second French cycle show advertised weights of 9·5 to 10 kg (21 to 22 lb). If we turn to the actual wheels we find that the cyclist's well-being, and his enjoyment of cycling, had been vastly improved by the 'invention' in 1888 of the 'hollow rubber tube inflated with air'. The 'inventor' was John Boyd Dunlop, of Belfast, but in fact the principle had, as we have seen, been invented by R W Thomson, in 1845, although it had been a failure at the time.

More and more cycle races were run as the 19th century drew to a close and more and more champions emerged. Some competitions took the form of long-distance races, while others were speed contests. Arthur Augustus Zimmermann, known as 'the flying Yankee', took part in European cycling events in 1892, 1893 and 1894, and was long considered to be the greatest racing cyclist of all time. Another famous name, the French soldier-turned-cyclist Edmond Jacquelin, made the hearts of the crowds beat faster at the turn of the century. Then Frank Shorland and Constant Huret, racing on both sides of the Channel, broke the 24 hour record again and again, while Charlie Miller, who in 1897 got married on the sacred track centre of Madison Square Garden, proved himself to be the ace cyclist in individual six-day contests.

An increasing number of national and international trials were held on the roads – most of which were in appalling condition. The contests got tougher and tougher and faster and faster, with the contestants paced by individual pacemakers, by tandems, by groups of three or four cyclists, by motorised tandems or by cars. But the best of them, however plucky, were never as popular as 'the stars of the track', some of whom made a mint of money.

We have been describing the golden age of the bicycle, in those far-off days when Paul Bernard ran the Buffalo cycle-racing track in Paris and his friend Toulouse-Lautrec was recording Zimmermann's turned-up nose with three deft strokes of a pencil.

That far-sighted journalist Richard Lesclide had died in Paris on 15 May 1892 at the age of 67, but a new generation had emerged. In the year of Lesclide's death an athlete of 27, who had only just learned to ride a bike, was beginning to make his name. It was this man, Henri Desgrange, who was to set up a new unpaced speed record the following year. On 11 May 1893 he achieved a distance of 35·325 km (21·9 miles) in an hour, verified by official timekeepers. Poor Dodds and his rivals were well and truly forgotten by this time and by public acclaim Desgrange, who was later to found and edit the sporting daily L'Auto, was popularly hailed as the first 'Unpaced Hour record-holder'.

Yet in those days no one – not even Desgrange himself – would have cherished the absurd dream that one day racing cyclists would be taking their places on the starting-line of a race that would take them on a 'Tour de France'.

*A 'portrait-card', by sporting artist Pellos, of Henri Desgrange, founder of the Tour de France. Pellos sees Desgrange's 'Tour' as having everything – the cobblestones of northern France, Alpine and Pyrenean mountain passes, the Riviera, Atlantic coast, Brittany, Normandy, and the Eiffel Tower.*

The programme of the first Paris six-day race, 13–19 February 1913. It was won by the 'favourite' team of Fogler-Goullet in a final sprint from five other pairs who had all covered 2792 miles, a distance that was never beaten in the Paris race.

BELOW LEFT: *Lucien Michard, a great French sprinter of exceptional tactical skill. As an amateur he was world champion in 1923 and 1924, and also won the Olympic gold medal in 1924. Later Michard was unbeaten in professional world championships from 1927 to 1930.*

*The American star Joe Fogler, winner of nine six-day races at a time when riders were on the track for the full 144 hours. Fogler took the New York 'Six' five times with various partners between 1905 and 1913, and in 1913 also triumphed in the first 'Six Jours de Paris' partnered by Alf Goullet (Australia).*

# Races and champions

The aim of this book is to lead you through the varied adventures that are liable to occur in the small world of the cyclist, and competition cycling is only one approach to the subject – albeit the most obvious one. This holds good both for the eager crowds lining the roads in Europe, North Africa, Mexico or Canada; for the television viewers trembling with excitement at the spectacle offered by 'the box' when the most important cycling events are on; and most of all for the children or teenagers who demonstrate, in the most natural way possible, an urge to pit their strength against each other as soon as they start going out with their friends – perhaps struggling to get to the top of a steepish hill first, or to beat their mates to a village sign or a county boundary. One fine day these young bike fans will find themselves perched on a roadside bank, gazing wide-eyed at the colourful spectacle of motorcycle outriders clearing the way; the motley *peloton* of pedallers; the cars weighed down with gleaming bicycles and wheels spinning uselessly in space. They will become autograph-hunters, pressing their noses against the windows of hotel dining-rooms, clutching autograph albums in their hands. They will want to try their luck for themselves, for the Yellow Jersey appears constantly in their dreams.

So whether we like it or not, there's no doubt that competition cycling has great drawing-power, like the mirrors used to trap larks – it is a moving shop-window for the sport. It has a true history, made up of a mixture of human courage and human endurance; it also has a legendary history invented by journalists, though by sincere journalists. Pressmen – and their radio and TV colleagues – are easily carried to epic heights as, in cars or on motor-cycle pillions, they mingle with the riders on mountain climbs and dangerous descents, or watch them battling over flat, cobbled roads. Reporters find 'colour' in a frenzied sprint for first place and also in a hard-luck story of a courageous rider, injured in a crash, finishing half an hour behind the winner.

Many thousands of racing cyclists have taken part in many thousands of races since cycling began – on racing tracks and on roads, in all weathers, summer and winter. To sketch in the most important facts and the major champions of the last 75 years means leafing through the family album of cycling – and we all enjoy commenting on familiar or not-so-familiar-snaps, some of them faded over the years. It also involves a conscious effort to understand why the contemporary bicycle is what it is, and why and how the feats performed by some unknown cyclist benefited from improvements to his equipment.

A quick run-through of the history of competitive cycling offers the best introduction to the sport as practised today, no matter what form it takes. There is, of course, absolutely no reason why you should 'go down on the drops' when sauntering along on your bike. If we are honest about this, however, can any of us, even if we only ride an ordinary sit-up-and-beg bike, truly say that we've never had a stab at seeing how fast we can go? People may talk about the 'ethereal' cyclist who rides serenely on, without the slightest urge to accelerate – but I do not believe that such a creature exists.

## Racing cyclists with silk jerseys

In the Edwardian era the track sprinters were idolised by the crowds. The major heroes were a Dane called Thorwald Ellegaard, who wore a checked jersey and sported a droopy moustache, and Frank Kramer from the USA, with his underhung jaw; though men such as Emile Friol of France who could always put on a spectacular 'jump', would sometimes create a great stir. Thanks to his prowess in this respect Friol managed to win three Grands Prix de Paris – probably the most sought-after cycling trophy of the pre-First World War era.

In the immediate postwar period the Australian cyclist Bob Spears, with his strange handlebars, seemed to be invincible. But soon a new reign began, with the throne occupied by the giant Dutchman Piet Moeskops. His successor was the brilliant Lucien Michard, who had a good brain as well as being a great athlete. Michard's reign lasted from 1926 to 1931, when he was deprived of his fifth consecutive world title by what was quite clearly an error on the part of the chief judge. Then came the Belgian champion Jeff Scherens, known as *Poeske* – 'the Cat' – who always managed to get past his opponent in the last few yards. He was the best of a first-class bunch that included the bespectacled Dutch cyclist Arie van Vliet and 'Toto' Gerardin of France.

Two great names stand out from the period 1949 to 1964: the British cyclist Reginald Harris, who recently made an amazing come-back to regain his British championship title at the age of 54; and the Italian Antonio Maspes, who donned the professional champion's Rainbow Jersey no less than seven times. The Parisian cyclist Michel Rousseau had a meteoric rise to fame, becoming Olympic champion only a few weeks after his first race. That was at Melbourne in 1956 and he went on to be world champion three years running, one of them as a professional. The art of sprinting has fallen off since 1965 and perhaps the most gifted sprinter, the Belgian Patrick Sercu, has been forced to turn to six-day races and road races in order to earn his living, which has inevitably taken the edge off his speed.

On the other hand the 'amateur' cyclists, those who are entitled to take part in the Olympic Games, are becoming increasingly competitive, because the countries of Eastern Europe are constantly throwing up new champions to add to the pool of talent available. Outstanding in this category is the French sprinter Daniel Morelon, with his long face and amazing self control. He was amateur world champion seven times between 1966 and 1975 and has won three Olympic gold medals, including one for the tandem in Mexico City, partnered by 'power-house' Pierre Trentin.

## Whirling dervishes and human stopwatches

Six-day team events began in the USA in 1899. They were introduced because individual races were encouraging cyclists to commit dangerous excesses as they tried desperately to cope with as little sleep as possible. In 1898 Charlie Miller had covered 3368 km (2105 miles) on his own. In the following year Miller and Frank Waller, racing as a team, covered over 4398 km (2750 miles) in Madison Square Garden, New York in the same six-day period – the Anglican Church strictly forbade racing on the Lord's Day. This type of competition thus became known on the continent of Europe as racing à l'Américaine and in Britain as 'Madison racing' although events did not always last the full six days. Sometimes they were only 100 km (62·25 miles) in length, or even less. Such races were particularly popular with spectators at indoor cycle-racing tracks.

The most famous teams and specialists in this field included the American cyclists Eddy Root and Joe Fogler and the Australians Alf Goullet, Alf Grenda and Reggie MacNamara, all of whom were well-known figures in the prewar period as well. MacNamara held the record for the greatest number of six-day race victories for many years, ending with a total of 19. At that time 'sixdaymen' rode at a steady pace and the result would often be decided by the one and only sprint in the last laps of the race.

Gradually this rhythm changed. As the number of 'primes' offered increased and series of sprints for points were introduced (these points were used to separate teams finishing equal on distance), slack periods began gradually to alternate with sessions of a stronger tempo, generally in the evening. Then came the Swiss Oscar Egg; the Belgians – Gérard Debaets, Emile Aerts, Albert Buysse and Albert Billiet; the Canadian William ('Torchy') Peden; Frenchmen – Georges Wambst and Charles Lacquehay, Paul Broccardo, Marcel Guimbretière and Alfred Letourneur; and finally the Dutch expert Piet van Kempen, who took over from MacNamara at the top of the tables, winning 32 six-day races.

After the Second World War the six-day rider's day was gradually shortened and the total distance covered had little significance because during the 'chases' or 'jams' competitors would 'gain' and 'lose' several hundred laps every evening. The outstanding figures now were four Belgians – Rik van Steenbergen, Achile Bruneel, Patrick Sercu and Emile Severeyns; a German, Klaus Bugdahl; an Italian, Ferdinando Terruzzi; and a pair of Swiss cyclists, Fritz Pfenninger and Armin von Büren. Once they had proved that they were better than their rivals some riders assumed the role of 'Track Boss', dictating the speed and duration of the 'jams'. Examples here are the famous Dutch cyclist Gerrit Schulte, who acted in this capacity from 1945 to about 1959, and his compatriot Peter Post, who still heads the list, with 65 six-day race wins under his belt. On the other hand some of their colleagues were little known outside cycling circles, as was the case with Lucien Gillen from Luxembourg.

During the last two six-day trials in Paris, held in the Vélodrome d'Hiver in 1957 and 1958, teams of three riders, instead of the usual two, took part. The winners each time were Terruzzi and Darrigade, whose repertoire was based on speed, and Jacques Anquetil, whose thoroughbred pursuiting style was a joy to watch.

Although dating back from the 1890s, individual pursuit racing became firmly established in the inter-war period. It is the toughest test of all, with each contestant attempting to catch up his rival, who has started on the other side of the track. It brings out the really top-class racing cyclists, such as the French expert André Raynaud, but it was not granted official recognition until 1946, when the first world titles were awarded.

Star pursuit riders are among the most widely accepted of all cycling champions, because there is no room for weakness in their chosen field. For many years now the professional titles have been fought out between Italy (Fausto Coppi, Antonio Bevilacqua, Guido Messina and Leandro Faggin) and Holland (Gerrit Peeters, Gerrit Schulte, Hank Nijdam, Tiemen Groen and Roy Schuiten) and occasionally Belgium (Ferdinand Bracke and Dirk Baert). However, a few other nationalities do manage to snatch the occasional victory. There was the Australian 'Sid' Patterson, who was capable of finishing with a sprint, the brilliantly talented Roger Riviére, from France, and Rudi Altig from Mannheim in Germany. Then the British cyclist Hugh Porter wore the champion's jersey four times between 1968 and 1973.

Nowadays pursuits rarely last longer than 5 km (3 miles), but the effort demanded is roughly comparable with that of the rider attacking the world Hour Unpaced, that record forming a cross-roads where roadmen and trackmen meet and whose possession can be one of the finest jewels in a racing cyclist's crown.

## Under the leather crash-helmet

In distinct contrast to pursuit riding are motor-paced races in which the cyclists' speeds are enormously increased. People would flock to the turnstile to see these modern gladiators, carried away by the noisy racket of the big motorbikes. Once the pace-making system had been perfected – tolling the death knell of the motorised tandems of the early days – some remarkable racing cyclists emerged. They included the talented American 'Bobby' Walthour and the French cyclists Georges Parent and Paul Guignard, who sported a small moustache. It was Guignard who made the onlookers yell with mingled delight and terror when he broke the 100 km 'barrier' by covering 101·63 km (63·15 miles) at Munich-Milbertshofen on 15 September 1909, to regain the paced Hour record taken from him the previous year by A E Wills (Britain) who had become the first cyclist to ride 60 miles in less than 60 minutes. Then there was Louis Darragon, whose tragic fall at the Paris Vélodrome d'Hiver in April 1918 added yet another name to the endless list of martyrs to this branch of the sport. The onlookers were always aware of the risk the 'stayers' had accepted, and it was part of the fun, whether or not they admitted it openly.

After the First World War this branch of the sport was all the rage. The figures at the top of the tree were Georges Sérès (France), the famous Victor Linart (Belgium), known as 'the Sioux', and 'Toto' Grassin (France), the 'king of indoor racing'. Linart was world champion four times and even at the age of 42 he still managed to take third place in the 1931 battle for the Rainbow Jersey. These men were followed by three Frenchmen – Georges Paillard, Charles Lacquehay and André Raynaud – who fought it out with three Germans – Walter Sawall, Erich Metze and Walter Lohmann. Germany was the Promised Land for motor-paced specialists. They were paid big money by track directors and their spectacular racing drew huge crowds of enthusiastic spectators.

*Star performer of the great days of motor-paced racing, Victor Linart of Belgium. He was showing good form before the First World War, spent the 1914-1918 period racing in North America, and in the 1920s won four world motor-paced championships in Europe.*

But the number of racing cyclists trying their luck at paced racing started to dwindle. Even the best rider cannot win if his pacemaker is not up to the job or has done an illicit deal with one or several of the rival pairs. Yet the pacemakers themselves, who grew old in the service of the sport, since they usually owned their own equipment and felt little inclination to hand over to someone else, were partly to blame for the decline. There were, however, still some excellent competitors in this field, such as Raoul Lesueur from Nice, Adolf and Theo Verschueren and Leo Proost from Belgium, and Guillermo Timoner from Spain.

The motor-paced race was on its last legs. The rhythm of cycling races had grown monotonous, with the standard length down to a mere 60 minutes, instead of 100 km (62·25 miles) as it had been for so long. The amateur world championships brought back into fashion by the International Cycling Union in 1958 have not managed to alter the problem in any way.

## The call of the road

They're spattered with mud; their legs, arms and faces tanned by the scorching rays of the sun beating down on them in other races; the pockets of their woollen jerseys are bulging; their water bottles are still half full, but they will be throwing them into the ditch a few miles before finishing to

*Octave Lapize (France) was one of the first roadman-sprinters of great class. He scored three notable 'hat tricks': Paris-Roubaix 1909-10-11, French professional championship, 1911-12-13; Paris-Brussels, 1911-12-13. Lapize also won the Tour de France in 1910 and Paris-Tours in 1911. He died on active service in 1917.*

lighten their load by a few grams before the final sprint. The roadracers are passing by.

The start of the first-ever Tour de France race took place at 3.16 p.m. on 1 July 1903, at Villeneuve-Saint-Georges in the south-eastern suburbs of Paris, on the Montgeron road. But it was no more than a curiosity. In retrospect the raised arm of the starter takes on a completely different significance. The balance of forces would seesaw, not immediately and not at a steady rate – there would be periods of economic crisis when some amateurs, on turning professional, would be advised to take up track racing, in 1925 for instance – but inexorably. Track racing would be eclipsed in

popularity by road sport with its much wider scene, varying from an exciting series of one-day classic promotions to major stage-race Tours which sent riders toiling over high mountain passes. Instead of journeying to a stadium and paying to see the racing, spectators were given a free show outside their own front doors by the 'giants of the road'. The indoor tracks nevertheless continued to play an important part in the sport. (They have an atmosphere all their own, compounded of cigarette smoke, loudspeaker announcements, catcalls floating down from the gallery, riders crashing heavily when speeding in a tight bunch round the steep bankings, sudden laughter, shouts, bursts of enthusiasm). When the road-racing season finished in autumn the winter velodromes became a refuge and a meeting-place for cycling fans. In 1976, however, road-racing is far and away more popular than track-racing in most countries.

I have already traced the 'true story' of the 'giants of the road', in my descriptions of the various periods in the history of the sport. We might sum them up as 'the heroic age' (1903–18); 'the classic era' (1919–36); 'the stormy period' (1937–48); the age of the indisputably 'great' champions (1949–55); the age of the two contrasting types – 'the "rouleur" and the "puncher"' (1956–65); and the solitary reign of the 'greatest champion of all' (1966–7?). Now let us take a look at the outstanding riders whose story best symbolises those 75 years of enormously varied road competitions.

## The last 200 metres

The road-racer's sprint, or turn of speed, is his decisive weapon. You could say that he has some kind of cross-bow built into his cranks which shoots him out of the madly sprinting field and sends him streaking like an arrow towards the line. Once in sight of the 'Finish' banner, however exhausted he may be, the sprinter always has a chance of winning because he is the only one who can make his legs spin fast enough, the only one who possesses the mysterious ability to gather all his forces together at the crucial moment. In the earlier stages his jittery spurts put his rivals to the test and sometimes enable him to 'find an opening'.

The sprinter is best suited to the classic races, to one-day events and Tour stages on flat roads. Any rider who has him on his tail up to the last 200 metres is bound to rue the day.

Some of the greatest champions hold this vital trump-card, which enables them to notch up wins at a remarkable rate. We might mention in this category the following riders, although several of them had other skills in their repertoire as well as the final sprint: Octave Lapize and Lucien Petit-Breton (France), both of whom were killed in the First World War; Costante Girardengo (Italy), the first *campionissimo*, who beat another thoroughbred,

*Fausto Coppi (Italy) who, until the advent of Eddy Merckx, was considered to be the greatest of all racing cyclists. His feats ranged from two world 5000 metres pursuit championships on the track, to five victories in the 21-day Tour of Italy road race; he held the world hour track record for 14 years, and was world professional road champion in 1953. Coppi's long list of triumphs include the Tour de France (twice), Milan-San Remo (three times) and the Tour of Lombardy (five times). He also won a sensational Paris-Roubaix in 1950. In 1960 at the age of 40 Coppi died from malaria after returning from a hunting expedition in Africa.*

Henri Pelissier (France), by a mere quarter of a wheel in the 1924 Grand Prix Wolber; Pelissier's intelligence and original views helped to advance the sport of cycling; another champion from the same period is Henri Suter (Switzerland). Then comes Georges Ronsse (Belgium), whose talent was revealed in the 1927 Paris-Roubaix when he was only 20; André Leducq (France), who for many years held the record for winning the largest number of stages in the Tour de France – 25 altogether; Charles Pelissier (France), Henri Pelissier's popular brother, a thoroughbred racing cyclist known as 'Charlot' or 'Charlie'; Georges Speicher and Roger Lapebie (France), the elegant Jean Aerts (Belgium) and his compatriot Eloi Meulenberg, a stubborn competitor in the same mould as the French cyclists René Le Grevès and Paul Maye. Then there were other Belgian fireballs, generally Flemish who had learned their trade in

the tough school of Kermesse road races. 'Rik' van Steenbergen, a giant of a man who was as effective as a road-racer as on the track; 'Brik' Schotte; 'Fred' Debruyne; 'Rik' van Looy, who towered over one-day events in the same way as the French 'rouleur' Jacques Anquetil did at the same period over long-distance stage races. And of course 'Ferdi' Kubler from Switzerland, with his fiendish grin; Miguel Poblet from Spain; the pale-faced, bespectacled Dutchman Jan Janssen; Marino Basso from Italy; Walter Godefroot, who specialised in races at record-breaking average speeds, Roger de Vlaeminck, known as 'the Gipsy', Rik van Linden and Freddy Maertens.

As we run through the list of these human arrows a whole world of dramatic finishes, of surging packs of riders, of collisions and crashes, rises up before us. How exciting it all is for spectators watching these furious ding-dong battles, which are nowadays contested at 60 km/h (35 mph)!

33

# The 'Rouleurs'

Though the 'rouleurs' only rarely use the explosive kind of speed favoured by the sprinters, they can keep up a very fast pace over long distances without worrying about their rivals. It is very difficult, indeed almost impossible, to outpace them if they are riding hard. On the other hand if they manage to open up a gap their rivals will be hard put to close it, no matter how seriously they combine forces as a chasing group. The next time we see them they will be clutching the victor's bouquet!

Maurice Garin, who stole the show in the first Tour de France, seemed indefatigable. He also won the second race between Paris and Brest and back, in 1901, displaying long-distance qualities that were shared by two of his successors, the cheerful Louis Mottiat (1921) and the excellent Australian Hubert Opperman (1931). Cyrille van Hauwaert, 'the lion of Flanders', and François Faber of Luxembourg were unusually powerful 'rouleurs', while no one could equal Gustave Garrigou's steady pace. Eugène Christophe (France), 'the old Gaul', was courage incarnate; Philippe Thys (Belgium), who won the Tour de France organised by L'Auto three times; Francis Pelissier (France) who specialised in the Bordeaux-Paris race; Gaston Rebry (Belgium), who bounced over the cobblestones like a little round ball in the Paris-Roubaix race which he won three times; Learco Guerra (Italy), world champion in a 170 km time-trial at Copenhagen in 1931 – they were like so many machines tirelessly churning out the kilometres.

In time trial events the contestants battle it out alone, racing against the clock and never enjoying the advantage of the support and shelter offered by the gregarious 'pack'. After the Second World War the majority of famous 'rouleurs' demonstrated their prowess against the watch, though Fiorenzo Magni (Italy) also performed splendidly on the slippery roads of the Tour of Flanders, which is a one day mass-start race on flat roads. Hugo Koblet, le pédaleur de charme; Ercole Baldini from the Romagna; the steady German ace Rudi Altig; the French cyclists Roger Rivière and Jacques Anquetil (Anquetil improved on his pre-

*The 'Angel of the Mountain', Charly Gaul of Luxembourg, rides through a snow-flanked corridor high up in the Dolomite mountains. He was a stage-race specialist who twice won the Giro d'Italia (1956 and 1959), and the 1958 Tour de France, through brilliant mountain climbing. Gaul sat very still on his bicycle, rarely moved out of the saddle, and rapidly twirled gears several inches lower than those of his rivals.*

*Jacques Anquetil (France) was the master time-trialist, but here he is seen battling on a mountain col, still with his stretched-out position on the bicycle. Anquetil is wearing the yellow jersey, symbol of leadership in the Tour de France which he won in 1957, and then every year from 1961 to 1964. That record of five victories has since been equalled by Eddy Merckx. Anquetil also twice won the Tour of Italy, and the Tour of Spain once.*

*Originally a track rider, Tom Simpson won an Olympic bronze medal with the British pursuit team in the 1956 Olympic Games. Then he went to Brittany to learn the road game. Turning professional in late 1959 Tom immediately finished fourth in the world championship, but had to wait six years before he took that greatest of all titles in Spain. In the meantime he had collected classic race victories such as the Tour of Flanders, Milan-San Remo and Bordeaux-Paris, and later added the Tour of Lombardy and Paris-Nice to his store. In 1962 Tom Simpson was the first (and only) British rider to wear the yellow jersey as leader of the Tour de France – he finished 6th overall. When Tom collapsed and died during a mountain stage of the 1967 Tour de France the sport lost not only a great competitor but one of its most respected and likeable characters.*

vious best every time he raced and his admirably pure style helped him to carry off the Grand Prix des Nations nine times); Felice Gimondi from Bergamo; Luis Ocana, a Spaniard from the Landes region of France; plus of course the amazing Eddy Merckx with his long string of wins – all of these athletes could ride on their own a minute or so ahead of the field, and not only defy the efforts of the chasers to 'bring them back' but even increase the lead when the pace slackened momentarily (the rhythm of a big pack of riders is punctuated by bursts of speed, followed by lulls). Two notable amateurs

from Eastern Europe should also be mentioned among the 'rouleurs', Gustav-Adolf Schur (East Germany) and Ryszard Szurkowski (Poland). Several of the professionals appear on the list of unpaced Hour Record holders which, as has been emphasised, contains only the names of outstanding champions.

## The 'kings of the mountain'

When the road starts to climb up towards the sky and to describe a series of hairpin bends, the forest gradually gives way to alpine pastures or gravelly marl and the air gets clearer and keener – the moment of truth is at hand. The 'climbers' soon appear at the front and then start drawing away from the pack. Sometimes they will be featherweights who are helped by an auspicious ratio of weight to strength, sometimes they will be athletes with long legs. Some of them really torture their machines, while others rest their hands on the top of the handlebars and never get out of the saddle, and others jerk forward by 'dancing' on the pedals.

The true 'hill climb', which is very short, is becoming increasingly rare. It is on the mountain roads of stage-races that the specialists have a chance to show their paces, either outside the overall classification (because they have lost too much ground on the flat) or by turning a tricky situation to their advantage and thus making sure of winning the whole Tour. 'Climbers' are few and far between but they are popular with the fans, who travel miles up the major mountain passes, applauding their heroes as they race ahead when all the others are suffering agonies.

The first 'king of the mountain' was René Pottier (France), who won the Tour de France stages over the Ballon d'Alsace in 1905 and 1906. Then in 1911 Emile Georget (France) reached the top of the Galibier pass in the Alps ahead of the field. In the twenties the aces were Ottavio Bottechia (Italy), Lucien Buysse (Belgium), the hero of the Bayonne to Luchon stage in 1926 which was run in a downpour, and Nicholas Frantz (Luxembourg), whose handlebars were bent downwards in the middle. Then came Alfredo Binda (Italy), whose climbing style was perhaps the cleanest ever, Antonin Magne (France), René Vietto (France), a prodigy at 20, the solid Sylvère Maës and his Belgian compatriot Félicien Vervaecke.

Gino Bartali (Italy) was unbeatable before the Second World War and reappeared when it was over. He held his own until he was beaten by the unforgettable Fausto Coppi. Jean Robic, with his famous leather helmet, did not accept defeat easily, and Louison Bobet, whose gifts as a sprinter and 'rouleur' were also far from negligible, carved out his successes in the 1953 and 1954 Tours de France on the Izoard pass in the Alps. The most characteristic exponents of this type of race since 1955 – and people are always saying that it is a dying art –

*Gino Bartali (Italy) was a great hill-climber and rival of Fausto Coppi. Their battles had Italy in a fever of excitement. It was feared that the Second World War had ruined Bartali's career – he had already won the Tour of Italy, the Tour de France and other big races – but he came back to gain even greater fame. Most notable were his wins in the 1946 Italian marathon and 1948 'Tour', in each case 10 years after his pre-war victories. They called him 'the old one', 'Gino the Devout', 'the iron man'. Here he is the mountaineer, riding in the Alps during his second Tour de France win in 1948.*

are the baby-faced Charly Gaul (Luxembourg), the temperamental Federico Bahamontes (Spain), known as 'El Picador', and his compatriots Julio Jimenez and José-Manuel Fuente, though their endurance was not as great as the man from Toledo's; Lucien van Impe (Belgium) and Raymond Poulidor and Bernard Thévenet (France), whose physique bears no resemblance to that of the 'mountain fleas'.

The hill-climber shines on those parts of the course where human effort is a stirring sight. Those who frequent road races, the professional camp-followers such as journalists and sports reporters, who might well be blasé about it all, are invariably gripped by the tension that dominates the scene. The moment when the 'mountain kings' take off, the magnificence of their exploits enhanced by the natural backcloth against which they take place, remains one of the most extraordinary moments in the sport of cycling – and those aren't just words.

A cycle race is a wonderful adventure, 'depending on the ground and the climate, the weather and the wind' – no one has ever put it better than Antoine Blondin. A cycle race is the joy of struggling to win, of overcoming pain and difficulty, full of colour and laughter. The racing cyclist experiences these emotions and feelings to an intense degree. But the spectator appreciates the true beauty of the race in his own way, together with the true meaning of the moving spectacle that flashes before him.

Once they have reached the finishing line the faces of the racers relax, no matter how weary they are. Or if this does not happen at once, it will a few hours later when they relive the tough moments spent 'in the saddle', either by listening to a commentary on the race or by thinking back to it.

The general public studies the champions carefully, catches a cap as it goes flying past, takes up a squashed bun with a thrill of delight because it has fallen from one of his heroes' lips, snatches at a comment here, begs for an autograph there, shows the way to the hotel or lays siege to the car in which the athlete has taken refuge.

Admirers male and female, cyclists, their relations and friends – they have all been taken out of themselves for those fleeting minutes snatched from the greyness of everyday life and have recaptured the essence of life – the salty taste of spring, youth and the glow of life.

In other words: freedom on two wheels.

*The bicycle, dream object, as seen by the painter Denis Rivière.*

# II
# THE WHOLE GAMUT OF CYCLING

OPPOSITE: *There are no problems when you want to park a bicycle in Denmark, but finding the right machine later is another matter. Most of the machines parked here are of the roadster or utility type which are still in great demand despite the increased popularity of the lightweight model.* ABOVE *is a Raleigh ladies' machine with a modern type of frame.* BELOW: *the Batavus Favoriet from the Netherlands has a loop frame, chain and dress guards.*

The 'open' frame is the most suitable design for women who do not take part in competition cycling. As well as giving increased rigidity, the twin stays running from the head tube to the rear fork ends also provide good anchorage for the brake.

# Every man his bike

'The first rays cast by the nickel on one's first bicycle are sweeter than the first rays of the dawn'. This sentence penned by some poet who hymned the bicycle surely remains true today in its naive and old-fashioned lyricism.

We have been dreaming of this first bicycle, hoping for it, waiting for it. But now that it is right there in front of us it is even lovelier than imagined and we can hardly believe it. 'Is it really mine?' 'Yes, it's all yours'.

The joy the small child feels when he discovers the tricycle, or the bicycle with stabilisers, that Father Christmas has left for him beneath the branches of the Christmas tree is one of the sweetest moments of all. But what about the joy of the small boy who, at the age of about twelve, steps into the local bike shop clutching his father's hand and leaves the shop trembling slightly, clutching *his* bike by the handlebars? 'Is it really mine?' 'Yes, it's all yours'.

Nowadays bicycles are being used less and less as a functional piece of equipment for getting to work. We go by public transport, or by car, not to mention the motorised bikes that boys and girls use for going to school. But cycling as a leisure activity has staged a comeback and bicycles are being used for outings, for touring and short races. The joy of the child whose first bike brought such happiness is complemented by the pleasure experienced by the adult who returns to his first love and acquires a lightweight, beautifully finished model that bears little resemblance to the sturdy roadster of his childhood.

You can find bikes to suit all tastes, all skills and every purse – ranging from the child's 'bike' to the champion's racing model, from the 'Dutch' version with raised handlebars to the fine 'Randonneur' models made to measure by a skilled craftsman. France has a 'stock' of approximately twelve million bicycles in 1976, or one for every five members of the population. The annual production figures for the main manufacturers with worldwide reputations are roughly as follows: USA, 10 000 000; Japan, 8 000 000; Soviet Union, 3 500 000; West Germany, 3 200 000; Great Britain, 2 750 000; India, 2 600 000; France, 2 500 000; Italy and Taiwan, 2 000 000; Austria, 1 250 000; Holland, 1 000 000. You can't help being struck by the number of bicycles recently put on to the market.*

## A young cyclist has to grow up one day

'Apparently I was a prodigy in the sense that I could ride a bike at 18 months. I can see you smiling.'

'With the help of stabilisers . . .'

'No! My father had taught me to keep my balance at an age when other children have only just learned to walk. Apparently, although I'd learnt to balance by now, and could guide my tiny bike down a slight slope, I hadn't yet grasped the point that I needed to push with my legs to move the contraption forwards. . .

'I've often been told that when I was barely two and a half I would go on six kilometre [three and a half miles] bike rides from Saint-Meen to Saint-Tonen, astonishing the local farmers as they watched a chubby-cheeked baby ride merrily past.

'My father was prouder than I was. He was like a dog with two tails. He showed me off to the whole village with touching pride.

' "Look at my Louison," he would say.'†

Not all the mini-cyclists become world champions like Louison Bobet, but their little legs somehow manage to pedal away on their very first bikes, helping to satisfy to their heart's content the instinctive need for activity and movement.

When they are very young they will ride 'baby models', with long seat pillars and ultra-adjustable handlebars so that the bike can grow with them. Generally stabilisers enable the child to start riding a bike without having to face the problem of keeping his balance (although stabilisers are not always as easy to adjust or as simple as the salesman makes out, without bothering to explain the system properly). Then one day, sooner or later, depending on the pupil's natural aptitude, the day comes when he has learnt how to propel himself forwards. The stabilisers are removed and the little boy or girl will soon be able to ride gaily off under the delighted, or suddenly nervous, gaze of their parents. The parents, although they do not fully realize it, are sometimes quite right to be anxious – the brakes may not work properly, especially as small children are not very good at handling them.

Who would ever have thought that 'fashion' would play its part in the field of children's bicycles?

*Figures by la Chambre Syndicale Nationale du Cycle et du Motocycle, Paris.
†Louison Bobet: *Mes vélos et moi*. Editions du Lys, 1951.

But it does. For instance nowadays the traditional handlebars seem to have been superseded by a new design that originated in Italy, with high grips and concave in the middle. In a few years this will doubtless give way to some new design.

The diameter of the wheels gradually increases. First it was 12.25 in and now it's as much as 16 or 18 in. The child's coming up to seven by now. In some cases he will already have experienced the thrill of pedalling on a sort of scaled-down version of a racing cycle. Opinion is divided on this subject, but it must be admitted that children do look adorable on them. And how many people realize that a five-year-old child, or thereabouts, is perfectly capable of covering a distance of up to 18 miles? He should take his time, of course, and be accompanied by his parents or by some other adults prepared to ride slowly and steadily and watch him all the time.

Bikes for ten-year-olds have a wheel diameter of 600 mm (24 in). Apart from this boys and girls have a choice of models that is almost the same as the range available for adults. Touring models, semi-racing models, even racing models – after all when they reach the age of 14 French boys can take part in beginners' events, while coaching classes give an introduction to competition riding to those not yet old enough to be issued with racing licences by the National Federation. At this stage, however, such activities are officially described as 'cycling games'. Across the Channel juvenile cycling is very well organised, with the English Schools Cycling Association supervising a wide programme of local and national events for boys and girls, including championships for road racing, time-trials, track racing and cyclo-cross!

The English-speaking countries are also responsible for the introduction of yet another type of bike. The new gadget is called a 'chopper' and some teenagers find it great fun, though it makes the purists shudder. It combines the principles of cycling with the sort of equipment needed, perhaps not for a car, but at any rate for a motorcycle – broad tyres, a huge saddle, a vague approximation to a shock-absorber, and a gear box.

Very little is usually said about all the various children's bicycles, but we should not neglect this aspect of the cycling industry. After all, although for many children a bike is just one more toy, for some of them 'my first bike' is a lovely memory. Such children will for the rest of their lives have a special affection for cycling.

## 'Carrier bikes' versus 'mini-bikes'

Napalm bombs, roads caved in, ultra-modern logistics – yet none of these has made a scrap of difference. After their country had endured the terrible ordeal of a modern version of the Thirty Years' War the Vietnamese went on going about their business – or, in many cases, fighting the war – perched firmly on a bicycle. A bicycle will stand up to anything, and as well as a heavy-weight rider can easily carry loads of 50 kg (112 lb) or even more. The bikes were more often pushed than ridden, but that does not alter the fact that right to the end of the war the Vietnamese peasants countered the air-lift with a bike-lift. This was, of course, taking things to extremes, but after all it was all in the spirit of the tradition whereby farmers struggle alongside roads or across fields with ancient bicycles, all rusty and caked with mud, but still rideable. As recently as 1971 a survey showed that 63 per cent of the families of French farmers owned bicycles. The figure for the families of semi-skilled workers and unskilled labourers was 48.6 per cent, and for foremen and skilled workers it was 43.5 per cent. These figures are striking, for they show that 'non-motorised' two-wheeled vehicles are still widely used as functional everyday objects. On this level we are talking on the whole about a bike on the classical model, with straight handlebars and a pretty basic design, and 'single speed' – approximately 10 per cent of the cycles produced in France in 1974 had only one gear.

The 'carrier-bike', used by licensed delivery boys and roundsmen of all kinds, is the typical urban example of this type of bicycle. It is still being made, though it is occasionally improved by being equipped with a hub three-speed gear – on the principle that the mechanism in the hub is protected against dirt, wet and any type of impact. The days when hordes of paper boys raced round Paris to deliver each edition as it came out, with their bundle strapped to the front luggage-rack, are over now. And the golden age enjoyed by carrier tricycles during the Occupation was short-lived. (Tricycle races were organised, the star performer being Marcel Cognasson.) But deliveries are not by any means a thing of the past and the bicycle is still competing with the light-weight motor-bike.

My reason for turning for a moment to 'standard' mass produced models is that there is a marked tendency to ignore the important part they played, and still play, in providing a means of transport in the 20th century. (Incidentally, firms such as Raleigh have recently managed to bring out 'standard' models that seem to be much more highly finished than before.) In direct contrast to these, showing the wide range of potential variants, are the mini-bike and the folding bike – of which a 'real cyclist' vehemently disapproves, calling them 'a heresy'.

'Heresy. The word isn't strong enough, sir! A book on bicycles should not even give house room to these scaled-down models, these half-breed variants . . .' That's all very well. Whatever I feel about them personally it would be unreasonable to cross them off the map altogether, for the fact is that mini-bikes have spread like wildfire over the last ten years, and have played their part in the revival of what you and I still believe to be the only true 'bicycle'.

In 1962 a British engineer called Alex Moulton presented a comic-looking curiosity to those who visited the London Cycling Show. It had 40 cm (16 in) wheels, and instead of being joined to the top of the fork at the base of the saddle stem the frame formed a central bar.

A few years later sales figures for the Moulton in the English-speaking world approached a quarter of a million. Its success was probably partly due to its remarkably good suspension, but chiefly to the fact that it corresponded to one of the requirements of the age by taking up very little space. On the continent of Europe research was beginning to go in this direction as well. When the political and social crisis erupted in France in 1968, resulting indirectly in a temporary halt on motor-fuel deliveries, the general public were forced to rush off to the cycle shops and buy up all the available stocks. Sales of mini-bikes went up dramatically, and folding models were particularly popular.

But it would be wrong to see these little bikes with articulated frames as a radical innovation. At the end of the 19th century the military bicycle ridden by one Captain Gérard could be folded up, and so could one of the models in the catalogue of a firm such as Gladiator, although in each case these were machines of standard size. For those of our contemporaries who have just rediscovered with something of a shock the once-familiar pleasure of getting about under one's own steam by sheer muscle power, the 'mini-bike', especially the folding variety, suddenly appeared, offering a panacea for all ills. There seemed to be little difficulty in finding somewhere to put it, even in the cramped quarters most of us live in today. And then there's the crunch argument – now that the car is forging ahead once again a folding bike can easily go into the town-dweller's boot when he sets off for a weekend in the country.

The craze for folding bikes soon spread to children's models, to the extent that in 1975 one major French manufacturer* stated that they were making 15 per cent folding bikes for children and 25 per cent for adults, with 550–600 mm (22 to 24 in) wheels. This was in spite of strong opposition from those who favour the classic design, and see the unstable mini-bikes, which aren't very pleasant to ride on a steepish slope, as a mere catch-penny or a trick to take in the public.

Yet the mini-bike manufacturers deserve credit for having enticed large numbers of adults back to the idea of cycling. They suddenly acquire a taste for the idea of pedalling merrily along and one fine

*'L'Officiel du cycle', September, 1975.

day they decide that they really must have 'a bike worthy of the name'. And so they join the band of people who own a touring or racing model, and we too – now that we have opened our readers' eyes to the mini-reality – will now join them.

## Touring and competition cycling

Although a fine bicycle does not necessarily make a fine rider, it does help him to look good, to ride efficiently and to enjoy himself. It is an amazing experience when you get on to a racing bicycle for the first time – you seem to be gliding along on the wings of the breeze, and the design seems to be so perfect that you hardly need to move a muscle yourself. Unless you are a trained cyclist however, a longish hill will soon make you feel heavy and unwieldy. You will find yourself in agony, gasping for breath, with a rasping sound in your throat and your legs like jelly. A fine bike will not do the trick on its own – but it is a great help.

Nowadays mass production means that anyone can buy a good high-efficiency model. All the same, the 'semi-racer' (the very term conjures up for many teenagers their first dreams about tearing away up a mountainside and splendid victories) is still inferior to the best and most up-to-date cycles from the point of view of finish, lightness and efficiency. People are amazed to find that the price of a bicycle can vary enormously, with the most expensive models ten times dearer than the cheapest (ranging, say, from £50 to £500 – though some go even higher than that). It is, perhaps, not so surprising when you realize that they vary enormously in the type of metal used, in weight-saving measures employed, in the quality of their accessories, and particularly in the time they take to assemble. On the assembly line there is no time to be lost or the daily production figures will drop – so if some part or other does not fit all that well, too bad, we'll just force it a bit and there she goes – next one, please!

In other words, although modern assembly lines do turn out goods of a high average quality, and most firms offer a very wide range of the various possible types of machine, it is still true to say that anyone who wants to buy a bicycle will always do better if (following the advice of an expert if he does not know enough about the ins-and-outs himself), he goes for a top-class model with high-quality accessories.

His choice will of course depend on whether he wants a touring or a racing model. The basic principles are the same when it comes to the crucial factor – the design of the frame. It is generally agreed that the frame size, i.e. the length of the tube running from the bottom bracket to the point where the seat pillar begins, should be 25 cm (10 in) less than your inside-leg measurement. In other words your overall size does not have any direct bearing

*A strange bouquet. Front forks ▶ by the hundred. Although technically part of the frame, forks move freely and, coupled to the handlebars, form the steering unit of the bicycle.*

While the annual output of the great cycle factories runs into millions of machines, the traditional 'lightweight maker' produces only two or three hand-built frames a week in a small workshop at the back of his business premises. When the main tubes, seat and chain stays have been brazed together the frame is subjected to alignment tests. ABOVE: a tracking jig is fixed to the bottom bracket to check that the main members are parallel. RIGHT: Touching the head and seat tubes, the long straight-edge has an adjustable piece which passes inside the lower rear triangle and verifies that the two 'ends' are correctly positioned. LOWER RIGHT: The front forks are given the 'roll' test which immediately reveals whether or not the two blades are parallel. As well as for checking new machines, these jigs are frequently used for assessing damage to frames involved in accidents.

48

*A link in the production chain. A naked frame is gradually clothed with transmission, mudguards, wheels, handlebars. The machine is packed and dispatched to the four corners of the globe.*

*Alex Moulton and his brainchild which in 1962 began the fashion for mini-bicycles. Unlike his imitators, Mr Moulton offered something more than two small wheels which, on their own, are less comfortable to ride than conventional 26 or 27 in wheels. The 'Moulton' had patented spring rubber suspension in the head column and in the swinging arm at the rear of the main tube.*

on the question – it's the length of your legs that counts. However, it is possible to lay down rough guidelines for someone with average proportions. The following generally accepted table will give the beginner an idea of what to look for before he finally makes up his mind and puts in a firm order.

| Height of cyclist | Height of frame |
|---|---|
| 160–5 cm (5 ft 3 in–5 ft 5 in) | 51–3 cm (20–21 in) |
| 165–70 cm (5 ft 5 in–5 ft 7 in) | 53–5 cm (21–21½ in) |
| 170–5 cm (5 ft 7 in–5 ft 9 in) | 55–7 cm (21½–22½ in) |
| 175–80 cm (5 ft 9 in–5 ft 11 in) | 57–8 cm (22½–22¾ in) |
| 180–3 cm (5 ft 11 in–6 ft 0½ in) | 58–9 cm (22¾–23 in) |
| 183 cm + (6 ft 0½ in and over) | 60  cm (24 in) |

The second factor you must bear in mind is the 'Trail'. This means the distance between a vertical line drawn down to the ground from the front-wheel axle to the vertical line you get if you follow the head tube down to the ground. All this may sound rather theoretical, but if you were to compare the bicycle as it was in 1925 with one of today's models you would realize straight away that its 'Trail' was greater, which explains why it had great stability when you were riding downhill but was hard to steer, as though you were running along fixed tramlines. Today's model, on the other hand, has a 'Trail' of the order of 60 mm (2·4 in) and is therefore more supple, which makes up for the fact that it does wobble more than its predecessors. This drop in the 'Trail' is accompanied by a corresponding drop in the distance between the front axles: i.e. from the front hub to the bottom bracket. This, too, makes the cycle easier to handle and helps the rider to shelter behind his rivals.

Of course, many other factors affect the design of the frame, but you will need to turn to a technical manual for full details. We recommend the work of the very experienced French author Daniel Rebour, with its admirably clear explanatory texts, and excellent sketches, for which he is rightly famous. In particular we recommend his most recent book, *Cycles de compétition et randonneuses* (Technique et Vulgarisation 1975).

The main difference between touring and racing bicycles is the owner's state of mind. The racing cyclist is looking for a fast, streamlined machine, while the touring cyclist needs to ride in the most varied conditions – and pretty rough conditions at times – so he is interested in things such as the lighting, the luggage-rack, wired-on tyres and the mudguards.

This is, of course, an over-simplification. When he is in training the racing cyclist is no longer the demigod who flew past admiring crowds – he's just an ordinary human being, bound by the Highway Code like anyone else and therefore compelled, for instance, to have proper lights, which are anyway extremely useful if he sets off at crack of dawn or

comes back after dark; once winter comes, unless he lives in a Mediterranean climate, he will need mudguards. Similarly, the touring cyclist is now and again 'bitten by the speed bug', particularly if he takes part in the *cyclosportif* type of trial and will have to pedal as hard as if he were in a proper race. If so, he too will want his machine to be as light as possible and some of the classic equipment is therefore pared down to the minimum.

Both in the racing and touring fields the designers and craftsmen have managed to perfect their techniques and to produce some really magnificent machines.

Of course, you have to know how to get the best out of them. Which explains why one word is so important: 'position'.

## Position

When the technical boys say that a racing cyclist has 'a good position' on his machine their faces light up because it usually follows that a rider's pedalling style will be as attractive as it is effective. Good positioning is a big step towards a good performance, for it is an effective way of combating tiredness.

This holds good for anyone who rides a bicycle.

So how should the beginner set about acquiring the correct position? First of all he must select a correctly proportioned frame, on the lines already discussed. All we need add by way of further clarification is that 'rouleurs' generally sit well back, because what they are after is streamlining, whereas hill-climbers specify a shorter top tube in proportion so that their centre of gravity is further forward.

Next, the position of the saddle. There is no point in having this pointing downwards at an eccentric angle, because you always would be sliding forward; on the other hand it is just as bad to have it tilted presumptuously skywards. Always stick rigidly to the horizontal position. As for the height, when you are seated on the saddle with your *heels* on the pedals and with one pedal depressed to its lowest point, the lower leg should retain its slight natural bend behind the knee. If it was completely straight you would soon start getting cramp if you rode for any length of time over difficult terrain. On the other hand if the knee was bent too far it would be very difficult to pedal smoothly, quite apart from the fact that it doesn't exactly help your breathing to have your knees bunched up into your stomach! Obviously you should make sure that you are not wearing ordinary 'town' shoes with any sort of a heel when adjusting your 'position' because this would completely ruin your calculations. When trying out a bike for size you can do it while stationary, by supporting yourself with one hand pressed against a wall, making sure the bike itself is parallel to the wall, then pedalling in space, doing the normal pedalling movement back to front, as it were. Alternatively you can test it while actually riding, but in that case you are liable to be distracted by other factors that need your attention and may go wrong in your calculations.

If the height of the frame has been worked out correctly, the seat pillar will protrude about 10 cm (4 in) from the seat tube, though this will be much higher for a tall man since a good frame should never be more than 60 cm (24 in). A saddle can, of course, be moved laterally as well as vertically; for the newcomer to cycling who is of average height, the saddle tip should be about 5 cm (2 in) behind an imaginary vertical line drawn up through the middle of the bottom bracket axle. The competition cyclist will study this matter much more scientifically, taking into consideration the length of his thighs and the type of competition he has in mind.

We now come to the position of the last major component, the handlebars, bearing in mind that for road-racing the top of the arc should be slightly lower than the top of the saddle. Considering that the saddle has already been adjusted more or less finally, it is only logical that the length of the handlebar stem should depend on the length of the cyclist's arms rather than his overall height. A racing cyclist about 1.75 m (5 ft 9 in) tall will normally need a handlebar stem about 10 cm (4 in) long, but if he has short or long arms he will go for a length of 9 cm (3.5 in) or 12 cm (4.75 in), as the case may be. In other words whether a racing cyclist gets 'down', on his dropped handlebars or holds them by the

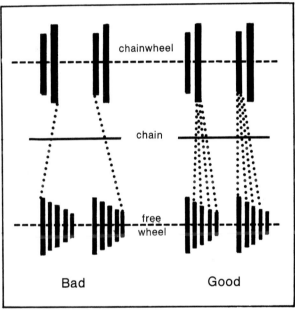

*The outline of a road frame with a 22·4 in seat tube and a bottom bracket 10·8 in above the ground. The tip of the saddle should be between 1·2 and 2 in behind a vertical line drawn up through the bottom bracket. Undue 'bending' of the chain should be avoided by users of derailleur gears.*

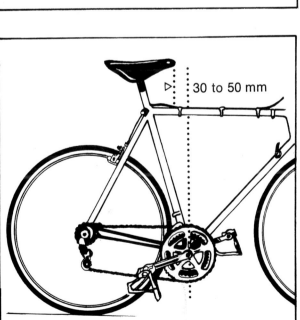

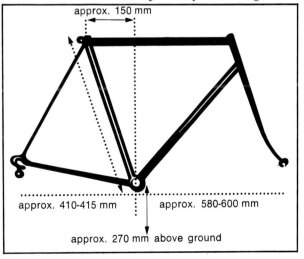

51

tops he must feel in complete control of his machine, be able to breathe easily or make an extra effort without having to tense his arms too much.

It should be understood that the right 'position' will only be found after a considerable distance has been covered on the bicycle, working on the principle of trial and error. It may be necessary to make certain alterations to suit the type of terrain covered. Eddy Merckx often takes a spanner from a jersey pocket and adjusts the height of his saddle when actually racing. Fortunately few care to imitate Eddy in this respect, for it would be highly dangerous if a big group of riders all decided to lower their saddles when descending a mountain road at 50 mph.

If the beginner follows the few simple guidelines we have just laid down he will avoid making serious mistakes, while the more experienced cyclist will be able to work out his correct position and decide whether or not a particular bicycle is right for him. Indeed, if his machine is equipped with a single fixed sprocket he will be virtually forced to find a positive solution to the problem, because the use of a 'fixed wheel' necessitates the smooth and regular pedalling action that can only be produced by a correctly-positioned rider.

So if you are going to enjoy your cycling to the full you must watch out for the three vital factors: the frame must be adjusted correctly to your own build and the saddle and the handlebars must be in the correct position. In point of fact these three factors are interdependent, although for the sake of clarity they have been dealt with separately.

'When my father came with me . . . that morning . . . to the foot of the first of the hills that occurred at intervals during the 20 km [12·5 mile] stretch between Castellania and Novi-Ligure I wasn't at all pleased. Or at least the only thing I was pleased about was the bike my brother Livio had given me; it was an elderly boneshaker . . . with a comfortable saddle; handlebars turning up at the ends just like my father's moustache and a lamp that rattled almost as loudly as the wheels did.*

And yet it was on this rattletrap that a skinny butcher's boy of 15 revealed his brilliant talent by pulling away from a bunch of racing cyclists on a training run. They never caught him for all their magnificent machines, their racing handlebars, their toe-clips and silk, tubular racing tyres.

There has only been one Fausto Coppi in the history of cycling. But there are bicycles available to suit every build, every temperament and every pocket.

*Fausto Coppi: *Le drame de ma vie*. Bibl. France-Soir, 1950.

# Bicycles For All

*In the following 12-page 'catalogue' of bicycles –
largely of French manufacture – prices are not given
because of fluctuating rates of exchange and import
duty. Comparable British machines range from £30
for children's models to £500 for hand-made super-
lightweights.*

# Racing and Trials

**LEJEUNE 110**

10 gears
Light brazed frame
Wheels: 700C two-colour tyres, chrome
    rims, 5-block freewheel
Chromium plated chainwheel
Front and rear derailleur
Mafac Racer brakes
Sponge covered plastic saddle
Pump, toe clips and straps
No mudguards; no lighting

**MOTOBECANE C1**

10 gears
Brazed frame
Wheels: Normandy quick release hubs,
    alloy rims
Alloy chainwheel
Alloy racing pedals
Side-pull brakes with alloy levers
Chromed racing handlebars. Four
    colours

**LEJEUNE 105 Interclub**

10 gears
Light frame, 20 to 25 inches, reinforced
    forks
Wheels: Record rims, quick release
    hubs, Wolber Junior tubular tyres
Chromium plated chainwheel set
Front and rear derailleur
Mafac Racer brakes
Covered plastic saddle

**GITANE Tour de l'Avenir**

10 gears
Racing frame, forks chromium plated
    Italian style
Simplex 'Prestige' derailleur
Wheels: Mavic alloy rims, Normandy
    Sport quick release hubs, freewheel
    16, 17, 18, 20, 22 teeth
Maxi Sugino alloy chainwheel set
Mafac Racer brakes
Racing saddle
Handlebar bend and stem

### PEUGEOT D.R.10L

10 gears
3 principal frame tubes Reynolds; Nervex lugs, Simplex ends
Stronglight alloy 49D double chainwheel, 42 and 52 teeth
Lyotard pedals with toe clips and straps
Front Simplex Prestige derailleur, rear Simplex 'Criterium'
Mafac Racer brakes
Ideale 80 saddle
Racing type pump

### RALEIGH Super Course

10 gears
All Reynolds 531 brazed frame with front and rear forks chromium plated
Wheels: 700C alloy rims, hand-made tyres, light metal large-flange quick release hubs
Alloy chainwheel set
Front and rear derailleur
Weinmann light centre pull brakes
Brooks leather saddle
Other features: Gear selection by 'Ratchet' system; Bluemels Super-light mudguards

### MERCIER Mont Cenis

10 gears
Three principal frame tubes Reynolds 531
Wheels: Chrome spokes, alloy rims, Campagnolo Record B quick release hubs; Tubular tyres
Stronglight Super 93 chainwheel set
Alloy racing pedals
Simplex derailleur
Mafac Competition brakes
Hide covered sponge saddle

### BIANCHI 423 Course Record 746

10 gears
Light frame, choice of sizes: 21.2 in, 22.0 in, 22.8 in, 23.6 in, 24.4 in
Wheels: extra light quick release hubs, Nisi rims
Ofnega chainwheel set
Campagnolo Nuovo grand sport derailleur
Universal 51 brakes
Chamois saddle
Alloy seat pillar and handlebars, forged stem
Weight $22\frac{3}{4}$ lb

### CILO 144 Professional

12 gears
Frame built from Reynolds 531 tubing
Shimano hubs
Clement tubular tyres
Shimano derailleur, chainwheel set and brakes
Sakae handlebars
Arius saddle
Shimano seat pillar

### MERCIER Tour de France

10 gears
All Reynolds frame, Cinelli fork crown
Primata Corsa tubular tyres, dural rims
Campagnolo chainwheel and headset
Nuovo Record Campagnolo derailleur
Campagnolo brakes
Hide covered sponge saddle
Alloy handlebars

## BIANCHI 511 Specialissima

12 gears
Frame in super light Colombus tubing
Super light Nisi rims with rustproof butted spokes
Regina Extra 'Oro' freewheel with 13, 14, 16, 18, 20, 22 teeth
Tubular tyres, 230 grams
Campagnolo gear
Campagnolo brakes
Chamois saddle
Super light handlebar and stem

## GITANE Olympic Record

12 gears
Light frame and forks
Extra light Mavic Montlhery anodised rims
Campagnolo gear
Campagnolo chainwheel set
Campagnolo brakes
Unica saddle
Cinelli handlebars
Impero pump
Supplied free: Gitane racing jersey and cap

## MOTOBECANE Tour de France

12 gears
Brazed-up frame and forks built with Reynolds 531 tubes
Wheels: Super Champion 'Arc en ciel' rims, Campagnolo 1035 wide flange hubs with 6-block freewheel, number of teeth to order. Clement tyres. Union chrome spokes
Campagnolo best chainwheel set, brakes and gear
Unicanitor saddle
Fluted Campagnolo seat pillar
Cinelli handlebars and stem

## BIANCHI
### Specialissima Superlight 430

12 gears
Frame built with Colombus extra light tubes
Wheels: Nisi extra light rims with butted rustproof spokes, special racing tubulars
Regina 'Oro' 6-block freewheel
Campagnolo Record Strada chainwheel set
Campagnolo Record Strada derailleur
Campagnolo Record Strada brakes
Chamois saddle
T.T.T. super light competition handlebars
Weight: 19.8 lb

## RALEIGH Team Professional

12 gears
Frame and forks all Reynolds 531 extra light, forks chromium plated, lightened Campagnolo ends
Vittoria silk tyres
Lightened bracket shell
Campagnolo Nuovo Record derailleur
Campagnolo brakes
Brooks Professional B17 saddle
Cinelli handlebars and stem

## LEJEUNE World Championship

10 gears
Frame and forks built with Reynolds extra light 531 tubes, chromium plated on copper
Wheels: Super Champion extra light rims, wide flange quick release hubs, chrome spokes, extra light silk tubular tyres
Campagnolo derailleur, brakes and chainwheel set
Brooks B17 Professional saddle
Italian handlebars
Toe clips, straps
Delivered with Lejeune professional jersey and racing hat

# Randonneur Bicycles

### LEJEUNE 54

3 gears
Brazed frame and forks
Wheels: 650 mm half-balloon white tyres
Chromium plated chainwheel and cranks
Plastic covered saddle
Handlebars with guidonnet brake levers
Aluminium mudguards with coloured bands
Lighting set
Chromium plated front and rear carriers
Pump, bell

### MERCIER C.T. 10

10 gears
Brazed frame and forks
650 × 35 two-colour tyres
Cottered chainwheel and cranks
Huret derailleur
Dural brakes with guidonnet levers
Semi-racing supple saddle
Other features: lighting set, Uginox mudguards, rear carrier and clips, front Randonneur carrier, Randonneur handlebars, tool bag and tools

### C.N.C. 247-8

8 gears
Steel frame
650 mm half-balloon tyres
Steel double chainwheel
Huret or Simplex gear to order
Mafac brakes
Supple plastic and foam saddle
Front and rear carriers
Lighting set

### MOTOBECANE St. T

10 gears
Brazed frame
White 650 × 35B tyres
BSA bottom bracket
Huret Allvit derailleur
Centre-pull alloy brakes with coupled levers
Chrome Randonneur handlebars
Racing saddle
Rustproof mudguards

## PEUGEOT PX 8L

10 gears
Chromed frame and forks
700 C wheels, alloy wide flange
Quick release hubs. Free wheel 14, 17,
  19, 21, 24 teeth
Chromed pedals and toeclips
Simplex Prestige derailleur
Mafac Racer brakes
Plastic saddle
Front carrier

## RALEIGH Rialto

10 gears
Brazed up frame with 20–30 Raleigh
  tubes
Light wide flange hubs with quick
  release
Raleigh three-arm steel chainwheel
  with chain protecting disc
Front and rear derailleurs
Weinmann centre-pull brakes
Brooks saddle
Rear carrier with clip

## GITANE Paris-Nice 1442

10 gears
Light frame with front and rear ends
  chromium plated
Wheels: Mavic alloy rims, Clement
  700 × 28 tyres, Maillard wide-flange
  quick release hubs, freewheel 14, 16,
  18, 21, 24 teeth
Chainwheel Sugino DJX 2 Custom
  Black with 42 and 50 teeth
Simplex Prestige derailleur
Mafac Racer brakes
Semi-racing saddle
Other features: Alloy racing handle-
  bars, Bluemels plastic mudguards,
  lighting set, toeclips and straps, pump

## GITANE tandem Paris-Brest GS

10 gears
Chrome fork ends
Chainwheel 36 and 52 teeth
650 × 35 wired on tyres, steel rims
Huret Super Allvit derailleur, handlebar
  control
Mafac brazed-pivot brakes

## PEUGEOT PX 60

10 gears
Frame built with Reynolds tubes,
  chromed forks
Wheels: 700C, Normandy wide flange
  hubs quick release
Stronglight alloy 99 chainwheel set
Simplex 'Super Competition' front derailleur, 'Criterium' rear
Other features: Anodised alloy handlebars and stem; Simplex seat pillar,
  toeclips

# Touring Bicycles

### MERCIER R.L. 10

10 gears
Steel frame, half-chromed forks
Wheels: 700C, alloy rims, Normandy
  Sport wide flange quick release hubs
Stronglight chainwheel set
Mafac Racer brakes
Padded saddle
Front carrier
Alloy mudguards

### LEJEUNE Fédéral

10 gears
Frame size to order
Wheels: 700C Wolber open sided tyres,
  Super Champion alloy rims, quick
  release hubs
Mafac Racer brakes
Competition saddle
Other features: Alloy handlebars and
  stem, Uginox mudguards, lighting
  set, special 'cyclo' chrome front
  carrier, pump

### RALEIGH Super Tourer

10 gears
Frame built with Reynolds light 531
  tubes
Special Raleigh chainwheel set with
  chain protector
Raleigh front and rear derailleur
Weinmann Symmetric brakes
Brooks saddle

### LEJEUNE Fédéral 16

10 gears
Three principal frame tubes Reynolds
  531
Wheels: 700C Wolber open sided tyres
Stronglight 93 or TA chainwheel set
Atom No. 600 pedals, toeclips and
  straps
Mafac Racer brakes
Leather covered plastic or leather
  competition saddle
Bluemels mudguards
Special cyclo chromed front carrier
Racing pump

## GITANE Fédéral 1335

15 gears

Frame built with Reynolds tubes, front and rear chromed fork ends

Wheels: 700 × 26C Clement tyres, Mavic alloy rims, Normandy Competition quick release hubs, freewheel with 14, 17, 20, 24, 28 teeth

Stronglight Super 99 triple chainwheel set with 36, 45, 52 teeth

Lyotard pedals

Huret Challenger derailleur

Mafac Racer brakes

Ideale 2002 saddle

Other features: alloy handlebars and stem, spoke protector, toeclips and straps, racing pump, Dynamobloc lighting set, Bluemels 'Classique' mudguards

## PEUGEOT PY 60P

10 or 15 gears

Frame entirely hand made with Reynolds tubes, ends chromed, Nervex crown, Simplex ends

Wheels: Small or wide flange alloy quick release hubs, alloy rims, 700 × 28C 'tubular style' wired-on tyres, 5 block freewheel with 13 to 28 teeth to choice, chromed tied and soldered spokes

Stronglight 99 alloy double or triple chainwheel set with teeth from 28 to 53 to choice

Front and rear Simplex Super LJ derailleurs

Mafac anodised 2000 alloy brakes

Ideale 2002 saddle, Simplex pillar

Stronglight Super Competition headset

Forged alloy handlebars and stem

## MOTOBECANE Fédéral

15 gears

Three principal frame tubes Reynolds 531

Wheels: Alloy Super Champion rims, Wolber super sport 700C tyres, wide flange Luxe competition quick release hubs, 5-block freewheel

Alloy TA Professional triple chainwheel set

Steel semi-racing pedals with approved reflectors

Huret Super Allvit rear derailleur, Allvit front

Mafac Criterium brakes brazed to stays and forks

Ideale DR saddle

Cyclotouriste handlebars with Phillippe alloy stem

Polished steel Uginox rustproof mudguards

61

# Junior and Ladies

### MOTOBECANE B.E.

Children 2–5 years
Inside leg approx 15–20 inches
Single gear
Robust girder frame with built-in
    carrier
White tyres
Rubber pedals
Chrome front brake
Supple saddle
Other features: fixed rear sprocket;
    adjustable handlebars with hooter;
    mudguards; chain guard

### MERCIER C 600

Children's 'semi-racer'
3 gears
Steel frame and forks
600 mm wheels
Steel pedals
Huret derailleur
Steel cranks
Alloy brakes
Supple saddle
Other features: chromium plated rear
    carrier; Uginox mudguards; racing
    handlebars and stem

### LEJEUNE 'Semi-racer' 45

Children 5–10 years
3 gears
Welded frame and forks
Chromium plated rims and brakes
'Racing' saddle
Other features: Racing handlebars, rear
    carrier, alloy mudguards, pump, bell

### BIANCHI Junior Racer

10 gears
Light steel racing frame and forks
Wheels: Nisi rims, light quick-release
    hubs
Chromium plated steel chainwheel
Campagnolo Valentini derailleur
Universal 68 racing brakes
Chamois-covered saddle
Other features: bottle carrier, toe-clips
    and straps, pump, alloy handlebars

### LEJEUNE H.S.

Single gear
Welded frame
Chromium plated rims and hubs,
    650 mm half-balloon white tyres
Steel pedals
Chromium plated brakes
Other features: Trials chromium plated
    handlebars, aluminium mudguards
    with coloured bands, chromium
    plated cranks, chain guard, lighting,
    chromium plated front carrier

## MOTOBECANE C10M

Ladies' 'Randonneur' type
10 gears
Brazed-up open frame and forks
Wheels: Normandy quick-release hubs; 700 mm alloy rims
Alloy chain set
Huret Allvit derailleur with handlebar stem control
Alloy centre-pull brakes
Padded racing saddle
Other features: rust-proof half-mudguards; chromium plated handlebars; front and rear carriers with clips

## MERCIER R.L. 30

Ladies' 'Randonneur' type
10 gears
Steel frame
Front forks half chromium plated
Wheels: 700 m two-colour tyres, alloy rims, Normandy quick-release hubs
Stronglight 49D chainwheel
Simplex 'Prestige' derailleur
Mafac Racer brakes
Padded saddle
Other features: Dropped handlebars, lighting, front and rear carriers, alloy mudguards; Also available (at extra cost) with triple chainwheel giving 15 gears

## RALEIGH Ladies' Grand Prix

Ladies
10 gears
Open brazed frame of light Raleigh 20/30 tubes
Front fork ends chromium plated
Light quick-release hubs
Alloy chainwheel set
Weinmann centre-pull brakes
Brooks saddle

## PEUGEOT PA 65

Ladies' cycle touring
10 gears
Light triangular sport frame
Simplex fork ends
Wheels: Normandy light metal quick release large-flange hubs with 36 spokes, light metal rims, 700 mm light wired-on tyres
Bluemels mudguards
Simplex Prestige front and rear derailleur
Stronglight 49D double chainwheel, 48 and 36 teeth, alloy cranks
Freewheel with 14, 17, 20, 24 and 28 teeth
Lyotard chrome steel pedals
Mafac Racer brakes
Soubitez dynamo lighting

## GITANE Super Evry 1234

Ladies' sports
10 gears
Frame all Reynolds 531 tubing
Chromium plated front forks
Wheels: freewheel with 14, 16, 18, 21, 24 teeth; Mavic alloy rims; Clement 700 × 28 C tyres; Normandy quick release hubs
Stronglight super 93 chainwheel set
Huret Challenger derailleur
Mafac Competition brakes
Semi-racing saddle
Bluemels Classique mudguards

63

# Utility

### MERCIER PH

Single or 3 gears
Steel frame and forks
650 × 35 two-coloured wired on tyres
Chromed chainwheel set
Alloy brakes
Supple saddle
Other features: Lighting, rear carrier with clip, Uginox mudguards, toolbag and tools

### MERCIER Longchamp

Folding model
Single or 3 gears
Steel frame and forks
550 two-coloured tyres
Chromed chainwheel
Alloy brakes
Supple saddle
Other features: Removable handlebars, rear carrier with clip, stand, Uginox mudguards, lighting

### PEUGEOT N.S.M. 22

Single gear
'Mixed' frame with oval section tubes
550A wheels, half-balloon two-coloured tyres
Light metal hubs
Inox chainwheel set
Scissor type brakes
Sprung saddle
Other features: stand and front and rear carriers chromed, with clips and elastic hooks, instant saddle adjustment
Also available in 5-gears, and folding models

### BIANCHI Viaggio Lusso

Ladies'
Single gear
Frame in strong steel, 50 cm
Alloy hubs, steel rims
Steel chainwheel
Bianchi brakes
Sprung saddle
Steel mudguard with chromed chain guard

## BATAVIUS Favoriet

3 gears (hub)
26 × 13.8 wired on tyres
Pedals with reflectors
Rear back-pedalling brake; front rim brake
Special features: this typically Dutch model with distinctive frame, dress and chain guard, also has mudguards, carriers, electric lighting, padlocks, rubber hooks and bell

## RALEIGH Ladies'

3 gears (hub) with handlebar control
Light frame and forks
Raleigh rims and hub
Chaincase
Automatically adjustable cable brakes
Brooks saddle
Carriers, stand, headlock

## BATAVUS Cambridge

Models for men and women
3 gears (Sturmey-Archer hub)
Inox rims, 27 × 14 wired on tyres
Pedals with reflectors
Rim brakes, or hub brakes, front and rear, cable operated
Sprung leather saddle
Other features: enamelled mudguards, chromed carriers with clips and elastic fasteners, 'Nordlicht' lighting set, dress guard, chain guard, lateral support, light metal pump, lock, mudflap, bell

## KATAKURA SF 4D

5 gears
Steel frame and forks
Freewheel with 14, 17, 20, 24, 28 teeth
Chainwheel with 48 teeth
Suntour derailleur
Hydraulic rear brake, disc front
Plastic Katakura saddle
Other features: this is a 'gadget' bicycle with winking front and rear lights, direction indicators, klaxon, battery transistorised electric circuit, dynamo front and rear lights, lateral stand and lock

*Gear-box of the modern lightweight bicycle – the derailleur and multiple free-wheel block.*

# To have or not to have

Once started you will soon be hooked. You will fall in love with 'fine equipment' – either deliberately tracking down the best or following, sheep-like, the latest fad.

Once you have sorted out the basic principles of construction you are faced with a large assortment of components. A bicycle is made up of many different parts and I shall discuss the most important in this chapter, though I certainly do not claim to cover the subject as comprehensively as an author such as Daniel Rebour, since in this book we are not only interested in bicycles but also in the way they are used. I would like to give the reader some idea of the wide range of possible combinations available.

'To have or not to have' – that is the question both the racing cyclist and the tourist are constantly coming up against. It depends of course on what they are after – and on the size of their purse.

## The frame: strong but light

It is easy to imagine a painting by a great artist without a frame. Not so a bicycle – the frame in this case is the skeleton or framework and all the various components have to fit on to it.

Here, as with the various components, we are concentrating mainly on the lightweight road model. Most of the research done in this field applies both to the construction of a track 'iron' – stripped down to the bare essentials – and to that of the touring model. This has not prevented touring cyclists from being responsible for improvements that the competition rider initially viewed with suspicion, and presenting a convincing case for them. A good example is the introduction of derailleur gears.

A bicycle frame is made up of a series of tubes which, in the old days, were welded together by a type of solder that formed slightly rounded joints. Welded frames generally lacked rigidity and are rarely seen on the continent nowadays, but apparently they are coming back to fashion among amateur enthusiasts in Britain and North America. Nowadays the vast majority of good quality cycles have 'brazed up' frames, the component tubes being coupled together by 'lugs' which are filed and lightened beforehand.

The 'walls' of cycle tubing vary in thickness; builders select a 'gauge' suitable for the type of machine they are making. In a non-technical book like this it would be confusing to list the various gauges available, particularly as some tubes are 'plain' (of uniform thickness) and others 'butted' (slightly thicker at the ends where they are brazed into the lug). Furthermore, one gauge may be used for the top tube of the frame, and another for the seat and down tubes.

The most popular alloy steel tubing – not only in Britain but throughout the world – is the famous Reynolds 531, a remarkable 'all rounder' used in the construction of road, track and touring machines. A road-racing frame built from these tubes weighs between 5.5 lb and 6 lb according to the amount of weight-saving treatment given by the builder; several ounces can be trimmed off by filing the lugs, and by cutting out sections underneath the bottom bracket. By using very thin plain gauge tubing the weight of a frame can be reduced to about 4.25 lb, but this will not be rigid enough to withstand really fierce pedalling.

Technicians have always been searching for something lighter and stronger than steel. Frames made of duralumin became all the rage during the inter-war years at the time of the keenly contested competitions organised from 1933 onwards, initially under the impetus of the dynamic touring cyclists of the Groupe Montagnard Parisien. Another material, introduced recently, is titanium, which was first brought to the notice of the general public in 1973 when it was used for some accessories by the popular French rider Raymond Poulidor, while during that same year Spanish star Luis Ocana rode a British-built titanium frame for time-trial and uphill stage finishes in the Tour de France in which he was the overall winner.

It might be supposed, therefore, that anyone who can afford it should buy a machine made from the lightest possible tubing. In fact, this would be an error because of the discrepancy that so often crops up between the 'ideal solution' and the limits imposed by the material. An ultra-light frame can be a good thing for road time-trials in which the contestant is on his own and tries to pedal at a regular speed, without frequent and abrupt changes

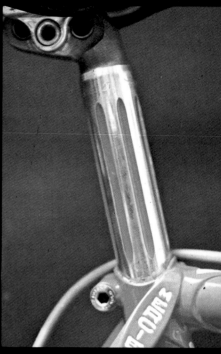

*The bicycle, wonderfully simple –
simply wonderful!*

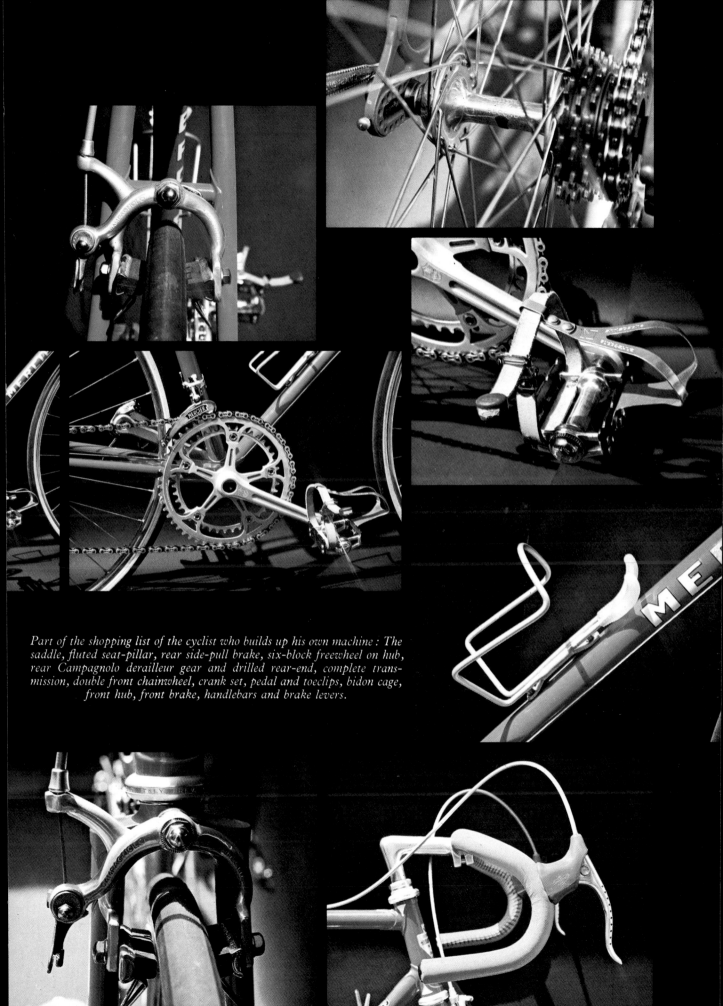

*Part of the shopping list of the cyclist who builds up his own machine: The saddle, fluted seat-pillar, rear side-pull brake, six-block freewheel on hub, rear Campagnolo derailleur gear and drilled rear-end, complete trans-mission, double front chainwheel, crank set, pedal and toeclips, bidon cage, front hub, front brake, handlebars and brake levers.*

*Since the First World War there have been many attempts to build frames with aluminium alloy tubing. They were costly and lack of rigidity made them unsuitable for hard competition purposes. Recently great progress has been made, and now the type of frame illustrated is being successfully used on road and track in world and Olympic championships. Although for technical reasons the lugs are plain and substantial, there is a saving of nearly 2 lb over the conventional alloy steel frames.*

of rhythm. In a normal road race the frame must be strong and rigid to stand up to the violent impact of sudden accelerations. The same applies to track models where the rider produces explosive efforts, and for touring models which have to make long runs with perhaps quite a load of luggage. For the moment very light tubes are used only in special circumstances. This does not mean that in a few years' time the perfect solution, combining strength with lightness, will not be found. Who knows, the ideal material might even be plastic – with which an American manufacturer recently claimed to have made a workable free-wheel!

Once the tubes have been fitted together one or two precautions have to be taken, in particular the legendary small cylinder of hardwood that has to be fitted tightly into the lower part of the steering column. This has prevented generations of cyclists from having serious accidents when their fork-crowns snapped. I was surprised to learn that this simple precaution is not taken by British manufacturers.

Now the time has come for the frame to be enamelled, unless it is a light alloy, in which case it is just polished. The beginner may well be lured into buying a machine for its bright colouring rather than its intrinsic qualities. There are colours to suit all tastes – midnight blue, pillar-box red, sea-green and so on. Although chromium plating looks very attractive if it is done properly, such precautions have to be taken that technicians strongly advise against it. In spite of this, you must bear in mind the psychological factor – a chromium-plated bike looks like a glittering jewel, which explains why track experts like the French sprinter Daniel Morelon and his friend Pierre Trentin, who specialises in the standing-start kilometre trial, often use chromium-plated machines and have won many of their greatest victories on them. The chromium-plating process had indeed been carried out under very special

conditions, which only goes to prove that it is no ordinary technique – and incidentally it is very expensive.

## 'The wheel, the wheel!'

When a racing cyclist hears these words yelled at him from behind, either by one of his team-mates or by a rival who is temporarily his ally by force of circumstances, even if he is glassy-eyed and grey-faced with exhaustion he somehow manages to summon up the last ounce of energy to stamp on the pedals and catch the fellow who was trying for a surprise breakaway. The wheel is the very symbol of cycling – ever slipping away and being pursued, leaving an impression of lightness and speed on the spectator's retina as it flashes past. When a puncture suddenly forces a racing cyclist to bounce along on a flat tyre, throwing him off balance and putting the final result in jeopardy, you should just see him leap feverishly from his machine, a wild look on his face, unclamp the offending 'hoop' and brandish it aloft, yelling in his turn, 'A wheel! a wheel!' to attract the attention of those he hopes will help him out.

In the centre of the wheel is the hub, which is hollow so that a fast-locking spindle can be slid into it. Racing wheels made on this system are gradually being used for touring models as well, supplanting the old-style wing-nuts which used to be a source of considerable irritation and a waste of time for the cyclist struggling to screw them equally tight – especially if one of them had been lost in the grass. The track cyclist does not have to mend his tyre right away if he has a puncture and the whole wheel can be replaced on the spot. Plain 'track nuts' are used to lock the wheel in position and, having no projections, they cannot cause injury in the case of an accident.

The spokes which are in stainless steel or chromium plated, branch out from the hub. In Britain many bicycles still have 40 spokes in the

*A wheel begins to take shape.*

*The principal elements of a wheel. Two types of hub are shown, one with small 'flanges', the other with large. These are the drilled discs in which the spokes are threaded, and a builder selects the right type for the kind of riding proposed. Where rigidity is essential (track racing, time trialing, or road racing on good surfaces) large flange hubs are specified, while small are favoured by those who have to compete over bumpy roads. Also shown is the simple but effective quick-release (and quick-locking) spindle device.*

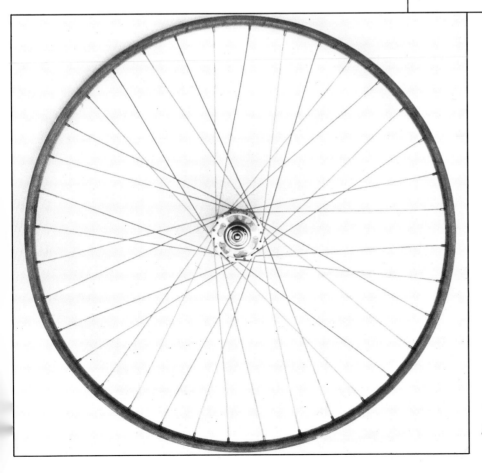

*A rear wheel built with large flange hubs and spokes 'crossing 4', that is each spoke crossing four others on its own side of the hub. 'Stiff' wheels of this type are used for track sprints and Madison races.*

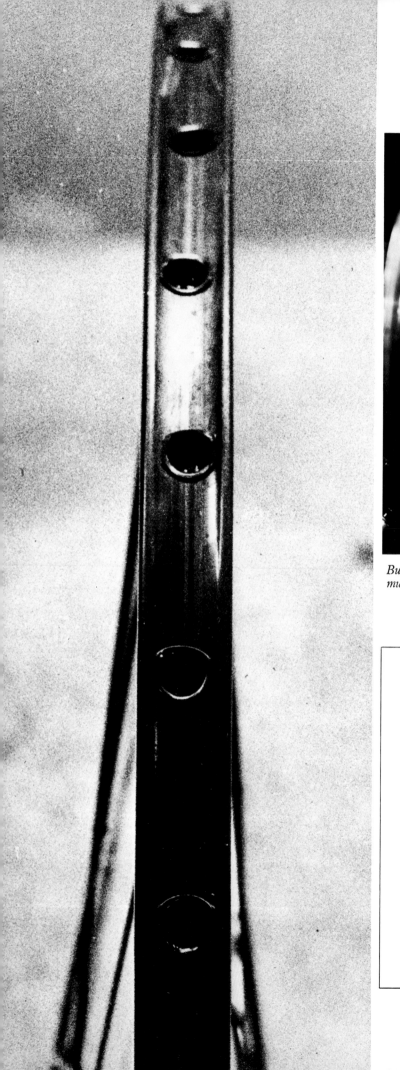

*Building a wheel is not the end of the job. The spokes must be given just the right tension with a spoke-key so that the revolving rim runs straight and true.*

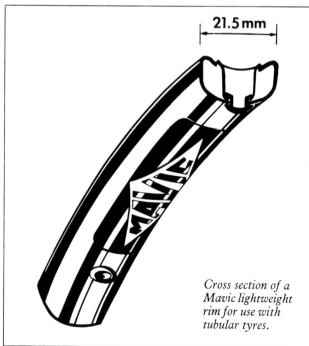

*Cross section of a Mavic lightweight rim for use with tubular tyres.*

back wheel and 32 in the front, while in the rest of Europe 36 spokes in both wheels is usual. Some experts favour a system whereby the spokes are laced 'crossing three', each single spoke crossing three others between the spoke and the rim. This system is normally used for mass-produced wheels with a small-flanged hub. Others prefer having the spokes grouped in fours – there are endless arguments over this! The dry rattle of a loose spoke is a highly disagreeable sound, as it means that the wheel will buckle. This is a painful moment for the cyclist whose efficiency suffers because the offending wheel is running out of true. Now it seems that the system with the spokes grouped in fours greatly reduces the risk of broken spokes. The use of large-flanged hubs means that the wheel is more rigid, which is an advantage in track racing or time-trials. On the other hand if the road surface is bumpy, or just plain bad, a small-flanged hub will cut down the risk of breakages because it is more supple. The experts, always on the look-out for ways of saving weight, and especially of simplifying the mechanism of the rear wheel, sometimes go for wheels with 32 spokes, or even 28 – not to mention 24! These are used only in special cases, particularly, once again, for races 'against the watch'. Nowadays the technique of tieing and soldering the spokes where they intersect is confined to competition cycles.

The spokes join the hub to the rim, which is a metal tube (steel on cheaper models and alloy on 'classics' jobs) with flat parallel sides. In some cases the weight of the rim has been reduced to as little as 250 g (8.75 oz). For the moment models weighing 70–80 g (2.5–3 oz) more than this should be chosen, as they are definitely safer. A split rim is fit only for the scrapheap and is bound to collapse in time.

The French have an expression 'I'm on the rim' *(je suis sur la jante)*, meaning I'm on my beam ends, down to my last halfpenny – and it is obvious where the metaphor comes from because that is exactly how a cyclist feels when 'riding on the rim'. It is essential that the perimeter of the wheel should be surrounded by a tyre, so that the bicycle can move smoothly forward!

Let us start with a few words about the 'wired-on' tyre, used for the majority of cycles in use today, because its very thick vulcanised rubber outer casing reduces the risk of a puncture to a minimum. When you *do* have a puncture you need tyre levers and a puncture-outfit to mend it and this can take some time if the 'hole' is hard to find. Wired-on tyres consist of an inner tube and an outer casing and can be 'fully rubbered' or open-sided. Nowadays the type of wired-on tyre used by sporting tourists is not all that different from tubular racing tyres used in competition – both have light inner tubes and hand-made covers.

The racing cyclist obviously cannot squat down by the roadside and patch up a puncture. He carries a spare tubular tyre that is, for those with the knack, easy to change. An expert will have the job done in little over a minute, but fumbling fingers could take much longer – especially if the spare tyre is completely new.

In the old days it was apparent at a glance whether a bicycle was fitted with tubular or wired-on tyres. Today it is not always so easy to decide. Large-section tubulars ('hose-pipes' in cyclists' jargon) used for winter training sessions are almost the same size and weight as the lighter wired-ons used by the touring cyclist, i.e. about 460 g (16 oz). When it comes to the lighter racing tyres, however, the difference between the two types is marked. These are handmade and may weigh as little as 250, 220 or even 160 g (9, 8 or 6 oz). The 'super-whistler', as racing cyclists call it, consists merely of the fabric and rubber tread.

Tubular tyres designed for racing on first-class tracks are very thin and light, weighing about 150 g (5 oz). They are inflated to a pressure of up to 120 lb/sq in, whereas road-racing tubulars need to be between 75 and 100 lb/sq in according to the surface. Cyclo-cross tubulars are bulky, with 'knobs' or studs to stop them slipping on difficult terrain.

The racing cyclist must take great care of his tyres, keeping them in a dark, dry place and always mounted on a rim. Whereas the beginner is glad enough to have just one spare pair by him, the top-class professional hoards them by the dozen.

Tubular tyres are stuck on to the rim with rubber 'cement'. Adhesive tape is also used, but is less satisfactory, because if you have to change a tyre hurriedly in a race, or when training, the tape often comes away with the tyre, whereas if 'cement' has been used some of it remains on the rim and the new tyre will grip satisfactorily.

## Propulsion

So we have got the frame on one side and the wheels on the other – inert masses, a cycle without a soul. Now let us slot the front wheel and the rear wheel into their grooves. The thing still will not move! So what do we need to make it move, which is after all the object of the exercise? What makes a bicycle go forward at all?

The answer lies in what is called the drive, which is worked by the chain, the chain-wheel set, the pedals and the 'gear'. Without them the bicycle will never come alive.

Toulouse-Lautrec's two cycling posters, drawn in 1893, were commissioned by a chain manufacturer called Bouglé, whose pseudonym was 'Spoke'. One of the posters, painted in magnificent colours, depicts Constant Huret riding behind a 'multiple machine' – a tandem or a three-seater. The second is no more than a sketch, though at a fairly advanced stage. It shows the Welsh Champion Jimmy Michael during a training session, a toothpick clenched in

his teeth, while his manager, 'Choppy' Warburton, spurs him on. 'Spoke' did not like the way Lautrec had drawn the bicycle and rejected his poster. Yet he had faithfully copied the bicycle chain, which was made by Simpson. It looks grotesque to us today, or at any rate pretty surprising, because unlike modern chains this one had teeth, which engaged with the sockets in the front chain-wheel.

Attempts have been made to use all sorts of transmission systems. The day of the 'chain war' is over, and so is the day of the chainless cycle, although it had its moment of glory. The old type of 'block chains' once used by track-racers has all but disappeared. Modern road bicycles with derailleur gears are usually equipped with $\frac{3}{32}$ roller chains, the links being $\frac{3}{32}$ in wide, while track machines – which have to stand up to such violent efforts – have $\frac{1}{8}$ in roller chains.

The chain winds round the chainwheel. The bottom bracket shell houses the mechanism of the two 'cups' and their 22 ball bearings, and axle to which the cranks are fixed. A commonly-used method of joining the chainwheel to the right-hand crank was by three 'arms,' but nowadays fitting by the 'five screw' method gives a more rigid and efficient assembly. (The Japanese cycle industry has recently introduced a narrower and lighter chain, the use of which will obviously require modifications to the rest of the transmission – front and rear sprockets, and gears.)

The cranks are only rarely less than 17 cm (approx. 6.75 in) long nowadays, except possibly on track models, where the speed at which the rider's legs turn is a vital factor. On the other hand the big gears used by road-racers means 'power pedalling'; a contributory factor is the use of cranks of 175 or even 180 mm (approx. 7 or 7.25 in) if the competitor can manage them. The pedals are fitted on to the ends of the cranks and are very light nowadays. For competition cycling fairly small 'rat-trap' pedals are used. These pedals are equipped with toe-clips, which are a useful accessory because they stop the foot slipping forwards, while the accompanying straps prevent it slipping awkwardly sideways. Combined, 'toe-clips and straps' enable the rider to pull up the pedals with one foot, while the other is pressing down.

The chainwheel, which can be single, double (normal for racing models) or even triple for touring machines, enables the rider to benefit from a very wide range of gears. At the front the chain winds round the chainwheel and drives the rear wheel by means of one or more sprockets built into the freewheel. Track-racing models and machines used by roadmen resuming training after a short winter break have a fixed sprocket, which means that the rider has to 'use his legs', even going downhill, and find his rhythm and suppleness all over again. Otherwise the normal system is to have a freewheel

carrying several sprockets. This necessitates a gear-change or derailleur system on the chain. On German and British models the gear mechanism may be inside the rear hub, which has the advantage of ensuring that it is protected from outside factors liable to clog it with dirt or generally make it deteriorate.

A great deal could be said about the development of the derailleur gear system, that magic instrument enabling the rider to adapt his pedalling rhythm to the terrain, to the direction and strength of the wind, and to the pace of his companions or his rivals. In the old days you had to get off the bike and 'turn the wheel' – the hub was threaded on both sides. It might strike you as extremely odd that racing cyclists were suspicious of the derailleur for so many years; they were fairly set in their ways, and were also worried that, as the mechanism was somewhat fragile, they might be jeopardising their chances of winning. Nowadays, the system has won complete acceptance.

When we return to the actual practice of cycling, on the third stage of our journey, we will be taking a look at the range of gear ratios available. There is a wide variety, following a logical pattern according to the extent to which the rider has to exert himself.

Gear tables used by cyclists on the continent of Europe are meaningless to their counterparts in Britain, North America and other parts of the English-speaking world. To take an example: a French rider of a 27 in wheel machine is using a 50 tooth front chainwheel and an 18 tooth rear sprocket. He consults his 'gear table' and finds his *développement* is 5.93 m, and knows that this is the distance his bicycle will travel with one complete revolution of the pedals. An English cyclist looks at *his* table and sees that 50 × 18 with 27 in wheels gives a gear of 75 in. This is *not* the Imperial equivalent of 5·93 m.

To understand what 75 in means in gear terms we have to go back to the days of the 'penny farthing' when the size of the front wheel a rider could straddle was determined by the length of his legs. Only a tall man could ride a 60 in wheel. When the safety bicycle arrived the short man was no longer at a disadvantage. By choosing the right combination of teeth on the chainwheel and sprocket he could help himself to a 'gear' which would take him as far, with one complete revolution of the pedals, as if he were making the same effort on a 'penny farthing' of enormous size. This system of expressing gears is still used a century later. Our man on a 75 in gear turns the pedals full circle and travels 75 × 3·14 which is the circumference of a 75 in wheel. Let us say that while the metric gear table is more realistic, the British system – printed overleaf – is more romantic!

Most cyclists will find suitable gear ratios within this table. Competition riders (who use chainwheels up to 60 teeth) and mountain tourists (rear sprockets up to 34 teeth) need an enlarged version. Chainwheel sizes do not come in even numbers alone – 'odd' teeth like 49, 51, 53 are also available.

If you have no full gear table available, you can work out your own ratio by this formula:

Multiply the *number of teeth on front chainwheel* by the *diameter (in inches) of road wheel* and divide the result by the *number of teeth on rear sprocket*.

$$\text{E.g.} \quad \frac{49 \times 27}{15} = 88.2 \text{ in.}$$

The free wheel screws on to the rear hub. On 'single gear' machines it carries only one sprocket – 18 teeth perhaps – but the derailleur system permits the use of 'blocks' of several sprockets. There are three sprockets on many inexpensive utility machines, five or more on sporting models. Professional roadmen and top amateurs now invariably have free-wheels carrying six sprockets, but while the additional 'gear' is useful, technical problems crop up owing to the increased width of the unit.

Today's rear derailleur systems are not based on the horizontal sliding motion of an axle, but on a much more flexible 'parallelogram' action which allows a wide difference in the number of teeth used on the front and rear sprockets, giving an extensive range of gears suitable for all circumstances. The weight of the rear derailleur mechanism has now been reduced to a startling 130–350 g (4·5–12 oz).

Although our bicycle is not yet complete, we can make sure that the 'drive' is working properly by hanging it from two hooks and pedalling with one hand, while the other works the derailleur controls. The levers are usually placed about four inches from the top of the 'down' tube, the one operating the front chainwheels being on the left, and the more frequently used lever working the main derailleur mechanism on the right. Small adjustments with a screwdriver will have to be made to the front and rear changing mechanisms before the chain runs smoothly over all the cogs but does not travel *too* far in either direction and jam against the spokes or against the end of the chain-stay tube. A chain so jammed may take only seconds to extricate – or it could take an hour.

## The supports

We have the frame, the wheels, the transmission, which includes one of the cyclist's 'three points of contact' with his machine – the pedals. Still missing are the two other points, the saddle and handlebars.

Not so long ago a racing cyclist would transfer 'his' saddle and 'his' handlebars from machine to machine over the years, keeping the same ones for most of his career. With the increasing number of races organised this custom has changed and a top professional cyclist will use as many as 15 different bicycles in a single season. The fact that the material the saddles are made of has changed over the years

| Chain wheel | 36 teeth | | 38 teeth | | 40 teeth | | 42 teeth | | 44 teeth | | 46 teeth | | 48 teeth | | 50 teeth | | 52 teeth | |
|---|---|---|---|---|---|---|---|---|---|---|---|---|---|---|---|---|---|---|
| Wheel size | 26″ | 27″ | 26″ | 27″ | 26″ | 27″ | 26″ | 27″ | 26″ | 27″ | 26″ | 27″ | 26″ | 27″ | 26″ | 27″ | 26″ | 27″ |
| 13 | 72·0 | 74·8 | 76·0 | 78·9 | 80·0 | 83·1 | 84·0 | 87·2 | 88·0 | 91·4 | 92·0 | 95·5 | 96·0 | 99·7 | 100·0 | 103·8 | 104·0 | 108·0 |
| 14 | 66·9 | 69·4 | 70·5 | 73·3 | 74·3 | 77·1 | 78·0 | 81·0 | 81·7 | 84·9 | 85·4 | 88·7 | 89·1 | 92·6 | 92·9 | 96·4 | 96·6 | 100·3 |
| 15 | 62·4 | 64·8 | 65·9 | 68·4 | 69·3 | 72·0 | 72·8 | 75·6 | 76·3 | 79·2 | 79·7 | 82·8 | 83·2 | 86·4 | 86·6 | 90·0 | 90·1 | 93·6 |
| 16 | 58·5 | 60·7 | 61·7 | 61·4 | 65·0 | 67·5 | 68·3 | 70·9 | 71·5 | 74·3 | 74·4 | 77·4 | 78·0 | 81·0 | 81·3 | 84·4 | 84·5 | 87·8 |
| 17 | 55·1 | 57·2 | 58·1 | 60·3 | 61·2 | 63·5 | 64·2 | 66·7 | 67·3 | 69·9 | 70·3 | 73·1 | 73·4 | 76·2 | 76·5 | 79·4 | 79·5 | 82·6 |
| 18 | 52·0 | 54·2 | 54·9 | 57·0 | 57·7 | 60·0 | 60·7 | 63·0 | 63·5 | 66·0 | 66·4 | 69·0 | 69·3 | 72·0 | 72·2 | 75·0 | 75·1 | 78·0 |
| 19 | 49·3 | 51·2 | 52·0 | 54·0 | 54·7 | 56·8 | 57·5 | 59·7 | 60·2 | 62·5 | 62·9 | 65·4 | 65·7 | 68·2 | 68·4 | 71·1 | 71·2 | 73·9 |
| 20 | 46·8 | 48·6 | 49·4 | 51·3 | 52·0 | 54·0 | 54·6 | 56·7 | 57·2 | 59·4 | 59·8 | 62·1 | 62·4 | 64·8 | 65·0 | 67·5 | 67·6 | 70·2 |
| 21 | 44·6 | 46·3 | 47·0 | 48·8 | 49·5 | 51·4 | 52·0 | 54·0 | 54·5 | 56·6 | 57·0 | 59·1 | 59·4 | 61·7 | 61·9 | 64·3 | 64·4 | 66·9 |
| 22 | 42·6 | 44·2 | 44·9 | 46·6 | 47·2 | 49·1 | 49·6 | 51·5 | 52·0 | 54·0 | 54·4 | 56·4 | 56·7 | 58·9 | 59·1 | 61·4 | 61·5 | 63·8 |
| 23 | 40·7 | 42·3 | 43·0 | 44·6 | 45·2 | 46·9 | 47·5 | 49·3 | 49·7 | 51·6 | 52·0 | 54·0 | 54·3 | 56·3 | 56·5 | 58·7 | 58·8 | 61·0 |
| 24 | 39·0 | 40·5 | 41·1 | 42·7 | 43·3 | 45·0 | 45·5 | 47·3 | 47·7 | 49·5 | 49·8 | 51·7 | 52·0 | 54·0 | 54·2 | 56·3 | 56·3 | 58·5 |
| 25 | 37·4 | 38·9 | 39·5 | 41·0 | 41·6 | 43·2 | 43·7 | 45·3 | 45·8 | 47·5 | 47·8 | 49·7 | 49·9 | 51·8 | 52·1 | 54·0 | 54·1 | 56·2 |
| 26 | 36·0 | 37·4 | 38·0 | 39·5 | 40·0 | 41·6 | 42·0 | 43·5 | 44·0 | 45·7 | 46·0 | 47·8 | 48·0 | 49·8 | 50·0 | 51·9 | 52·0 | 54·0 |

*A metric Gear Table will be found on page 217*

Although not generally as expensive, and never as light, as racing models, the modern 'Randonneur' bicycle used by hard-riding tourists is a well-designed, elegant thoroughbred of the road.

Bright colours on a carpet of dead leaves.

Early chain-driven Safety bicycles involved the plain rear sprocket. Then, at the turn of the century, the free-wheel was perfected. 'Fixed wheels' are still compulsory for track racing, and roadmen also use them for early season training. Before the general acceptance of derailleur gears with 'blocks' of three, four, five and six teeth, sporting cyclists used the double-sided hub. Although this example is fitted with a modern quick-release spindle it shows the principle – a fixed sprocket is fitted on one side and a free-wheel on the other. A cyclist taking the rear wheel out and reversing it was a familiar scene on the road 40 years ago.

Adjustment of derailleur gears is necessary from time to time. There are two screws governing the 'throw' of the chain. Tightening or loosening the top screw affects movement past the small sprocket, and the bottom screw the throw past the large sprocket. A few seconds of 'trial and error' with a screwdriver will have the gears running sweetly without the chain jumping off the sprockets into spokes or frame.

The component parts of a Campagnolo derailleur. Most cyclists use the 'down tube' controls as shown, but a few specialists – road sprinters and cyclo-cross riders – have levers built into the handlebar ends. This enables them to change gear rapidly without taking their hands from the 'bends'.

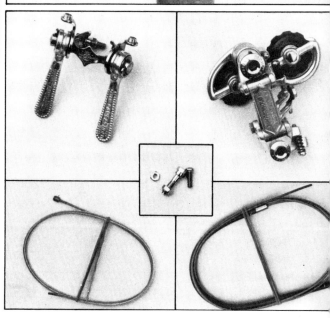

The obvious way of getting a very low gear on a touring machine is to fit a large rear sprocket – up to 36 teeth is sometimes used, but this adds considerably to the overall weight. An alternative method is to go no higher than 28 teeth on the free-wheel and use it in conjunction with a third small front chainwheel. Here is a typical triple set.

A Raleigh mechanic builds up a free-wheel 'block' with the sprockets a rider has chosen for tomorrow's race.

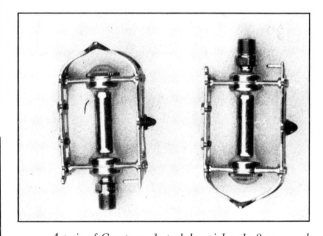

A pair of Campagnolo pedals weigh only 8 oz – and cost nearly £60! There is a small projection on the plate which enables the rider to 'pick up the pedals' rapidly after an enforced stop. On track racing pedals the curved portion is removed to give extra clearance.

A Stronglight 5 arm double chainwheel.

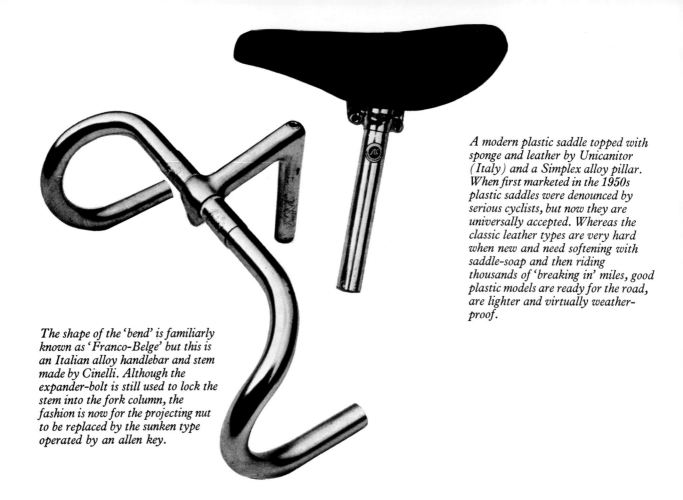

*The shape of the 'bend' is familiarly known as 'Franco-Belge' but this is an Italian alloy handlebar and stem made by Cinelli. Although the expander-bolt is still used to lock the stem into the fork column, the fashion is now for the projecting nut to be replaced by the sunken type operated by an allen key.*

*A modern plastic saddle topped with sponge and leather by Unicanitor (Italy) and a Simplex alloy pillar. When first marketed in the 1950s plastic saddles were denounced by serious cyclists, but now they are universally accepted. Whereas the classic leather types are very hard when new and need softening with saddle-soap and then riding thousands of 'breaking in' miles, good plastic models are ready for the road, are lighter and virtually weather-proof.*

has facilitated the switch from one bicycle to another. Not everyone has a whole 'stable' of bicycles however. So the choice of the right saddle and handlebars is still important.

If you look at a saddle made in the 1890s you will be staggered at its size. Our ancestors must have had enormous backsides, if you will pardon my saying so, if they really sat on that sort of armchair seat. In fact your saddle should not be too big, but neither should it be exaggeratedly narrow. Do not choose a 'mattress' type with coiled springs, because it will be uncomfortable over long distances. The leather saddle, fastened with copper rivets, that racing cyclists used to 'break in' during training sessions and early season races no longer is a 'must', but many experienced riders still swear by it for long one-day races and for multi-stage events.

Plastic saddles made their appearance about 15 years ago, and although looked down on at first, are now the most common type in use. They are flexible and light and cyclists do not experience discomfort in switching from one machine to another. Plastic saddles are often covered with basan. The saddle clip and serrated washer method that was in regular use for many years was always difficult to adjust with precision and has gradually been superseded by the combined seat pillar and saddle clamps which, besides giving more positive adjustment, also saves weight.

The handlebar stem fits into the head tube. The steering mechanism and its bearings have to work

harder and are used more often than most of the other parts of the machine.

The right handlebar width for a rider of normal build is 40 cm (16 in). This will allow him to breathe freely. Handlebar 'shape' is always a matter for argument. Some hill-climbers such as René Vietto and Raymond Poulidor prefer them to be 'round', because they like to place their hands on either side of the stem. The same goes for such 'rouleurs' as Jacques Anquetil, who grip the lower curve and get a stream-lined effect. The most popular style is the square handlebar, called Franco-Belge when introduced, which offers three main riding positions: on the lower part of the 'bend'; on the upper part; on the straight transverse section. Eddy Merckx prefers this type of handlebar, and so do many touring cyclists, together with the majority of track riders, who use an extra-long stem so that they have a streamlined posture on their machines.

Track racing bicycles are not fitted with brakes. The rider can to some extent control his progress by attempting to 'back pedal' the fixed gear, or by rubbing his gloved hand on the front tyre. If a fixed-wheel machine is ridden on the open road in Great Britain it must be fitted with a second brake – usually operating on the front wheel. All bicycles with free-wheels must have back and front brakes. A few models are still fitted with the once-popular back-pedalling unit built into the rear hub, and with some other type used for the front wheel. Hand-operated hub brakes on both wheels are favoured by those who do not mind a bit of extra weight. Hub brakes work well in rain, unlike those involving the action of rubber 'blocks' on the rim, which – controlled by cables – are the only type used on racing and lightweight machines.

The operating levers of the rim brake are attached by clips to a point slightly above the most forward curve of the handlebars. These clips are enclosed in a smoothly rounded alloy casing (which is further protected by a rubber sleeve) known in France as *cocottes*, and in Britain as 'the hoods'. As well as forming a comfortable grip for the rider when he chooses to ride 'on the tops' of the handlebars, he can make an emergency application of the brakes simply by stretching out his fingers and squeezing the levers.

There are various types of rim brake. Some work on the classic 'Mafac' concept, and use the centre-pull cantilever principle – which appears to be a logical system because the two arms of the stirrup work simultaneously and have an equal effect on both sides. The alternative system, which originated in Italy, is the side-pull calliper brake which, it must be admitted, also gives good results.

Once the brake levers have been installed the bend of the handlebars is covered with cloth tape. Plastic tape is sometimes used, but is slippery and does not give a good grip. The tape is wound round, starting from the handlebar stem and finishing at the bottom of the handlebars. A few centimetres more are then poked into the end of the handlebar and the opening is sealed off either with a cork stopper or with a special plug. However well you ride and however nimble you are, one of these days you will fall off, perhaps because you have been caught unawares by some unexpected obstacle or because some idiot in the pack knocks you over. As long as your handlebars are properly sealed there is no danger of the ends digging into you or another rider and causing a nasty injury. Also, you will deprive the race stewards of the pleasure of slapping a fully justified fine on you for neglecting this precaution.

## Accessories – vital pieces of equipment

With accessories or without?

The wide range of equipment available explains why cycle manufacturers' catalogues offer models at so many different prices. There is a huge difference between good old wing-nuts and a quick-release spindle; between wired-on tyres and ultra-thin tubulars; between steel and light alloys. Then again, as this can still be a craftsman's field, with refinements sometimes taken to excessive limits, a mass-produced piece of equipment can be modified so that, say, the bottom bracket casing is perforated, or the studs for the derailleur controls are brazed on the frame, or you have a fluted saddle stem and drilled brake levers – the search for greater lightness or elegance is never-ending.

The choice available gives rise to endless comparisons and lively discussions, with furtive glances cast at a machine fitted with some new gadget and everyone vehemently insisting that it's quite pointless – and then rushing off to buy it!

There are still quite a few items of equipment that do have a specific function. These are grouped together under the umbrella label of 'accessories',

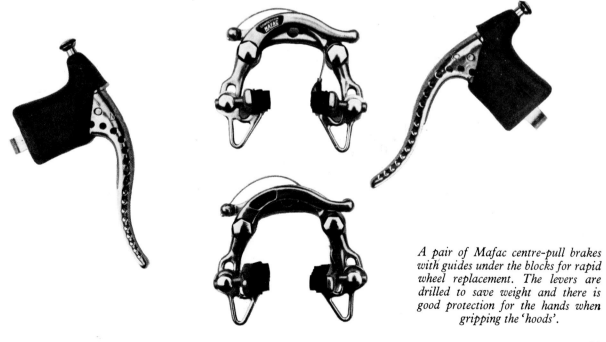

*A pair of Mafac centre-pull brakes with guides under the blocks for rapid wheel replacement. The levers are drilled to save weight and there is good protection for the hands when gripping the 'hoods'.*

81

though in fact they are essential for some specific types of cycling.

There are the mudguards, for instance. They provide essential protection against bad weather, both on training bikes – because the competition rider must never be forced to put off a trip that ought to be made straight away – and for touring models. They are one of the visible differences between touring and racing cycles. The front mudguard is extended downwards by a wide flap designed to stop your feet being splashed with water and getting frozen stiff in no time at all. Plastic mudguards are easy to fix, so the beginner, who often has only one cycle, will be well advised to use them. The bicycle frame will have little eyelets for fixing them, so when he enters a race the young cyclist can whip off the mudguards and his machine is all ready for action. On the other hand light metal mudguards are stronger and make it easy to fit an electric circuit.

This brings us to the point that for long runs the touring cyclist needs an efficient lighting system. In fact, all cycles must by law be fitted with lights, including racing cycles, though the law almost always turns a blind eye on the continent of Europe when they are used for racing.

The situation is different in Britain where all cyclists – even world champions! – are required by law not only to carry a white front light and a red rear light from half-an-hour after sunset to half-an-hour before sunrise, but the lamps must conform to British Standard specifications. Furthermore, these lamps cannot be stuck haphazardly to any old part of the bike as so many are in France, but must be firmly fixed within defined areas. In the USA, I understand that the legal requirements differ from state to state, and that in some parts the use of reflectors on the front, back and sides of the machine is also required. A red rear reflector is also necessary in Britain: most touring cyclists have theirs fitted to the end of the mudguard, but for 'stripped' machines used for training in the dark, or for long-distance competitions, a reflector built into the rear light is sufficient.

Electric battery lamps are used extensively and are satisfactory for short journeys, but long-distance night riders find they only give about six hours' continuous service before the batteries have to be changed. No such problems for the user of the dynamo system which, although 'dragging' slightly, gives a good light even when the machine is moving at little more than walking pace. Obviously a dynamo set gives no light at all when the road wheels are not moving, so the wise tourist carries a battery lamp of some sort in his kit for use in emergencies – such as consulting a map at a lonely cross-roads in the middle of the night. Tyre-operated dynamos cannot be used with light tubular tyres.

Unlike the racing cyclist who has pockets in his jersey or, when training, has a *musette* (light linen satchel) on his back, the touring cyclist needs a bag of some kind. On the continent of Europe the favourite method is the front *sac* supported by a lightweight carrier and attached to the handlebars in such a way that it is still possible to grip them in any position desired. If the rider is on a longer journey and needs more carrying space, he will have additional pannier bags suspended on both sides of the front wheel. Not until these areas of the bicycle have been used will the French tourist use the back part. In Britain the opposite is the case. Standard 'wear' for members of the Cyclists Touring Club is a capacious bag attached by straps to the saddle; if panniers are required they, too, are slung over the rear carrier. Handlebar bags are comparatively rare in Britain. In France it is contended that as the rider's weight is already depriving the back wheel of some of its driving power, it is better to carry luggage on the front.

Then there is the problem of thirst. In races or training sessions or on long-distance tourist trials the rider carries one or two *bidons* (plastic bottles) on his machine. Until the 1940s a wire cage carrying two bottles (then made of metal) was fixed in the middle of the transverse section of the handlebars, but nowadays they are carried singly in light clips fitted on the down tube as near to the bottom bracket as possible, thus effectively lowering the centre of gravity.

Another good place to carry a single *bidon* is low down the seat tube, but this makes it necessary to find somewhere else to fit the pump whose traditional place is there. The modern road-racer's pump does not have a separate rubber connection but has a built-in adapter which pushes straight on to the tyre valve. However top professional and amateur riders rarely have to pump up a tyre on the road – a following service car quickly replaces a punctured wheel.

The pump is nevertheless a necessary evil for the vast majority of cyclists and adds but a few ounces to the overall weight. Just how much a complete bicycle weighs depends, as we have seen, on the quantity and quality of the accessories, and how many weight-saving tricks the craftsman has been up to when building the frame. A 'stripped' track machine will scale around 8 kg (18 lb); a road-racing job with 10 or 12 gear, about 9·5 kg (21½ lb); a cyclo-sportif model for 'competitive touring', 11 kg (25 lb); a more robust tourer, 12 kg (27 lb).

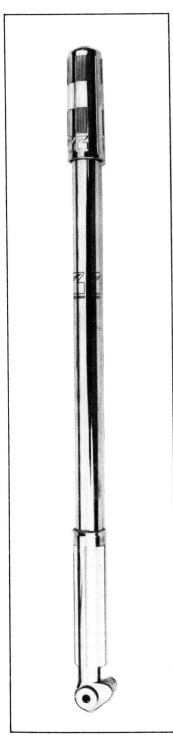

Inflation! Cyclists have lived with it for nearly 90 years. Everyday riders use a 'connection' to screw on to the valve. This competition model has a built-in adapter which clamps over it to save time.

Most 'cyclosportifs' in France ride by torch-light during the night. In Britain lamps must conform to British Standard specifications.

Three touring bicycles which at first glance seem identical. A closer look reveals several small differences (wing nuts and quick-release hubs, position of front lamps, type of front carriers etc.) and a major one. On the right is an open-frame ladies machine.

83

# III
# THE
# ADVENTURE

*Rallies are popular features of continental cycle touring. Though fitted with mudguards and front bags, many of the bicycles ridden are gems of lightweight engineering.*

FACING PAGE:
*City riding is not always so pleasant. A group of visitors enjoy a spin through the streets of ancient York during the annual rally which attracts tourists from all parts of the world.*

FACING PAGE:
*The rendezvous. In the early days of cycling club members wore uniform clothing. Today they tend to turn out in a wide variety of styles and colour.*

# On the open road

To set off into the unknown, roaming over distances that no one on foot or on horseback has ever covered, entering regions where the railway is unknown, taking no advice except that offered by your own stamina, reckoning only with your imagination – that's what a bicycle allows you to do.

These few lines by Maurice Barrès, which appeared in an article on the 'aesthetics of cycling', sum up the essence, and the charm, of cycle touring, or 'adventure on two wheels' as we might call it.

The first cycling adventure in history was clearly that experienced by a gentleman called Harry Kemp, in 1869. At that date, when people thought you were slightly touched if you set off to ride from London to Brighton, our touring hero managed to embark on a tour that involved following in the footsteps of Christopher Columbus as he set out to discover the fabulous Indies. But Kemp was luckier than his illustrious predecessor – who was driven to 'the Americas' by the hand of the Lord (or maybe by gale-force winds) – and actually managed to get as far as Hindustan. Regular reports of his odyssey appeared in the *Vélocipède Illustré*. The last telegram detailing his progress sounds like a leg-pull. It claimed that the British governor had been forced to intervene to rescue his compatriot, who had been locked up in a temple with his bicycle, by Hindus. They had taken him for a new god and started worshipping him! Well, it makes a good story! At any rate it was amazing to have got there at all, given the state of the roads in those days and the sort of machines available, and the intrepid Harry deserves to be worshipped by succeeding generations of touring cyclists.

Oddly enough, the tourist potential of the cycle, or rather the bicycle, was brought out by a long-distance horse trial staged six years later. A Hungarian lieutenant called Zubovitz had covered the distance between Vienna and Paris on his horse Caradoc in a fortnight and his feat put the 'bicyclists' on their mettle. Two of them set off from Paris on 12 October 1875 to show that the steel horse could outdo its iron-shod rival. Their names were Albert Laumaille, from Château-Gonthier, who had competed in the 1869 Paris-Rouen race and had been selected on this occasion to represent the Angers Cycling Club; and Henri Pagis, nominated by the Paris magazine *Véloce-Sport*. Pagis had an accident only a few hours off the target and never got to the Prater, but Laumaille managed to cover the 1245·5 km (780 miles) in under 12½ days. Three years later, this time accompanied by the young 'Emmanuel de Graffenried', he spent 16 March to 21 April on a magnificent 4000 km (2500 miles) odyssey that took him from Paris to Orléans, Bordeaux, Toulouse, Nice, Milan, the Simplon Pass, Vevey, Lausanne, Geneva and Troyes.

For a while tricycles were considered to be 'the ideal conveyance for the tourist', being stable and convenient for transporting luggage. Tricycle manufacturers went to enormous lengths to demonstrate the excellence of their machines. For instance the 'Coventry Lever Tricycle', a system which involved a rider sitting and standing at the rear of the machine, and steering and driving, while his passenger lounged back, managed to cover the 153 km (95 miles) between Coventry and London in 22 hours. This was in summer 1885. 'The tricycle carried a lady and nearly 50 pounds of luggage. The journey took place on a rainy and muddy night, which meant that the lady had to use an umbrella, though she slept for part of the journey, comfortably wrapped up.'

Group outings were becoming more and more popular. In 1887, for instance, one of the inevitable after-dinner speeches at a banquet held by the Lyon Bicycle Club described a splendid outing the previous spring, when 'eleven of us' covered the 230 km (142 miles) between Lyon and Chambéry and back in wonderful weather.

We can detect a difference here between the speaker's attitude and that of the racing cyclist, who would summon up all his strength with the sole aim of reaching higher speeds and beating his rivals. After all, although we cannot all be athletes, we can all experience the great joy of riding through the countryside at our own pace. The moment had clearly come to organise 'cycle touring'.

## Groups and individuals

As early as 1878 the Bicycle Touring Club – rechristened the Cyclist's Touring Club in 1883 – set the necessary example. The instigator was Stanley

Cotterell and his enthusiasm would soon bear fruit. Meanwhile the French Cycling Union (founded in 1881) though concentrating mainly on organising race meetings, did not neglect this side of the pastime. In January 1884 they published a list of 14 'regional delegates for Tourism', while the Federal Conference held in 1888 showed interest in a request put forward by a man called Panajou from Bordeaux. This 'concerned the setting up of standard symbols to be erected at the roadside' – an idea that was soon to gain ground. The road signs that line French roads today owe their existence to these early symbols.

Meanwhile the Cyclist's Touring Club was going strongly and in 1887 had 23 000 members. The CTC 'winged wheel' sign displayed by hotels and bicycle repairers was a guarantee of good service, and the Club's series of danger-boards such as 'Cyclists! This hill is dangerous' prevented countless accidents. The CTC was now recognised in the courts, in Parliament, and elsewhere as the champion of cyclists generally.

A Frenchman called Paul de Vivie, living in Saint-Etienne, realized that a similar touring organisation would be a good thing, though he himself declined the honour of setting up a French equivalent of the Cyclist's Touring Club. His idea soon came to fruition however, and on 26 January 1890 a group of seven friends living in Paris founded the Touring Club de France (TCF). It had 541 members in March 1891, 1500 by the end of the year, 20 000 in August 1895 and 100 000 in 1906. It had great influence, as we can see from the fact that in 1899 it gave the vital impetus to the plan for building a road across the Esterel Mass in coastal Provence. At about the same date it drafted a bill 'for protecting sites and providing panoramic tables, rustic benches and mountain paths'. It seems that ecology is not so new after all.

Large-scale migrations were soon taking place. For instance in 1891 'Docteur Vélo' organised two 'cycling caravans'. One of these embarked on a tour from Paris to Turin and back on 24 March, while the other left Paris for London on 15 August, returning on 1 September.

Individual jaunts, or small groups of friends touring together, continued to flourish. Some of these were fairly short, from Paris to Bordeaux for instance – one example is the tricycle expedition undertaken by Maurice Martin, Georges Thomas (chairman of the French Cycling Union) and Oscar Maillotte in 1889. Others covered vast distances, taking national boundaries in their stride. Asia always seemed to hold a particular fascination for the British. An intrepid Englishman called Thomas Stevens undertook a journey which dwarfed Kemp's extraordinary feat when, in 1886, he left San Francisco for London on a penny farthing, then continued across the continent of Europe to Afghanistan. He was barely 500 km (300 miles) from Hindustan when the police decided he was a Russian spy and forced him to withdraw to Persia. This meant that he had to make a slight detour of 1000 km odd (620 miles), but this did not stop him reaching India via Constantinople. Two American students called Allen and Sachtelben pulled off no less than a world tour. They, too, set out from San Francisco, in 1891, and the trip lasted three years. Their journey across Asia ended with a long meeting with the Chinese prime minister, the famous Li-Hung-Chang, who was more like a viceroy, with the destiny of a far-flung empire in his hands. They gave a faithful picture of this interview in the book they wrote about this part of their marathon, *Across Asia on a Bicycle*, which was published in New York in 1894.

Among other notable trips made in the 1890s were two by Robert Jefferson. One was from London to Moscow and back, 6890 km (4281 miles) at an average of nearly 160 km (100 miles) a day, the other a 10 000 km (6600 mile) trek across Siberia. He wrote books about his adventures, as did John Foster Frazer (later Sir John), who with two friends did a 32 000 km (20 000 miles) round-the-world tour in just over two years.

Travellers' tales were in fact beginning to appear thick and fast. So were maps and guidebooks aimed at cyclists. As early as 1869 specific itineraries were being studied and published. In France, for instance, routes between Paris and Chantilly and Paris and Chevreuse were worked out, while 1884 saw the publication of the first edition of de Baroncelli's *Guide des Environs de Paris* ('Guide to the Paris Area'). De Baroncelli was subsequently to collect and publish a vast amount of information about the various French regions, setting a fashion that was widely copied. He was the best as well as the first in the field, able to convey the delights of this type of touring holiday 'which presents no difficulties and costs nothing at all'. Needless to say the British adventurer awheel was well-informed on topographical matters. The cycling volume of the famous *Badminton Library* observed: 'The *Cyclists' and Wheel World Annual* and the earlier *Bicycle Annuals*, those especially of 1879 and 1880, together with as modern a copy of *Paterson's Roads* as may be obtainable will, with the aid of a decent map, enable the tourist to work out his route with sufficient completeness.'

Although the joys of touring on two wheels were fully appreciated from the start, they were limited to a small minority of enthusiasts. If their enthusiasm was to spread, clearcut principles would have to be laid down – principles that were applicable to everybody. There was also room for improvement in bicycles made for touring. In the early days tourists needed a leader who could remain aloof from the inevitable arguments, rivalries and dissensions that were constantly breaking out, and whom people would be happy to follow.

## Paul de Vivie

On a July Sunday more than 3000 cyclists have come from all over Europe, and even from Canada and the USA, to climb, on their bicycles, the Col du Grand-Bois above the French city of Saint-Etienne. Their exertions spread over a little under eight miles on a hill with a gradient that reaches 1 in 12 at its steepest point. When they reach the 1250 m (3800 ft) summit, they get their breath back and straighten up after pulling hard on the handle-bars as they toiled up the hill. They turn their heads slightly to satisfy themselves that the monument has not been moved since last year and is still sitting safely by the roadside, with the same circular plaque set into it. It bears a head and shoulders portrait of an elderly man with a vast walrus moustache, his expression amazingly alert behind his spectacles, which are held in place by the inevitable cord. The inscription has not changed either. The word 'VELOCIO' appears at the top of the column, with the following details beneath the plaque:

> PAUL DE VIVIE
> 1853–1930
> APOSTLE
> OF THE POLYMULTIPLIÉE
> HIS FRIENDS
> AND ADMIRERS

They cross over to the crowded clearing and sit down to enjoy their picnic. There is a great deal of noise and a few short speeches. Somebody lays a wreath. Old friends meet up again – they would not miss this reunion for anything in the world. People compare their performance today with last year's. Then when evening comes they all troop back to their own towns or countries; some live nearby, others have a long journey ahead of them, but they are all returning to their daily problems and their usual jobs.

On 11 June 1922 there were 163 of them who battled through the rain and the fog of the first 'Velocio Day'. Velocio himself played an active part – he came first in the 10th heat (for competitors aged 60–70), in 58 min 40 s! The event was such a success that it became a unique occasion and all touring cyclists felt they had to take part at least once in their lives. So Velocio has now become a sort of symbol. But what was so special about him? What exactly was his doctrine, based as it was on principles that were so sound they still hold good almost half a century after his death, with every touring cyclist, however unmethodical, putting them into practice, though he may not be aware of it?

The 'Apostle' of cycle touring, Paul de Vivie, alias 'Velocio'. Living in a mountainous area he was a pioneer of variable gearing based on the 'derailing' of the chain – or in this case the chains. Another of Velocio's favourites was the 'Retro' on which he pedalled forwards for top gear and backwards for bottom!

91

*The sport and pastime of cycling are not confined to a playing field or stadium. A bicycle ride can be a voyage of discovery in one's own country, across frontiers, all the way round the world.*

*Good machines, good pace, good style. The group of French cyclo-tourists is led by Jacques Faizant, well-known cartoonist of* Le Figaro *and author of* Albina and her bicycle.

Paul de Vivie was born on 29 April 1853 in Pernes-Les-Fontaines in the Vaucluse and went to live in Saint-Etienne in 1875 as a representative for a silk manufacturer in Lyon. Ten years later he turned to cycle-manufacturing instead, setting up the General Cycling Agency (Agence Générale Vélocipédique). He then started a magazine called *Le Cycliste*. In the first number, which appeared on 1 February 1887, he signed himself 'Velocio', which was destined to become his *nom de guerre* – although in fact he was always a very peaceable man.

In October 1954 André Rabault produced a remarkable booklet in which articles by Philippe Marre and Henri Chaix, backed up by a study by Professor Champin, were an essential contribution to the portrait of a simple, cultured and very generous man. In this book I shall simply pick out the basic points on which the practice of cycle touring still rests today.

'I call a touring cyclist,' said Velocio in 1911, 'anyone who is interested in tourism (as an end) and bicycles (as a means). Put a velocipede between the legs of the first person who happens to come along and you will foster in him a new way of looking at everyday life, of understanding and appreciating anything that happens to him, the people he meets, the things that come within his ken. He'll see them in a new light.'

Invariably practising what he preached, 'Velocio' led a frugal life, and pedalled all the better for it. He was passionately interested in the technical advances made on bicycle – brakes, freewheels, tyres and, of course, the various gear-change systems. It is hard to realize today that the very idea of gears aroused violent arguments once upon a time! And yet people did gradually see the light. For instance at Easter 1927 'during an unforgettable night of frenzied pedalling, with a gale behind us, from Valence to Avignon', Philippe Marre, then in the full flower of his youth, 'had difficulty keeping up with Velocio', who was 74 by then. This sort of experience is a lesson you learn straight away and never forget – the journey between Tournus and Les Baux covered over 400 km (250 miles)!

Velocio inevitably became the leader of a school of cycling and was soon surrounded by disciples and friends. Yet journalist Claude Tillet produced convincing evidence to show that there was no need to build up a whole 'Velocio myth'. The man was a 'potterer and a sportsman, a researcher and a dilettante, a superb leader who nevertheless loved being alone'. He was not just the head of a clan, 'of a church that was closed to all but a very small group of initiates'.

Those who meet every year to meditate by the Velocio grave in the Loyasse Cemetery in Lyon, like the large and merry crowd who picnic in the Grand-Bois, refer to his teachings constantly. Whether or not you know who Paul de Vivie was,

his doctrine can be summed up in seven guidelines, which will give you the key to the magic world of cycle touring. These passwords will never be outdated, and will remain both true and effective.

## With a light heart

Perhaps you are only 15 and setting out on a voyage of discovery. Perhaps you are three times that age and are returning to the bicycle you have hardly looked at since national service days.

While it can still be fun setting off hell-for-leather and generally disorganised, your pleasure in cycling will be more lasting and complete if you remember the 'catechism of the School of Saint Etienne', which has also been called 'The Seven Commandments of Velocio.' They run as follows:

1. Few stops and short, so as not to lose your 'drive'.
2. Eat little and often. Eat before getting hungry, drink before you are thirsty.
3. Never ride until you are so tired that you cannot eat or sleep.
4. Put on extra clothing before feeling cold, take some off before getting hot. Do not be afraid of exposing your skin to the sun, air and rain.
5. Do not drink wine, eat meat or smoke, at any rate while in the saddle.
6. Never rush things. Ride within yourself, particularly during the first few hours of a ride when you feel strong and tempted to force the pace.
7. Never pedal out of vanity.

That last rule is probably the most difficult of all to follow. Another aristocrat of cycling, Dr James Ruffier, commented that even the great Velocio did not always obey his own 'Commandments'. . . .

This is how he put it:

M. de Vivie, you tell us all about your outings and your tales are full of the pride you feel when you go on eating up the kilometres in spite of your age, getting the better of hills and wind and rain, setting a wonderful example, standing out from the rabble of cowardly and lazy people who make up the great mass of the human race. Come off it! You pedal on out of vanity, just like the rest of us. And why not? *

Instead of using the word 'vanity' Velocio's Seventh Commandment would have done better to use 'vainglory' – after all he wanted to make people realize that although to try to outdo your own performance is commendable, it would be a bad thing to play to the gallery, overestimating your own abilities.

The pleasure of cycling will come from exerting yourself, violently at times, but you must always be in control, so as not to exhaust your physical and mental resources too soon. The touring cyclist

*Docteur Ruffier: *Voyage à bicyclette*. Editions Physis, 1928.

*Although riding a touring bicycle, this enthusiast is obviously the sporting type who enjoys a good fast session of pedalling on his own, or with other members of the club.*

*Speed cycling has no attractions for this seasoned campaigner. He has plenty of time, a map on the top of his bag, and the open road ahead.*

enjoys life, enjoys looking at the countryside, enjoys every moment of his journey. He ambles slowly along a road, beside a winding river, perfectly content.

He does not necessarily pay much attention to which gear he is in or to his pedalling rhythm or to what sort of food he ought to eat and the distance he covers. Maybe he is a veteran who knows instinctively the right thing to do. Or maybe he is a beginner acting entirely on impulse. Yet these four things – gear ratio, rhythm, food and distance – are the four pillars of wisdom. How should you set about being a touring cyclist in order to experience its many delights? I must repeat that my aim in writing this book was to present a sort of fresco in which the cyclist of 1977 can see some concrete images and pick up useful tips on various types of cycling. I also wanted to trace the history of cycling and reveal its poetry, but I certainly do not claim to have exhausted the subject and covered the whole ground. Clearly cycle touring in itself would need several volumes. Others have covered the topic before me. Michel Delore, for instance, deserves credit for having devoted a study at the end of 1973 to exactly this theme of 'a sport allied to tourism, culture and nature conservation'. His book does contain some errors, as does another very recent book on cycling by the same author and the same publisher,* but it was no easy matter to attempt a synthesis enabling him to popularise the basic ideas.

*Michel Delore: *Cyclotourisme*. Éditions Amphora, 1973.

My aim, on the other hand, is to point out the main principles.

We have already seen what a touring cycle looks like. Now we are going to see it in action, bowling merrily through the countryside. What gears will the touring cyclist use? If he is not going far it may well be that a single chainwheel and three rear sprockets will do the trick. Generally speaking he will have a double chainwheel and a five – or even six – free-wheel 'block'. If he lives in a fairly flat area a suitable range of gears would be: front chainwheel with 50 to 40 teeth, with 15, 17, 18, 20, 24 sprockets on the free-wheel. (The gear table included on page 76 shows the ratios produced by these combinations.) A rider so equipped will be able to take advantage of a following wind or downhill stretch with the 50 × 15 or, at the other end of the scale, to tackle a short sharp hill on the 40 × 24 without having to dismount. In some districts the smallest gear is rarely used. In hilly country it is the one most frequently employed. In such conditions the same free-wheel block (15, 17, 18, 20, 24) could be used, with the number of teeth on the front chainwheels reduced to 49 and 32, giving gears from 86·4 down to 35·9 for really steep hills or long drags up mountain passes. If you indulge in the luxury of a triple chainwheel something like 52, 42 and 28 teeth might be chosen, again in combination with the free-wheel set already suggested.

The above are, indeed, merely suggestions to guide the newcomer in the right direction. As in the case of finding a good riding position, the ideal gear range will only be found after thousands of experimental miles. It must also be realized that while a cyclist may own a 10-speed machine, two of the gears should not be used! One of the early technical objections to derailleur gears was that the chain had to run out of line on some of the sprockets. In practice the loss of efficiency in the drive is negligible provided the chain is not 'bent' too much. It is advisable not to use the bigger chain wheel with the biggest rear sprocket, and neither should the smaller chainwheel be paired with the smallest sprocket. When a triple chainwheel is used it is even more important to avoid running the chain exaggeratedly out of line. In selecting their gear ratios, double chainwheel users should regard only eight of the ten gears as being effective, while 'triple' devotees should be content with only 12 – or even ten – of the 15. Touring cyclists have not shown much enthusiasm for the six-block free-wheel whose extra width causes various technical problems other than unacceptable chain-line.

Continental cyclists who go in for 'rough-stuff' riding on surfaces other than metalled roads, often use 650 mm (25·5 in) wheels, but their British counterparts stick faithfully to the 27 in variety. This is a good place to point out that while the same size (27 in) tubular racing tyres are used on both sides of the Channel, there is a small but critical difference in the dimensions of the wired-on type. A visitor to the Continent riding 27 in 'high pressure' tyres should take a spare cover with him if he feels there may be a need, because the 700 mm size will not fit his rims.

Having the ideal gear combination available is not everything. You must know how to use the derailleur system properly. This is where the concept of rhythm comes in. You should not have to twirl the pedals frantically or be forced to press them down heavily, swinging the shoulders and panting heavily at each movement. Pedalling rhythm should be smooth and supple. At the same time it must be reasonably regular. The experienced cyclist will not have to change gear every 100 yards or so, but will 'negotiate' changes in the terrain, in much the same way as racing drivers use their gearbox. When he comes to a hill he will 'derail' on to a more sensible gear – the hill sloping upwards beneath his wheels is of course an obstacle, but using a lower gear will allow him to make up for the greater difficulty by maintaining the same sort of rhythm as he was using on the flat. On a downhill stretch he will use his 'heaviest' gears – in this way he can keep pedalling, which means that his legs will not stiffen from the cold or comparative immobility, as they might otherwise, and he will still have complete control of the machine. Over the first few miles, when he has not really warmed up, he will take care not to tire himself out by using too high a gear – otherwise he may find the return journey tough going.

He might also find it tough going if – through carelessness or lack of experience – he had failed to plan his eating and drinking properly. As a matter of fact this problem is not confined to cycling. Anyone who advocates taking physical exercise, or indeed anyone at all, should remember that his daily diet must maintain the correct nutritional balance and include essential mineral salts and trace elements. Sauces should be avoided as far as possible, along with fried food, indigestible pork products and game, and of course alcoholic drinks.

The question of food is also important when you are not actually pedalling. Although you should not set off on an empty stomach, you must allow some time to digest your food before starting a ride. Racing cyclists are very strict about this, finishing their meal three hours before the start of a competition. Ideally the tourist, whose opening miles may involve the climbing of a mountain pass, should follow suit. Many would be quite willing to do so, but find it impossible. The proprietor or staff of a small country hotel or boarding house will hardly get up in the small hours of the morning to prepare a meal for a crazy cyclist who then rests in an easy-chair for two or three hours before starting his day's ride!

On the road there is an obvious difference between a short run of an hour or two and a whole-day outing. In the first case you will need nothing more substantial than some dried fruit, oranges, biscuits, and perhaps a *bidon* of drink. On a longer trip, first make sure you have a nourishing breakfast. If you stop for lunch at a restaurant avoid rich food and stick to grilled meat or fish with fresh vegetables. Do not drown your food by drinking too much with a meal. In the summer do not just drink anything whenever you feel like it. It is advisable to steer clear of iced drinks, which are refreshing for a moment but do not really quench the thirst – and are liable to cause an upset stomach.

Now what about the right *distances* to aim for when planning a cycling programme? The word 'programme' implies the idea of a carefully thought-out rate of progress. A man or woman using his or her cycle again after many weeks' inactivity will certainly not be up to a 100 mile ride straight away. Outings early in the season will cover less than half that distance and only the middle range of your set of gears should be used. Gradually you will find yourself getting fitter, and will be less out of breath, finding it easier to maintain a steady pedalling rhythm. A 100 km (62·25 mile) outing will not present any problem by now, if you are content to ride without over-exerting yourself – five hours at an average speed of 20 km/h (12·5 mph) will not tire you out. A circuit of 200 km (125 miles) or a return trip of 100 km (62·25 miles) each way, or a cycling holiday made up of a series of 'stages', will become a viable proposition. Keep an eye on the stamina of the youngest members of your party. Although it is perfectly all right for them to burn up excess energy, they are just at the age when lack of height and girth may have unfortunate consequences and make them give up cycling altogether after a few months.

What sort of timetable is best suited to the four key factors we have mentioned – distance, rhythm, the use of a sensible range of gears, and eating nourishing, easily digested food, on a little-and-often basis? If you are cycling alone you can please yourself and pedal happily at any time of the day and night, although in certain circumstances care must be taken. Ice on the roads can be dangerous at night, because it is difficult to see, while in summer it is best to avoid the hottest time of the day.

## The early birds

Individual touring at a speed that suits your mood is one of the most spontaneous forms of cycling, along with the odd 'spin' broken up by fairly frequent and lengthy stops. However, these only partly satisfy the keen rider's appetite for cycling. Indeed it would be childish to deny that other deep-seated motives often come into it – an urge to compete with others or to improve on your earlier performance or a feeling that you want to know what your own potential is and to surpass yourself. This leads to a very different form of cycling, known in French as a *randonnée cyclosportive*. This term is used to cover a wide variety of different events which were, until the last few years, unknown in Britain but are now gaining popularity as 'hard-riding tourist trials'.

There are a large number of 'Cycle Touring Federations' all over the world, many of them affiliated to the Cycle Touring Commission (CTC) of the Alliance Internationale de Tourisme (AIT), which has its headquarters in Geneva. The federations vary considerably in the number of their members, most of whom also belong to cycle clubs. Their main function is to co-ordinate, or in some cases to mastermind, a whole series of events which their members can take part in. These events vary enormously – in some countries speed is of no consequence, while in others it is the whole idea of the exercise. These latter tests are a controversial subject, as some people protest vehemently that cycle touring should be totally non-competitive. This, by the way, is the principle adopted by the most famous touring club of all, the Cyclists' Touring Club. They are by no means anti-racing. Indeed there is a feeling of pride that many world-famous competitors – Reg Harris for example – started their cycling careers as CTC members. With cycle sport

efficiently controlled by the British Cycling Federation and Road Time Trials Council, the CTC organise few or no contests in which speed cycling is all-important. They do however promote interesting touring tests in which 'brain rather than brawn' is called for – map reading, knowledge of countryside, weather lore, and so on.

Some continental events take the form of festivals or rallies of varying size, with organised cycle outings to explore a specific part of the country. Some of them last several days and are based on a 'star' system whereby you ride out in a different direction every day and return to base every evening. Cycle rallies generally involve an official start, either from a single starting-point or from several different ones, and a series of checkpoints at various places along the route where you stop to have a 'route card' stamped. Sometimes the object of the exercise is to get back to the starting-point within a given time, which is usually not too difficult.

Winter rallies are pleasant because they enable tourists to 'keep in touch' socially – and also to 'keep in touch' with pedalling. Some meetings are organised to commemorate a specific event, which may have happened years ago. Local cyclists and others from all over the country will get together at a fixed meeting-place. Gatherings of this kind are particularly friendly.

Then there are a wide variety of events in which every entrant who has come up to a given standard is awarded a certificate or badge. This type of test is called a 'standard ride' in Britain and a *brevet* trial in France and Switzerland, but most national federations organise their own trials. The French system covers a wide range of tests with some that have become world-famous. In recent years the number of entrants has suddenly shot up, as a result of the boom in cycle touring as a sport.

As a matter of fact the idea of crossing a country diagonally, from farthest point north to farthest point south or vice versa (or east and west), started in Britain almost a hundred years ago. In July 1880 H Blackwell and C A Harman took 13 days to pedal a 1440 km (900 miles) route from Land's End to John O'Groats. (Seven years earlier, starting on 2 June 1873, a 'quartet' comprising Messrs Spencer, Hunt, Leaver and Wood of the Middlesex Bicycle Club had taken 15 days to cover the 1040 km (650 miles) between London and John O'Groats.) It was not until the 1930s that the famous nine 'diagonals' began to be organised in France on a systematic basis. In April 1930 a pair of tandem cyclists, Georges Grillot and Roger Coiffier, rode from Brest to Menton, a distance of 1350 km (840 miles). To commemorate this long ride their brother-in-arms Dr Philippe Marre of the Groupe Montagnard Parisien thought up the nine 'diagonals', which he put forward in July 1932. They were: Brest-Menton, Brest-Strasbourg, Dunkirk-Hendaye, Dunkirk-

*Off the beaten track. At first glance, with riders in crash helmets and racing jerseys, it looks like some kind of competition. It is in fact a leisure outing, but as well as using the same kind of bicycle equipment as the racing fraternity, many tourists are now equally sporty in their dress.*

Menton, Strasbourg-Hendaye, Brest-Perpignan, Dunkirk-Perpignan, Strasbourg-Perpignan, Hendaye-Menton. Before the war these long-distance tests were not particularly successful, but in recent years hundreds of cyclists have been tempted into trying them. One or two brave souls can even boast of having covered all nine diagonals in both directions!

The French federation also has two other *brevets*, the Brevet de Cyclotourisme National (BCN) and the Brevet des Provinces Françaises (BPF). Successful entrants have to cover the whole of France, because the BCN includes checkpoints in each of the French *départements*, both on the mainland and in Corsica, while the BPF involves checking in at six compulsory checkpoints in each *département*. This takes us back to the long-forgotten feats of a pioneer called Maurice Martin, who was one of the founders of the racing cyclist's 'Derby' – the Bordeaux-Paris race – and for decades was more or less a permanent fixture as the 'starter' who gave the signal for the Classic to begin. In 1897 he had carried out a survey for the daily newspaper *Le Vélo* which involved travelling on his bike right through all the French *départements* south of the Loire. It took him seven months, from March to September, to ride 8900 km (5600 miles) at an average of 81 km (50 miles) a day. The roads were in terrible condition and he had to cover a lot of mountainous country.

Mountains are, or course, the supreme test of the cyclist's skill – he sees them as both friend and enemy, worshipping them one minute and scared of them the next. Covering very long distances, without even stopping at night, does of course demand a dogged approach to cycling and this is an admirable quality. However, the true symbol of the hard-won pleasures of cycle touring is the hill-climber pushing himself to reach greater heights, literally and figuratively, by the strength of his will and sheer effort as he tackles mountain passes and lifts himself manfully up the long haul to the very top. From this point of view, and thanks to the physical geography of France, the Brevet Cyclo-montagnard Français, which was set up at the instigation of the French Cycle Touring Federation in 1965, is a model of its kind. It takes at least four years to obtain, as you have to do one long-distance run a year over the four main mountain ranges, with a series of trials laid down by rule two. First come the Alps, leading to the Brevet de Randonneur des Alpes (BRA), or Circuit des Aravis, in alternate years. Then the Pyrenees, with Bayonne-Luchon in one year and the Randonnée des Cols Pyrénéens (RCP) in alternate years. Then the Massif Central, with the Randonnée Velay-Vivarais or the Randonnée des Pays. And lastly the Vosges: Brevet de Randonneur des Vosges, or Circuit des Vosges. All of these are very tough going. Yet in 1974 900 entrants lined up at the start of the RCP (founded in 1946) and in 1975 no less than

1917 of the 2138 entrants in the BRA (founded 1936) finished the 245 km (152 mile) course in the stipulated time. The BRA involved crossing the Lautaret (2058 m, 6752 ft), the Galibier (2556 m, 8386 ft), the Télégraphe and the Croix-de-Fer (2067 m, 6782 ft) mountains, the intrepid entrants setting off before dawn.

The French humorist Jacques Faizant, a well-known cartoonist and novelist, is a passionate devotee of bikes and a keen touring cyclist. He has described the thousand and one difficulties – and the thousand and one delights – experienced by anyone who tries for a *brevet* or certificate. In the following extract he is riding with Albina, 'a young and very attractive American friend of my wife's, who is living in Paris on the vague pretext of studying oriental languages , and who becomes a sort of *alter ego* for Faizant.

An unexpected visit to the Salon du Cycle – she thought is was an art exhibition – kindles in her a consuming passion for bi-cycles. Now Albina and her Pygmalion are toiling up the mountainsides of the Circuit des Vosges – which are a great deal less welcoming than the uninitiated imagine.

'When does it start going downhill?' panted Albina, bending over the handlebars.

'It never goes down! You'll just have to get used to the idea. The tests that count towards the Brevet Cyclo Montagnard never go downhill. The organisers attended a secret ceremony in the cellars of the Federation at which they crossed their hearts and swore to die if they ever let the course go downhill.'

'Don't talk so much,' said Albina. 'And anyway: if you've got any puff to spare you can push me!'

Things had actually started off well. The previous day hundreds of cyclists had converged on Saint-Dié, with their bicycles slung over their shoulders and their huge, innocent eyes alight with the anticipation of a healthy, little spin in the gentle foothills of the Vosges. 'Oh no,' some of the tenderfeet were saying, with the usual arrogance of the novice, 'the Vosges are child's play!'

Quite apart from being rather insulting, this remark was totally inappropriate and they got a few pitying looks from the old-timers who'd been tempered in the fires of all the roads of France and who knew from experience that cycling certificates aren't just handed out like free gift offers.*

And then there are the 'Audax' tourists. Under the direction of 'captains' who must not be overtaken, they ride in groups at a stipulated speed of 22 km/h (14 mph) between control points where route cards are stamped. At some controls stops are brief, at others hurried meals are taken, and in the long-distance affairs a few hours' sleep is possible. Audax certificates are awarded to those completing the course within the following time standards: 200 km (124·5 miles) 12 hr; 300 km (186·75 miles) 17 hr; 400 km (250 miles) 22 hr; 600 km (383·5 miles) 37 hr; 1000 km (625 miles) 71 hr. A booklet compiled by Bernard Deon in 1974 gives full details of such tests

*Jacques Faizant in *Cyclotourisme* No. 179, September-October, 1970

and also tells us that the Audax movement began in Italy on 12 June 1897. On that date 12 cyclists set out from Rome to cover 230 km (143 miles) to Naples, and nine of them managed to get there that same evening. In January 1898 the Audax Italiano was founded, electing as President the sculptor Vito Pardo who had led the historic Naples run. In 1902, 55 Audax members covered the 540 km (336 miles) of the 'March of the Giants' circuit starting and finishing in Turin, in less than 36 hr.

On 7 January 1904 Henri Desgrange took up a pet idea of his colleague Geo Lefevre – just as he had done the previous year in setting up the Tour de France – and formed the French Audax whose first run was held on Easter Sunday. Like the Tour de France, the Audax movement is still going strong, though it scarcely gets the publicity afforded the world's greatest road race. The Union des Audax Français is well-known for combining four different types of activity: cycling, walking (certificates for 100, 130 and 150 km); swimming (6 km in less than 3 hr) and rowing (80 km) in 12 hr. This admirable scheme gives the 'man in the street' the chance to achieve a worth-while athletic performance without undergoing a severe training programme.

Apart from the regular programme of cycling *brevets* special Audax trials are organised from time to time. Notable among these was the 1450 km (900 miles) run in 1960 between Paris and Rome, where the Olympic Games were being held. This was enjoyed so much by the 124 who finished the course – divided into six stages and crossing the frontier by the Mont Cenis pass – that a Paris-Munich trip was organised in 1972 during the 20th Olympiad. A year earlier a 'Eurodax' association was formed, the member countries being France, Belgium, The Netherlands, Luxembourg, West Germany and Italy.

The most famous of all Audax tests is the 1200 km (750 mile) Paris-Brest-Paris run founded in 1931 and run simultaneously with the great professional classic which had been organised every 10 years since Charles Terront's epic victory in 1891. That first Audax adventure was marred by bad weather and only 29 of the 81 starters arrived back in Paris within the time limit of 90 hours. The idea was to make the Audax Paris-Brest-Paris a decennial affair like the professional race, but when 1941 came Europe was at war and while a limited programme of road racing was carried out during the Occupation, the organisation of a giant event like the 'Brest and back' was out of the question. The scheduled 1941 events were eventually held in 1948 and the intended 10 year sequence resumed in 1951, by which time the Audax trial had become firmly established. So popular in fact that it was decided to promote Paris-Brest-Paris every five years instead of every ten for both tourists and professionals. Ironically the 1956 professional race was cancelled through lack of entries

and has never since been contested. The Audax trial however has been very well supported. In 1971 only 24 of the 328 entrants failed to complete the course in 90 hr.

It should be remembered that during that time the Audax riders rode in small groups led by a 'captain' who set a steady 22 km/h (14 mph) pace. Scheduled stops were made by *all* contestants for meals and brief sessions of sleep. This classic Audax formula suits one type of *cyclosportif* but not the one who is more competitively minded. Such hard-riders have become known as Randonneurs and have their own set of *brevets* over the same distances as the Audax riders: 200, 300, 400, 600 and 1000 km (125, 185, 250 and 620 miles) – and the 1200 km (750 miles) of Paris-Brest-Paris. Apart from compulsory stops at the control points to 'sign on the dotted line' and have their route cards stamped, the Randonneurs are free to make their own pace. Although some contestants undeniably 'race' and try to make as fast a time as they can, the man who rushes Paris-Brest-Paris in about 50 hours gets exactly the same medal as the more leisurely rider who has a good meal every 160 km (100 miles) and two sessions of sleep and yet still completes the 1200 km (750 miles) inside the 90 hr time limit.

Over the years there has been much rivalry between the Audax and Randonneur organisations, but now they are living together more happily. According to schedule both categories would have organised a Paris-Brest-Paris trial in September 1976, one starting the day after the other finished. To avoid congesting the roads for a long period, and to give riders a chance to take part in both types of test, the respective organisations amended their plans. The Randonneur event was brought forward to 1975, the Audax keeping to the original 1976 date, and the two trials will now be held every four years.

The 1975 Randonneur event over the Paris-Brest-Paris trail was a great success and to keep the field down to manageable proportions the organisers insisted on applicants proving their capabilities in a number of preliminary tests up to 600 km (375 miles) in length. Even so, an enormous pack of 666 set out from the western outskirts of Paris in September and 554 got back to Paris within the 90 hr. Three of them actually covered the 1200 km (750 miles) in a record 43 hr 27 min – two Frenchmen, Yves Cohen and Robert Truchi, and Hermann de Munck of Belgium. At the other end of the table was 71 year old Monsieur Maury who arrived back after 89.5 hr – and in between was Madame Suzy de Carvailho whose ride lasted 57 hr. Among 16 successful British club cyclists were four on tricycles and their skilled riding was a feature of the trial.

Before leaving the 1200 km (750 miles) Paris-Brest-Paris road, it is interesting to compare the 43·5 hr Randonneur record with the 'absolute' best of 39 hr established by Maurice Diot in winning the 1951 professional race, the last to be run. The difference of 4·5 hr is not great bearing in mind the fact that Randonneurs make 16 compulsory stops at control points, and that their bicycles must be fitted with mudguards.

## An intelligent pastime

This does not mean that we should mix up cycle touring and competition cycling. You cannot call it racing when various associations work out itineraries and offer them to the public,* or when two vegetarians from India pass through Paris in January 1975 having covered 73 000 km (45 000 miles) travelling in the opposite direction from Kemp, Stevens, Allen and Sachtleben from India via Afghanistan, Iran, Bulgaria, Yugoslavia, Italy, Switzerland, Austria, West Germany, the Netherlands and Belgium, then on to Spain, South America, North America, Japan and Australia. It is not 'racing' when you bowl gently along as the mood takes you. Some people do try to be both things at once and play at being racing cyclists, but the vast majority of those who like an occasional 'scrap' on the road or a ride against time are content to take things easily on their bicycle rides.

Instead of racing they will be true cycle tourists, visiting new places or returning to those which hold happy memories for them. Now and then they enjoy putting their speed and their strength to the test, but they are just as happy, just as *completely* happy, enjoying the mild air of a spring morning, the sun caressing their cheeks, a chat with a friend, the beauty of a view that suddenly unfolds, the infinite variety of sensations offered by the bicycle, which is a true source of 'intelligent pleasure'. You can savour this pleasure best if you work out an itinerary right away from the main roads, where the endless stream of cars makes cycling dangerous, to say nothing of spoiling your pleasure.

> However far afield you go a journey by bike will teach you to see right into the heart of nature and its flora and fauna ... It will help you to understand the local people and the local customs ... to delve into the history and folklore of the various regions you pass through ... In other words it will draw out latent urges and characteristics ... cycle touring means setting off in daylight ... whatever the weather ... reaching hilly country ... riding through forests and valleys on the lookout for picturesque villages and rural beauty spots ... filling your lungs with fresh and sweetly scented air ... It also means setting off for a holiday in the open, laden with luggage or camping gear, finding out about all the various aspects of a region ... nibbling away at mountain passes ... intoxicating downhill runs that seem to go on for ever ... coming home with a beautiful tan and a rich crop of memories caught for ever in a series of excellent photographs.

This commentary is made up of extracts scattered throughout letters written by a man who was a shining example to all cycle tourists – Charles Antonin

(1888–1967), who was much loved in France and abroad. It appeared in a most attractive book of some of his splendid photographs, which were collected and published as a gesture of affection by the Amicale Artistique du Département de l'Ain.†

If properly understood, cycle touring should arouse your intellectual curiosity – in fact, this is an essential part of the whole process. It is the enemy of lazy thinking as well as physical laziness. The cycle tourist must know how to use his eyes. He must try to look beyond appearances, for after all he can come much closer to the heart of a region than the car driver roaring along in his glass-walled box and eating up the miles with no other thought in his head but to get from A to B as fast as possible. The cycle tourist, on the other hand, will be quite happy temporarily to forsake his bike to do some sightseeing in a town or to visit a picturesque spot. He will want to get close to the heart of man and of nature – and he will take back a whole series of visual memories, either in his head or in his camera.

The link between cycling and photography goes back a long way. The very first page of the very first issue of the Bordeaux magazine *Véloce-Sport*, published on 5 March 1885, contained an article by the editor, the distinguished cyclist Fernand de Lados, drawing his 'dear reader's' attention to this very subject:

> Any excursionist will be happy to bring back these delightful souvenirs of his travels. One day he will be struck by the sight of a magnificent old *château*, with graceful architecture and imposing turrets. Another day he will take a smiling valley with a river meandering slowly through it, sparkling in the last rays of the setting sun. Or he may have a wonderful view between a pair of hills, and then find a village square surrounded by some old houses built in an unusual style, or an old church with a medieval porch and belfry.
>
> Nature offers our young photographer an inexhaustible mine of delights. And how delightful for you, dear reader, to be able to preserve the image of these everchanging and infinitely varied scenes in a permanent visual form, instead of just in your thoughts or written down on paper! What a magnificent haul our intrepid cyclists will be able to bring back!
>
> We are convinced that you will answer our call, and that when he has read the learned articles by our colleague Monsieur Sun, every cycle traveller will be eager to put our friend's useful tips into practice.

Needless to say, many a spoilt film, many a mediocre snap, many a failed sunset have resulted from this advice over the hundred years since then. This method of improving on the human eye has also produced some intensely pleasurable experiences and has helped to make both those who instinctively like the idea and those who show little interest in it – maybe even those who hate the whole business – appreciate how cycle touring helps you to acquire an intelligent knowledge of the world we live in.

---

*Example: *La France à bicyclette*. 74 itinerary checked by le Touring Club de France, Flammarion, 1975.

†*L'Ain vu par Charles Antonin*, 1969. Copyright: L. & J. Antonin, 4, rue du Dr-Nodet, Bourg-en-Bresse.

*It is April and the 'form' is gradually coming back. But mileage is still only moderate and the riders are not yet ready for long-distance 'raids'.*

*Unlike the racing cyclist who is constantly trying to break away from his companions, the tourist is content to ride at a regular speed.*

*Young British cyclists on an Adventure Week exercise. Now for the next objective, and there are no signposts to show the way! But with good visibility and a large-scale map that is no problem at all.*

*A lone tourist with well-filled saddlebag, riding on the left of the road – where else but in Great Britain? Unlike professionals in competitive tours who speed down mountain tracks, this real amateur is in no hurry on the Lochinver road in north-west Scotland, with the twin peaks of Suiven and Caspin dominating the peaceful scene.*

Then there is also the question of trying to get your impressions down on paper, which is never an easy matter when it comes to conveying a simple pleasure that has been experienced so intensely. I have to admit that few descriptions or stories of cycle rides, some of them humorous, some lively, others less so, have managed to penetrate beyond a small circle of readers who are already converted. Yet some of them are full of instructive glimpses of the way the sport has developed, stressing, for instance, the fact that the appearance of the motorcar and the speed with which it caught on slowed down the progress of cycle touring to a remarkable extent after 1900 – cycle touring as a way of travelling over long distances, that is. And yet a few lines picked out here and there tell you more about the deep-felt pleasure of cycling than a long and weighty speech.

Tourists pedal along a cliff-top path – British tourists! They carry their goods and chattels in large saddlebags, whereas continentals prefer sacs attached to the handlebars.

Although bicycles are built to be pedalled on the open road, it is fun now and then to get off the tarmac on to simpler tracks – a river tow-path for instance.

*British cycle tourists are fond of leaving the beaten track and pedalling 'far from the madding crowd'.*

# The realm of the dropped handlebars

There are 60 of them, riding in close formation as they struggle up the first hill climb. Their weaker brethren gradually drop back. Now there are 40, but the multicoloured thread stretches taut and any minute now it will snap. Near the front, the champion rides on at a steady pace, led at this stage by one of his team mates, who acts like a pilot fish carving out a path for him, until he takes matters into his own hands once and for all. The others can't match his speed and give up the unequal struggle, dropping back in their turn. Only 17 left. The champion races on like one possessed. Eight riders, the best of the bunch, manage to keep with him by drawing on their last reserves of strength and courage. A close-up now. His face is tense with concentration, glistening with beads of sweat; his body is squeezed into a closely-fitting jersey – pink if it is the Giro d'Italia or yellow in the Tour de France – as he fills our field of vision, with the countryside gliding past down below. Now there are only four left. More hairpin bends, more sharp turns, and the road still climbs. This time the moment of truth has come – a young 'challenger' launches a single-handed attack on the 'title-holder', duelling with the man who is the king of cycling, the undisputed master of his art. Will the tamer be tamed? Some experts have been predicting for years that he is due to be toppled from his throne. For a split second a pine forest hides the two men.

Not today. When the trees give way, first to scrubby grass, then to gravelly marl, and the crowd of spectators grows thicker – the racers are almost at the top now and it is still the champion in the lead. He is way out in front, already riding under the banner proclaiming that this is the summit of the *col* counting in the Grand Prix de la Montagne competition. He is already snatching a newspaper from a team helper and tucking it under his jersey to protect his chest on the icy cold descent that follows the blazing heat of the climb. He is already tearing downhill, rolling like a marble round the hairpin bends. The *cognoscenti* have clicked their stopwatches to determine his lead over the next men to reach the top. They argue whether or not he will be able to maintain his lead to the end of the stage, and if so how far he will finish ahead of the second man. They marvel how 'he' managed to remain the

The first climbs of a mountain stage have already split the field. On a comparatively flat intermediate section the leaders observe a brief truce. The race leader in his yellow jersey is well in the picture, while in his red and white car the Race Director has a close-up view.

Early miles in the 14th stage of the
1975 Tour de France. The riders take
things quietly through the Massif
Central, preserving their strength for
the last tough climb to the summit of
of the Puy de Dôme mountain.

The quintessence of road racing,
the lone breakaway in the mountains.
The rider is Bernard Thévenet
(France) who by decisively winning
this stage went into an unbeatable
overall lead in the 1975 Dauphiné-
Libéré race. Six weeks later
Thévenet had an even greater
success – victory in the
Tour de France.

*Mountain racing is not confined to the big Tours of France, Italy, Spain and Switzerland. Alpine passes figure prominently in the route of the seven-day Dauphiné-Libéré circuit promoted by the Grenoble newspaper of that name.*

*There is no aspect of road racing in which Eddy Merckx of Belgium does not shine. Here is Merckx the Mountaineer.*

master hill-climber by fighting tooth and nail when challenged.

Splendid images these, and the film-maker Joel Santoni brought them magnificently to life in his film *La course en tête* ('At the front end of the race') which centred round the figure of Eddy Merckx, but also went beyond him to capture and recreate the epic of cycle racing. For, although leisure rides and organised touring can offer the most intense pleasure, there is no doubt that competition cycling opens up a different world – a world in which ambition and the will to win are all important; a world in which the racer must accept good luck or bad with equanimity and always be ready to face up to himself.

What does this world look like, when the sport of cycling is pushed to its furthest limits? Its appeal is universal; so many fields of action are possible; so many types of competition; so many ways of racing.

My aim is to provide a rough sketch map of this world without restricting myself to a geographical description. I want to point out the 'rules of the game' – how to train, how to plan your race, realizing that there is no point in riding like mad at the head of the pack, supposing that you can win that way. Technique and tactics play an important part in any race.

When it comes to the field of action, there are both amateur and professional races, road races and track races, plus the hard grind and switchback fortunes of 'cyclocross'. Yet a number of general principles can be established. Some of them are applicable to all types of cycle racing, while others only concern specific aspects of the sport.

## Up hill and down dale

### Amateurs

In some countries, particularly in Eastern Europe, all sportsmen are 'amateur' because the idea of professional sportsman is rejected. This means that their best racing cyclists can ride in the Olympic Games, which adhere to the rules of admission laid down by the International Olympic Committee. Even in Western Europe, the stronghold of the 'pro', few cyclists become professionals – there are a few hundred of them, as against tens of thousands of amateurs. This is not really surprising, because you need to be exceptionally good even to take part in professional cycling, let alone making a go of it. At the beginning of their careers at any rate, the professionals started along their chosen road by taking part in amateur races. Those who made the grade then joined the small, select party who are paid monthly salaries by commercial sponsors to ride in their teams. In other words the ABC of cycling is amateur competition.

The grass-roots unit is the club, affiliated to a regional 'division' which is itself answerable to the National Federation. The beginner's first move is therefore to join a club. If he is a continental he will have become interested in cycling through the media which give considerable space and time to racing, or perhaps through the enthusiasm of a friend. In Britain the latter is more likely since cycle-sport does not get mass coverage in the press and on radio and television. Each country has its own age limits, though the Fédération Internationale des Amateurs Cyclistes (FIAC) has stipulated that 18 is the upper age limit for junior world championships.

Except for races for the very young, where restrictions may be set on the number held in any one week, the distance covered and the gears used, the standard distance in the lower categories is (in France) about 100 km (62·25 miles). So we can study a number of different aspects of the sport on this basis.

First, training. In the old days all, or almost all training, took the form of actual cycling. The French ace Louison Bobet may have been the first to show how important general fitness is. In 1955 he published a book called *En selle* ('In the saddle'), in which his basic precepts were organised into a coherent programme by his brother Jean. From then on it has been generally accepted that although a racing cyclist may scarcely touch his bike during the winter he will follow a strict daily programme of physical exercise, with particular emphasis on breathing and abdominal exercises. He will also join fellow-members of his club for group training sessions once or twice a week. It is important to be conscientious about this, but it should be fun too. During the group sessions, which will be attended by a qualified instructor, our beginner will tone-up his muscular system by training with moderate weights. He will also take part in cross-country runs, which will not always be a picnic because the whole point is to improve the cardio-vascular system, which is what counts in cycle races. At this stage a weekly run on his bike should be enough, generally on Sunday and preferably with a fixed wheel. This will keep his legs in cycling trim, and also teach him how to ride in close formation with a pack of cyclists. He will soon realize that if he swerves, even very slightly, or if he loses concentration for just a moment, he may well fall off and perhaps cause a general 'pile-up'. He feels frightened at first when in such tight formation, but he gradually gets used to having his front tubular right up close to the wheel of the chap in front and to someone leaning on his shoulder. This type of apprenticeship is an essential part of his training.

February is the month when cycle training proper takes up most of the preparation time, at any rate in countries where the racing calendar starts in mid-March. General physical training gradually starts taking second place, though it should still be part of the daily routine. Stick to shorter and less intensive exercises at this point. I recommend a recent book by Anquetil, Chany and Scob called *Cyclisme* ('Cycling'), which is very good on this preparation period, as well as on many other points. It includes a series of tables showing different types of training suitable for young riders and backs these up with an explanation of the modern theories of endurance (for extended periods of exertion), resistance (for short and sharp bursts of speed) and strength.

As the weeks go by he will be covering longer and longer distances, and, more important, he will step up his rhythm and increase his gears. Once he has really found his form he will follow a series of alternating training sessions, concentrating on specific aspects such as hill-climbing, how to make a quick get-away, how to pedal a big gear. Monday and Friday will invariably be rest days. At one time the idea of resting on Saturday, the day before the race, was sacrosanct, but nowadays it is acknowledged that a short run at a relaxed pace is an excellent way of preparing your system for the next day's exertions.

The basic principle behind all this is that each week you should follow a pattern of intensive effort followed by an 'easy' time to allow the body to recover. A new concept called 'interval training' has been borrowed from athletics and now features in all training programmes. It involves alternating no more than a minute of maximum stress with about a minute or a minute and a half of deceleration. Your cardiac rhythm is strictly controlled to make sure you don't overdo it. If this tough training is properly organised it will greatly improve any racing cyclist's performance.

Once the season is really under way, four runs a week (on Tuesday, Wednesday, Thursday and Saturday) is the ideal programme to follow. There is no need to cover long distances (except possibly on Wednesday), because the factors that count are maintaining a steady rhythm, the terrain you have chosen and the extent to which you exert yourself. Equally important is the enthusiasm with which you accept the necessary constraints imposed by training and by the need to develop an iron will – you really must go through the mill to find your form and keep it. You learn to know yourself, you toil away, make strides, then reach saturation point and feel the need to cut down on your training for a while. To put it in a nutshell – what you are doing is perfecting the amazing mechanism of the human body, which always has greater resources than you imagine, and at the same time gradually soaking up the rules of the game.

For instance, you will learn the need to warm up at the beginning of each session before extending yourself fully; about the need to ease a bit before the end of a run; about the advantage of choosing a route where the wind will be behind you on the return journey, so that you finish with a burst of speed as you would in a race.

Training is the key to success. Without it no

Waiting for the start of any race is an anxious time. Today there is particular tension. Competitors are not riding for themselves, or for a club, but for their country. This front row will have the privilege of being the leaders – if only for a few seconds – of the 1975 world amateur championship contested by a field of 180 on the Mettet circuit, Belgium.

Calories? Carbohydrates? Glucose syrup levels? This young hopeful is not yet concerned with dietetics. He's just hungry!

117

*Winter preparation is the key to summer success, the programme including climbing, descending and group riding. Some riders prefer training on their own; this is excellent for stamina but does not produce the 'zip' necessary for fast road races. Comparatively heavy wheels and tyres are used for these off-season outings, as well as warmer clothes.*

The start of another season and the
familiar routine of massage and pinning
on race-numbers. Established stars are
determined to enhance their reputations;
newcomers dream of story-book victories.

sportsman will ever win his battle against inertia, laziness and dejection.

Now it's time for the actual race.

As starting time of a race approaches the atmosphere is tense, even though some riders seem relaxed enough on the surface. There is always the joker of the pack making his wisecracks as competitors file up to the officials' table to draw their race numbers, or in the changing rooms, or during the 'roll call' that summons entrants to the starting line. This is what they have been preparing and planning for all those months – so that they could experience these few highly charged hours, bright with excitement and colour. They had trouble getting to sleep last night. They thought of all the things that can happen during a race, wondering about their bicycles, about their team mates and their rivals, known and unknown. They wondered what kind of form they would be in tomorrow, remembering what sort of a show they had put up in last Sunday's race, and how they were going in mid-week training runs. Soon they will know.

The starter's flag drops. The pack shoots forward as though the race would only last a few minutes and not two or three hours. You try to get near the front. That is the best place to be. There will be less danger of falling for one thing, and you will be able to keep an eye on things, whereas you might not be able to spot a vital move if you are boxed up in the middle of the bunch. That bunch, inevitably, will split in two or three pieces. If you are in the front part, you are still in business; if in the second your position is difficult; if among the tail-enders, pretty hopeless.

After this tumultuous beginning the race moves into a country lane. This, remember, is a comparatively small amateur competition. No huge crowds of spectators line the route as in a professional classic, no long lines of press cars and service vehicles. As Antoine Blondin* has put it, this is one of those low masses early in the morning, where the swish of the tyres, the stuttering sound of the gears changing, the hoarse pants of the cyclists, the words of advice shouted to your partner, and the invectives hurled at rivals can easily be heard, like chairs scraping or sidesmen whispering to each other in a half-empty church. But meanwhile the cyclist is having his great adventure A shudder runs up his spine as he aban-

dons himself utterly to the race, looking tensely round him, his mind racing and his expression solemn, even if he is secretly jubilant at being part of the fun once again.

A beginner will be surprised by the fast speed at which road races are run. A more experienced road-racer will already be scheming how to be well positioned when the final outcome of the race is decided. If he wants to start a breakaway he will do so from the 'blind side' and try to surprise his rivals. If he finds the going hard he will avoid the temptation to change gear every few seconds and do his best to maintain a steady pedalling rhythm. He will choose a big enough gear so that he does not have to twirl his legs and almost suffocate with the effort, but not so big that he is left high and dry in the middle of a steep hill. Nowadays the following gear ratios are widely used for road racing: 52 and 42 on the front chainwheels, a 5 sprocket free-wheel of 14 to 18 teeth, or a 6 sprocket of 13–18. If the course includes a tough hill, the 18 tooth sprocket will be replaced by a 20 or even 22 if the gradient is severe.

It is essential to be wide awake for every second of the race. Brute force will give way to a 'race sense' which will enable a rider to judge that this time a breakaway attempt is really going to pay off. It will not necessarily happen on the steepest point of a hill. It may come just after the summit when the field is strung out and some riders are slackening their pace, thinking the worst is over. Or maybe it will come during one of those moments when the pack slows down for no apparent reason, perhaps because the weather is heavy, or because they have just finished a hard 'chase' after a dangerous-looking group which had broken away.

Although attempts at lone breakaways are constantly being made, the 'aggressors' usually hope that a group of eight or ten riders will form to share the pace-making and keep ahead of the chasing pack. For various technical reasons not all members of the group may be willing to do their fair share of the work, so those who are active must not throw their strength away. They must maintain their pedalling rhythm and it is also important to pick the right position in the 'relay' of pacemakers and avoid riding

*Jean Durry: *La véridique histoire des géants de la route.* Prèface by Antoine Blondin: Editions Denoël, 1973.

Professionals race over much longer distances than
amateurs, except in one type of event : the road team
time-trial. Instead of 100 km events on flat roads and a
few turns, professional tests are usually about 10 kms,
contested on short and often hilly circuits, with many
corners. In such conditions perfect formation riding is
difficult. The front man of this Spanish team during a
Tour de France test is too far ahead of the second member
to provide effective shelter.

Unlike British amateur time-trial riders who must
not be accompanied, each professional in a big
continental test 'against the watch' has a following
car carrying spare wheels and bicycle.

immediately in front of the strongest member of the party. As the race nears the finish and you swing out after doing a hard turn in front of the group, the strong man behind you may decide this to be the moment to forget the gentleman's agreement to maintain a steady pace and sprint away to win on his own.

Now we have reached the last few miles of the race. Riders prepare for the sprint. It is too bad if you have not got yourself up among the leaders because at that speed – approaching 40 mph on a flat road – there is no hope of winning. When should the decisive attack be made? As late as possible – but before somebody else has the same idea! Easier said than done . . . If the finishing line is on an uphill stretch a rider will not, of course, sprint in his biggest gear. Fast pedalling is more likely to give victory in the last yards over an opponent who is hampered by a 'big windmill' gear.

Even if it is only a minor race, the thrill of knowing your front wheel has crossed the finishing line first is quite extraordinary. It makes up for all the strenuous efforts made in training, for resisting the temptation of late nights and rich, heavy meals and 'drinks with the boys'. A moment of great satisfaction.

You have slowly worked your way up the ladder, winning several races. You are learning to stay the distance, moving up from 100 miles to 120 and even 150 miles if you've tackled the amateur Paris-Roubaix which is now contested over a modified version of the notorious professional classic course. Then there are the stage races, varying in distance and importance between local 'loops' of two or three days' duration and national amateur promotions like the Milk Race Tour of Britain and the Tour de l'Avenir. This latter event was modelled on the professional Tour de France and was designed to give amateurs a chance to try their hand at racing over the great Alpine and Pyrenean mountain passes. Most important 'marathon' of all is the 14 day 'Peace Race', first contested in 1948. This is staged over the Warsaw-Berlin-Prague triangle (though not always reaching the capitals in that order) and attracts huge crowds. It brought fame to Gustav-Adolf Schür who was later to be a member of parliament in East Germany, and to Ryszard Szurkowski from Poland who won the race four times (in 1970, 1971, 1973 and 1975). Victory in the Team Race category of the 'Peace Race' is considered by East European nations to be even more important than winning individual honours.

## When every second counts

We now come to the most important international road competitions for 'amateurs'. There are the Olympic Games, of course, which take place every four years, and the world championships. All the contestants are bound to be in splendid physical shape and a high level of technical competence is normally reached.

One event on the World and Olympic programme is a very different type of race from the mass-start variety, which is the only kind we have looked at so far. In individual time-trials it might be supposed that brute force is all that matters. In fact this is not so, as we shall see later. In professional cycle racing road team time-trial events are rarely held as a test in their own right, and are only incorporated in stage races, either as a 'curtain raiser' or as a mini-stage during the competition proper. The one included in the 1976 Tour de France was indeed a 'mini', being only 4 km (2·5 miles) in length! For amateurs, however, 100 km (62.25 mile) team time-trials are a feature of world championships and Olympic Games and are one of the most exciting and exacting parts of the cycling programme. For this type of racing you need higher and higher gear ratios – a chain wheel with 54, 55 or even occasionally 56 teeth. From the technical point of view the team's relay technique and timing must be absolutely top-notch. The Swedish team, made up of the four Pettersson brothers – Eric, Gösta (the team leader), Stüre and Tomas – had got this down to a fine art and were more or less unbeatable from 1967 to 1969.

It really is terrible if you are not on such good form as your three team mates when the great day comes. You will be struggling right from the start, getting in their way, making them turn in a performance below their best and upsetting the carefully timed relay technique. You will go through hell, both physically and mentally, and finally you will pack up exhausted, leaving your three team mates – who will be furious and thoroughly fed up by this time – to finish the race in a hopelessly disorganised fashion.

Team time-trial riders never let up for a single moment. Bending low over ultra-light machines for more than two hours of intensive effort the four team mates streak away like arrows. In the 1974 World Championships in Montreal there were barely two seconds between the Swedish team who took up the mantle left behind by the Petterssons and their Russian rivals. Only two seconds.

The 1975 championships in Belgium marked the decline of Western Europe in favour of Eastern Europe, though it is not necessarily a permanent decline. Only Eastern Europeans are willing to put in the long and painstaking work needed to prepare for this highly athletic type of cycling, which is more appreciated by connoisseurs than by the usual crowds who enjoy watching cycling events.

## Ladies first

In the Montreal World Championships a solidly built woman cyclist with powerful legs but a friendly smile climbed on to the rostrum at the end of a road race and swapped her red-white-and-blue vest for the champion's rainbow jersey. There have been road and track world championship events for women since 1958. At Montreal in 1974 Geneviève Gambillon had just won back the title she first held two years earlier.

The athletic standard can never be as high as it is for men, as you can see from the fact that in some countries adult women are allowed to take part in races for boys of 15 and 16 – and the women rarely come out on top even then. Geneviève Gambillon's average speed was just under 33·457 km/h (21 mph) over a distance of 60 km (37 miles) whereas Eddy Merckx covered the 262 km (163 miles) of the professional event at 38·176 km/h (24 mph). The careers of Elsy Jacobs from Luxembourg, world champion in 1958, and Beryl Burton from Britain, who took the title in 1960 and 1967, both of whom were still racing in 1975, suggest that there are not enough good women coming up to take their place.

The British are rightly proud of Beryl Burton, greatest in a long line of women champions. Beryl is the Anquetil of the feminine world of wheels, for like the great Normandy rider she is an incredibly strong time-trialist. Indeed in 1968 she came to Paris at the invitation of the organisers and rode the Grand Prix des Nations course an hour ahead of the professional time-trial. On the starting line Beryl said her ambition was to cover the 72 km (45 miles) at an average speed of 40 km/h (25 mph); she did much better, storming round the tricky roads at 41.853 km/h (26·170 mph), loudly applauded by the admiring roadside crowd. Of course her speed was well short of that of the professional winner Felice Gimondi (Italy) who did 47·518, but Beryl was almost as fast as those in the lower places. Since that convincing proof of her unpaced riding ability we have not been surprised, on the continent, to hear that at nearly 40 years of age Beryl Burton could still not only beat all the home women in time-trial competition, but most of the men as well – even at 100 miles! Of course some girl will eventually take over from Beryl – and it could be her daughter Denise who has been pedalling since a tiny tot.

There are families all over the world who, like the Burtons, provide an effective answer to those who say that competitive cycling is too tough and violent for women.

## Professional racing

Few cyclists are good enough to turn professional (though many want to), and even fewer find fame and fortune in doing so. Yet the most famous road races, the ones that have become legends in the history of the sport, are almost all for professionals. Cycling is the professional's livelihood, so he spends all his time cycling, racing on the road from mid-February to October. He sometimes uses a motorised pacemaker in training to get used to pedalling big gears at high speed. Professionals normally enjoy exceptionally good health and can perform feats that seem astounding to ordinary mortals.

Many amateurs with a brilliant record of wins have never managed to make a go of it in professional cycling. By the time they turned professional they were already worn out by their amateur careers – they should have made the break sooner. Some never managed to get accepted in a business full of little cliques and customs. Above all, the rhythm of professional races is completely different from what they have been used to. Professionals may start off more slowly, but by the end they are going at breakneck speed, and they keep it up for mile upon mile.

In the last few years 'open' road races between amateur and professional teams have been permitted by the international governing body. These have shown that, on the whole, the position is as one would expect it to be: second-class professionals are better than top-rate amateurs. Occasionally, however, there is an upset when the spirit and dash of ambitious youngsters has taken them over the finishing line ahead of well-known 'cash men'.

## One-day races

At the beginning of the 20th century very few road races were run, and no one could have foreseen the huge number that are organised today. Of course there are races and races. For instance, there are those early-season events promoted on Mediterranean coast roads which, although taken seriously by up-and-coming professionals, are treated merely as training rides by established stars. Then there are the criteriums – short-distance afternoon or evening promotions on a small 'round-the-houses' circuit in the middle of a town or village. These are particularly popular immediately one of the major Tours has finished because the paying spectators have a chance of seeing such stars as Eddy Merckx, Raymond Poulidor, Bernard Thévenet etc. who have been so much in the news for nearly a month.

None of these will ever create such interest as the 'classics' – the races with a long history behind them and an equally long list of famous winners. A description of these major events will give a good picture of the very different but most typical facets of cycling, as well as providing some striking examples of the situations that may arise.

## The 'Primavera' and the 'Autumn Leaves'

On St. Joseph's Day – San Giuseppe – which falls on 19 March, a tightly knit pack approaches the *capi* zone skirting the Italian Riviera. The first big race of the year, the 270 km (170 mile) Milan-San Remo, marks the beginning of spring. It was first raced in 1907 and for many years the real battle started on the Turchino pass 130 km (80 miles) after leaving Milan. It has had some famous moments in its history, such as the terrible agony suffered by Eugene Christophe, the 1910 winner – only he and two other poor wretches finished the course. For many years the race seemed to favour *stranieri* (foreigners), but

Women's road racing is gaining in popularity. There was an entry of 44 for the 1975 world road championship and eight nations were represented in the first 15 finishers.

Geneviève Gambillon (France) wins the sprint at the end of the 1975 world road championship – but has not retained her title. A few yards ahead is Trintje Fopma whose satisfaction is clearly shared by third finisher, No. 37, another Dutch girl, Cornelia Van Hoosten-Hage who earlier in the week had won the track pursuit championship.

Beryl Burton of Britain, universally acknowledged the greatest-ever woman rider. Winner of scores of British championships at time-trial, road and track racing, Mrs Burton has also won six world titles, two in the road race and four in 3000 metres track pursuits. The results of the 1975 world series in Belgium showed 'D Burton' as bronze-medallist in the pursuit race – Beryl's 18-year-old daughter Denise. These two photographs are of Beryl (in a 100 mile event) and Denise (in a 50 mile) taking part in British time-trials.

it later became the exclusive glory of the *campion-issimi* and their rivals. Between 1914 and 1953 only two foreigners managed to break the spell – the tough Jeff Demuysere in 1934 and Louison Bobet in 1951. Since then the tables have been turned again, and apart from Michele Dancelli, who wept for joy when he won in 1970, and Felice Gimondi (1974), the honours list has invariably shown Belgian, Spanish, French, German or Dutch names – and one British one, Tom Simpson. In 1964 popular Tom proved a splendid winner of Milan-San Remo, which was one of the most important in his collection of 'classic' victories.

The standard has constantly risen, and so has the entrants' physical condition, for most of them start the race two or three days after competing in tough stage events such as Paris-Nice (called the 'Race to the Sun') or the Tirreno-Adriatico (the 'Two Seas Race'). As a result, the days are over when Fausto Coppi could leave Lucien Teisseire standing as soon as they reached the Turchino pass, with Teisseire only too delighted to be in second place, 14 min behind the winner! It's tough going at the heart of the moving throng who cross the three *capi* in close formation, in the usual friendly uproar that characterises races in Italy.

The field is still compact at the foot of the Poggio, a very steep climb deliberately chosen by the organisers to enable a final weeding-out process to take place – the top of the climb is barely 5000 m (3 miles) from the finishing line. It looks as if the race will be decided by a massive, dangerous sprint. Yet from such a position in 1976 Eddy Merckx notched up a *seventh* Milan-San Remo classic victory, having already succeeded in 1966, 1967, 1969, 1971, 1972 and 1975 when he equalled Costante Girardengo's long-standing record of six wins. In the 1976 race Merckx attacked on the Poggio climb and then, switching over to his biggest gear, pedalled all-out on the helter-skelter descent. Only one rider was able to stay with him, his young compatriot Jean-Luc Vandenbroucke, but the 'boy' could do no more than put up a token resistance in the two-up sprint and the 'master' won his seventh Milan-San Remo. Half a minute later the rest of the pack came yelping in to fight for third position.

At the end of the season, in October, comes the Giro di Lombardia, which is raced in a very different atmosphere. The roads are already strewn with autumn leaves, but more than that the mountainous terrain means that the winners are bound to be fine hill-climbers, who are still going strong at the end of the season, whereas a lot of roadmen take part only to make up the numbers – they're already worn out by a difficult season of cycling. Mass sprint finishes are rare in this October race founded in 1905 and won by Giovanni Gerbi, the *diavolo rosso* or 'red devil'. Fausto Coppi's record of five wins, four of them in consecutive years (1946–9 and 1954), still

has not been broken.

Alfredo Binda won it four times and Gaetano Belloni, Girardengo and Gino Bartali have each appeared on the honours list three times, along with Henri Pelissier, whose wins in 1911, 1913 and 1920 are often forgotten, though he in fact made his name on the roads of Lombardy. The average speed is usually under 40 km/h (25 mph) because of the hilly nature of the terrain. This race marks the end of the international road season.

### Hills of the 'low country'

> Suddenly I saw a completely straight road stretching out in perspective ahead of me, lined on both sides by a row of tall poplars with their branches towering over the road to form a splendid gothic vault.*

That was how a young country lad from Moorslede, the son of a farm labourer and brick-maker called Leonard van Hauwaert, discovered the roads of his native Flanders, when he set off on his first major outing on a bike that the local blacksmith had knocked up for him in three weeks. In the pre-First World War period Cyriel van Hauwaert, the first of all Belgian champions, was to cover thousands of miles of road, but he never forgot that first exciting moment, or the time when he set off for Roulers one February morning and rode over icy roads to Thourout, then on to Bruges, then, carried on by his own momentum, to a town he didn't know.

> Ahead of me the road climbed to form a small steep hill. I climbed up it and suddenly I saw ahead of me the vast green plain of the sea, which merges in the far distance into the blurred line of the horizon . . . Neighbours had often told me about the sea, when they came back from their train excursions. I was proud of my little bike for carrying me as far as this magic sight.

What he was looking at was Ostend and the North Sea.

Flanders is cycling country if ever there was one. In every little bar or café people are discussing the hopes and chances of the local cycling ace and at every village crossroads you are liable to be stopped by police controlling the traffic to allow a 'Kermesse' race to pass by. Every paving stone has felt the touch of a bicycle wheel clad in a racing tyre. Near the North Sea the sand dunes offer little protection against the fearsome winds. But some 'Mountains of Flanders' rise up from the plain and for racing cyclists they are not a bit like molehills.

After Cyriel van Hauwaert (the 'Lion of Flanders') the second 'father of Belgian cycling' was Karel Steyaert, better known by his pen name of Karel van Wijnendaele. He it was who founded *the* Flanders race – the 'Ronde van Vlaanderen' (Tour of Flanders), which started in 1913. Apart from a win in 1923 by Henri Suter (Switzerland), the Belgians managed to shake off all foreign competition right down to 1949, when Fiorenzo Magni, the powerful

*Cyrille van Hauwaert: *Ma carrière*. Menin, 1911.

*Flemish hills are short but tough. For the first time the narrow Koppenberg 'wall' was included in the route of the Tour of Flanders in 1976, and was climbed 60 miles from the finish of the 150 miles race. Climbing on his own here is Marc de Meyer, but his team-mate Freddy Maertens has already reached the top. Then come Walter Godefroot and Francesco Moser who have avoided the crash that forces many others to 'cyclo-cross' tactics.*

Italian cyclist, put an end to their absolute reign. Since then Belgian and foreign entrants have won a roughly equal number of times. It is a great feat to win a race in Flanders.

For the first part of the race you are lashed by the sea winds, and it is essential to be aware of the danger right at the start. The kingdom of wind is also the kingdom of the *echelon*. This device protects road racing cyclists against their most inexorable enemy – the wind that saps their strength, slows their rate of progress to a standstill and disheartens the weak. The echelon changes direction depending on the wind. If it is blowing from three-quarters left, for instance, the man leading the group rides on the extreme left of the road. The second man places himself close alongside, but slightly behind so that his own front wheel is parallel with the rear wheel of the leader. The third member of the party takes up a similarly 'staggered' position until the whole of the road is occupied. Only the leading rider therefore is getting the full force of the wind coming at him diagonally, and that 'wind breaker' is constantly changing. After the front man has led for about 200 metres he eases his effort and drops back to take the last place in the formation which has moved over by the width of one bicycle during the change. The 'drill' continues like clockwork for as long as the wind maintains the same direction in relation to the road.

The above description is the echelon in its simplest terms. There may, however, be only room for 12 riders – and about 30 trying to get in on the act! It is a kind of Noah's ark and the struggle to enter is fierce; part of a professional's craft is the ability to 'slam the door' to any unwelcome visitor. All the top teams have a couple of 'lockers up' on duty who ride at the back of an echelon to make sure that no intruder slips in. A rider who fails to gain admittance will have to ride on the extreme edge of the road, behind the last man, but getting no shelter at all. He is said to be 'riding in the gutter', and obviously is fighting a losing battle. If he looks round to find that half a dozen others are immediately behind him the correct drill is for the lot of them to join forces and form a new echelon 40 metres behind the first. With luck the course will change direction, or the wind will drop, there will be no further need for this kind of formation riding, and the various leading echelons will merge to form one big group. On the other hand . . . well, let me give you an example: in 1962 Rik van Looy's famous Flandria-Faema 'red guard' formed an impressive echelon immediately after the start of the 1962 Tour of Flanders. Of course it was impossible to confine it exclusively to members of his own team, but they dominated the 20 or so involved. The race was virtually over with 150 miles still to be covered and the other competitors did not see the leading men until they got to the showers!

Then the so-called 'low country' suddenly starts writhing and twisting and the race has come to the 'Flanders Mountains'. They have fierce-sounding names like Kwaremont and Kruisberg, and the most notorious of all is the Grammont, a steep 'wall' of large cobble stones – known to road-racing cyclists as 'barnums' because they appear to leap about like performing fleas or circus acrobats. The vocal applause from the cheering crowds is not as melodious as that of Italian cycling fans, but it is just as loud. The enthusiasm of the Flemish crowds is unmatched anywhere else in the world. They line the roads in their lumber-jackets and caps, leaning forwards with knees bent so that they can get closer to their heroes, who almost touch them as they race by. They are out there watching in all weathers, even if it is pouring with rain or the roads are covered in snow as they were in a recent Ghent-Wevelghem race. The Ronde is not of course, the only international race in Flanders. There are the 'Het Volk' and Ghent-Wevelghem circuits, and others not so well-known, but contested on the same kind of roads passing through a land where cycling is far and away the most popular sport.

## Top of the tree – Paris-Roubaix

Take any road-racing cyclist during the winter break when, although his legs are resting his mind is very active planning a campaign for the next season – and ask him one question: 'Which is the greatest one-day race – the one you'd give anything to win?' Virtually all of them would reply without a moment's hesitation 'Paris-Roubaix'. Every year, as they scrape a thick layer of mud or black dust off their weary bodies, the losers chant a gloomy refrain. Five punctures; three crashes; a derailleur gear that jammed; a saddle-pin broken; a pair of handlebars worked loose; a broken pedal – and the team's service car stuck in the mud on a narrow track and unable to get up with a spare bike. Yet every year the result speaks for itself, because though the favourites may fall in Paris-Roubaix, an 'outsider' never wins this most coveted of all classics. You hardly ever hear the stars complaining. They have their bits of bad luck like anyone else, but their strength, clear-headedness and skill tip the scales in their favour.

Nowadays the race starts in Chantilly, 25 miles north of Paris, but the route to Roubaix is still 275 km (170 miles) and approximately the same length as when the race was first run 80 years ago. A big pack of 150 riders speed along good wide roads in the early stages, with perhaps the odd skirmish here and there as lone riders, or small groups, sprint out in front of the action, perhaps hoping to get a mention in the papers or on the radio, or even have their picture on the TV screen. Generally speaking the field keeps pretty close together for the first 128 km (80 miles), knowing full well that they are rapidly approaching the gates to the 'northern hell', a journalist's cliché that has become a household phrase. This road through the black cycling country is paved with rough cobble-stones. Back in the old days it was impossible to miss this *pavé*, but about 20 years ago Paris-Roubaix was in danger of becoming just another road race, so thoroughly had the French Highways Department replaced the main road sections with strips of smooth concrete. To preserve the character of the race, and to maintain the legend of the northern hell, the organisers sent out reconnaisance parties to discover the worst roads possible and string them together to form a diabolical final stretch for Paris-Roubaix. Accordingly the modern route cuts across fields and through forgotten villages and if a rider runs out of road on a corner he is quite likely to find himself in the middle of a farmyard!

For many years Paris-Roubaix was the 'Easter Race' and some starters in the pre-1900 races had to attend the religious service held near the Porte Maillot at one o'clock in the morning, or the locals would have stopped the race going through. This race has seen many feats since Josef Fischer from Germany, a sturdy, strapping fellow with a moustache, a goatee beard and wearing a smart coat, won the inaugural race in 1896. He had already notched up major wins in 1893 (Vienna-Berlin) and 1896 (Milan-Munich and Trieste-Vienna). Charles Meyer from Denmark and the pint-sized Maurice Garin from France came in second and third. Fischer had covered 280 km (174 miles) in 9 hr 17 min (the 1976 winner Marc de Meyer of Belgium took 6 hr 37 min for 277 km (172 miles)).

Speeds have increased, but the human courage demanded is the same, and so is the necessity to ride *la course en tête* – to keep as near the front of the race as possible. Otherwise the unsettling mixture of stretches of tarmac alternating with tracks made up of what cyclists call 'big sugar lumps' and 'bowler hats' will prevent your catching the long string of front runners and overtaking them one by one.

Some of Eddy Merckx's greatest feats have been performed on the road to Roubaix. He has won the race three times (1968, 1970 and 1973), which puts him on a level with Octave Lapize (France: 1909, 1910 and 1911), Gaston Rebry (Belgium: 1931, 1934, 1935) and Rik van Looy (Belgium: 1961, 1962, 1965). Some observers claim that Merckx has been even greater when losing Paris-Roubaix than when taking the victor's bouquet. In 1975 he certainly did amazingly well to finish second after puncturing with only five miles to go. After having a wheel-change from his following service car Merckx made a mighty effort to get back up with the leading trio of riders. The great classic race finishes on the cement track at Roubaix and his supporters still believed that he could win. That epic pursuit had taken its toll, however, and he could not match the powerful

finishing sprint of his great rival Roger de Vlaeminck who swept by to win and so join Merckx as a member of the select 'club' of cyclists who have won Paris-Roubaix three times.

Nearly all the Paris-Roubaix races have reached a very high standard and deserve to be remembered. In 1913, for instance, François Faber managed an average speed of 35·333 km/h (22·083 mph). This record was not broken until 1931. Then in 1921 Henri Pelissier beat his brother Francis into second place, while in 1927 the 20-year-old Georges Ronsse of Belgium made his mark with a winning sprint – in those days the finishing point was on the Avenue des Villas. There was no doubt in the judge's mind that he had beaten Jean Curtel from Marseilles, but the French spectators thought otherwise. That was only one of the many 'incidents' that have occurred in Paris-Roubaix. For instance there were the times when Jean Maréchal and Roger Lapébie were disqualified (in 1930 and 1934); the year when André Mahe and Serse Coppi were declared joint winners (1949) after the riders had entered the stadium by different routes because of a mistake by an official. Then there was Emile Masson's lightning comeback in 1939; the great Fausto Coppi's only win in 1950; and the record average speeds clocked by Van Steenbergen 43·612 km/h (27.257 mph) in 1948 and by Peter Post from Holland 45·129 km/h (28·205 mph) in 1964. Since 1957 the winners have been equally divided between Belgium and Holland. The only exception was Felice Gimondi (Italy) who was unbeatable in 1966 – he was more than four minutes ahead of his nearest rival. It is more than 20 years since a Frenchman won Paris-Roubaix, the last successful riders being Jean Forestier (who won in 1955) and Louison Bobet (1956).

Of all the feats that have stood the test of time the 1952 battle between Rik van Steenbergen and Fausto Coppi is probably the most colourful. The best account is Van Steenbergen's own, containing as it does the essence of cycling as a sport – athleticism, the will to win and that exceptional quality that the sport can bestow on a few privileged moments in man's existence.

It was a hot day and just as the race was running into the 'hell of the north', the Belgian sprinted away from the main bunch of riders with the obvious intention of catching a breakaway group of four, one of whom was Fausto Coppi. Van Steenbergen was obviously hoping that two or three other strong men would join him so as to make an effective 'working party', sharing the pace and making his task easier. Nobody came. The front man of the pack was still 30 metres or so behind. There seemed no future in the enterprise; Van Steenbergen was about to give up the fight, but then . . .

I don't know what happened but suddenly I told myself that if I didn't try to chase him, if I let myself be caught, they'd all say that Coppi had me beaten,

On the Neuvilly hill which marks the beginning of the
'northern hell' of Paris-Roubaix, the cobblestones have
been covered with a thick layer of mud. Dangerous going
for the field of 150 in the 1975 race. Soon most of them
will be off their bikes and 'cyclo-crossing' as best they can.
Many at the tail of the field realise the position is
hopeless and quit the race. Others like Roger Swerts, the
champion of Belgium, courageously struggle on
although delayed by crashes, punctures and mechanical
trouble.

*The rough cobblestones are over at last. Only 10 kilometres of good road before the finishing line on the Roubaix track. A sprint ending to the drama seems inevitable. Two of the four leaders sit up for a short breather, Hennie Kuiper in world championship jersey is followed by Francesco Moser.*

*The final sprint of the 1976 Paris-Roubaix was similar in many ways to that of the previous year. In 1975 (above) world champion Eddy Merckx attacked too early and Roger de Vlaeminck sprinted past him in the home straight, with André Dierickx third and Marc de Meyer (on the inside) fourth. In 1976 (right) it was De Vlaeminck who made his effort too early. Moser looked a likely winner but left a gap through which De Meyer sped through to victory.*

133

*For most riders Paris-Roubaix is a long and useless pursuit over good roads and bad. But stars like Felice Gimondi (Italy), the 1966 winner, seem unaffected by the frequent changes from smooth macadam road to stretches of the infamous cobbles of the 'northern hell'.*

that I wasn't as good as him. He beat me in the 1950 Paris-Roubaix. He dominated the Flèche Wallonne two years earlier and all our last clashes had clearly been in his favour. People were beginning to say that he was much better than I. I realized in a flash that this final stretch of Paris-Roubaix was my last chance to confound the critics and show them that I was in fact better than Coppi.

It was sheer madness, like a piece of bluff in poker, to think that I could catch up the four leaders all by myself – they were well ahead and pedalling at over 40 km/h [25 mph]. It was ridiculous. I was all alone but I really wanted to do something. I told myself it would be better to die on the road than to admit that Coppi was the better man and slip back into the anonymity of the pack. I felt slightly better after I'd been chasing them for ten minutes when I saw four Belgian journalists waiting by the roadside taking a time-check – they looked stupefied at my comeback. A bit later I saw press and official cars ahead, and I knew the leaders would be just in front. Another 200 or 300 metres and I passed Baldassari who had been 'dropped' by them, and then Jacques Dupont punctured. That left only Coppi and Kubler. A couple of kilometres further on – I'd been chasing for about ten kilometres – I caught Fausto and Ferdi. A bit further on Kubler, who was completely done in, gave up, and I was alone with Fausto Coppi. He looked daggers at me. A look full of resentment. The same look he gave me in Copenhagen during the 1949 world championship when he realized he could not shake me off. So a 'fight to the death' began between us, over the last few kilometres of hell. Coppi tried to break away several times. I suddenly felt terribly weak. Staging that comeback all by myself had really knocked me out, and I was terribly afraid that I'd have to quit. But I clung grimly on to his rear wheel and he could not gain so much as a metre. Before we raced into the stadium Coppi had already given up any idea of winning. He knew that when it came to the sprint I was bound to beat him, and in fact I had no difficulty in streaking three lengths ahead of him in the home straight.

That was definitely one of the greatest wins in my career. And it gave me – and my team manager Antonin Magne – more pleasure than any of the others. I collapsed on to the track. I was 'dead', unrecognisable. Magne promptly sent for a bottle of milk. I swallowed it down in one go and then was sick on the track before doing my lap of honour. I was in a pitiful state, but I'd done what really mattered – I'd won Paris-Roubaix for the second time and, more important, I'd caught Coppi and beaten him.

## The Ardennes

Although the Flèche Wallonne and the Liège-Bastogne-Liège races feature on the international calendar only a few days after Paris-Roubaix, they mark a transition, a turning-point as it were, in the cycling season. The classic specialists, the Spring men, still predominate, but both races are run over hilly country. The long stretches with the wind behind you, when you can use a high gear, the cobbles that strike fear into the hearts of some riders, are no more. Sometimes the fir trees in the Ardennes are covered with snow and the roadmen have to weave about all over the road, their features pinched with the cold. It was like that for the painful Liège-

Bastogne-Liège race in 1957, for instance. On other occasions the pack may be pedalling through the year's first heat wave, their faces streaked with sweat. Water bottles are being handed round and summer is clearly on its way. Soon the stage races will be coming up thick and fast and a different rider will begin to surface, with different tactics and different aims. Traditionally this is true of the French, who always see the Tour de France very much as their major objective.

Although the Liège-Bastogne-Liège race is still the 'senior' Belgian race, because it started as early as 1892, when Léon Houa outstripped another Léon – Léon Lhoest – it was not until 1919 that it was restricted to professionals. Its status was not confirmed once and for all until 1930, when Hermann Buse from Germany pulled off the first win by a foreigner. (He also won the Tour of Germany that year.) In fact it was not until Camille Danguillaume (France) won it in 1948, and still more when the long-nosed Swiss champion Ferdi Kubler pulled off the double in 1951 and 1952 that this testing race acquired the fame it deserved. Since then Eddy Merckx has dominated the race. In 1975 he caught Bernard Thevenet in the final miles through the outskirts of Liège. Thevenet had boldly tried to surprise him after his compatriot Jean-Pierre Danguillaume had himself attempted a solo breakaway, but had been overtaken when less than six miles from the tape. This was Merckx's fifth win, his earlier successes being in 1969, 1971, 1972 and 1973.

The Flèche Wallonne was started in 1936, but did not achieve international status until after the Second World War. Marcel Kint, known as 'the Black Eagle', won the race three years running (1943–5). From 1950 to 1964 it was officially coupled with its elder brother Liège-Bastogne-Liège and the combined classification became known as the 'Ardennes weekend'. All the great Belgian road men have tried to put the 'Walloon Arrow' into their quivers, and in 1963 the French expert Raymond Poulidor showed that he was just as good at climbing short hills in one-day races as at scaling long mountain passes in the Tour de France. In 1975 the final sprint brought together the three most recent winners: André Dierickx (1973) won by a hair's breadth from the tough Frans Verbeeck (1974) and Merckx himself (1972).

The fearsome series of hills that is a feature of both races – Wanne, Stockeu, the Rosiers, the Redoute des Forges – means that gears have to be used intelligently. You must not use too high a ratio on the flat stretches immediately before the hill climbs or you will not be able to find a rhythm on the 'bumps' themselves. On the other hand if you use too low a gear for the climbs you run the risk of proceeding at a mere crawl and running completely out of breath. The best bet is to tackle the climb out in front, either so as to impose your own speed on

*In some countries competitors stopped by a closed level-crossing have no redress; it is just too bad if a good lead is wiped out. In Belgium race officials time the arrival of various groups and re-start them at the same intervals when the barriers are raised. The leading group in the 1976 Flèche Wallonne is held up, with Van Impe in the rear.*

the others, or, if you find yourself in difficulty, so that you can let yourself be gradually overtaken, but avoid losing touch by keeping with the last riders of the group. The energy conserved will enable you to respond to the sudden acceleration that is bound to occur when the summit has been reached. There are usually two sides to a hill – up and down! This truism means that the downhill specialists have their moment too. Racing downhill is an art in itself. As well as being cyclists the men have to be acrobats, especially if the roads are wet. Brakes do not work well in the pouring rain, and the danger of ultra-light tubular tyres skidding is increased. With a little daring and the right sense of balance a breakaway can be established on a downhill stretch. It is obviously a dangerous exercise which can end disastrously if you bungle it by taking a bend at the wrong angle, or the brakes are applied too soon – or too late.

### 'The finest of all': Bordeaux-Paris

By 1975 all the long-distance road races in which competitors set off in the dark had disappeared – all except one 'the finest of all', Bordeaux-Paris. Nowadays no one has the time to take over traffic-infested roads, or the patience to follow long hours of monotonous pedalling before the real battle begins. Modern star riders show little liking for road marathons of this kind; they would rather ride the shorter, well-paid Criteriums which only last for a couple of hours or so. The days when the chief quality de-

manded of a racer was extraordinary stamina have long since passed.

All the other long French races – Paris-Belfort, Paris-Rennes, Paris-Nantes, Paris-Monceau les Mines, Paris-Clermont Ferrand, Paris-Limoges – have sunk into oblivion, though every now and then we read that one or other will be revived. But where could you find the organisers prepared to take a risk like that? So there is only Bordeaux-Paris left – a living monument to the Stone Age of cycling.

Did I say 'a *living* monument'? In the old days the eve of *le départ* went by in a fever of excitement and the race itself was called 'the Derby', or even 'the world road championship'. Nowadays the end-less ribbon of white dust is covered with tarmac, and the race no longer finishes in the Parc des Princes (the track was demolished in 1967). Since then *l'arrivée* of Bordeaux-Paris has had no fixed abode and has been staged at the Piste Municipale at Vincennes, at the new Rungis covered market near Orly airport and at 'new town' complexes on the out-skirts of the capital. In 1976 the final part was ridden within the factory grounds of a car manufac-turers at Poissy to the west of the city.

The chief difficulty confronting the organisers of a modern Bordeaux-Paris is not so much finding somewhere for the race to finish, as finding riders to start! That means sacrificing lucrative contracts and training behind motorised pace-makers and building up an harmonious relationship with them. It means following a special diet. Team sponsors are shy of

# Riding in

# Echelon

The small top picture shows a leading group of riders who, after 50 miles hard racing, are a minute or so ahead of the main pack. The riders are, from right to left: Verbeeck, Van Springel, who leads Maertens, Zoetemelk, Dierickx, Merckx and Godefroot. In accordance with the rules of the Belgian cycling federation everybody is wearing a leather crash helmet.

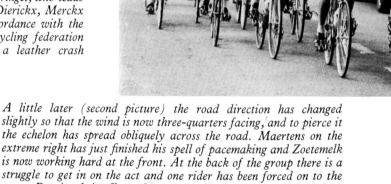

A little later (second picture) the road direction has changed slightly so that the wind is now three-quarters facing, and to pierce it the echelon has spread obliquely across the road. Maertens on the extreme right has just finished his spell of pacemaking and Zoetemelk is now working hard at the front. At the back of the group there is a struggle to get in on the act and one rider has been forced on to the grass. Despite their efforts this group will shortly be overhauled by their pursuers and there is a brief truce in the battle.

Then (third picture), after another sharp attack, and with 70 miles still to be covered, a group of 11 are firmly established in the lead. The road is wide enough for everybody, and Merckx is leading the smooth working echelon.

Later (fourth picture), Merckx has gone off duty and is already dropping back. Zoetemelk is now the driving force. Although wearing the colours of various sponsors the riders are temporarily allies in a common cause – to reduce wind resistance and to leave the rest of the field behind. Nearer the finishing line, however, it will be every man for himself!

Then (final picture), Zoetemelk has moved over to allow Maertens to come through to do his bit, and he in turn will be successively relieved by the rest of the front line members, Van Impe, Opdebeeck, Dierickx and Godefroot. As they move steadily forward to their left, the second line are dropping back to their right, thus forming an endless chain of effort. Length of spells at the front vary according to circumstances, but 20 seconds is a fair average for continental professionals. In a group of 11 each man, in theory, rests for about $3\frac{1}{2}$ minutes before finding himself in the lead again. In practice nobody has an easy ride in an echelon and riders frequently drop out because they cannot stand the pace. In this 1976 Flèche Wallonne seven men will lose contact 30 miles from the finish and then finally one man – Zoetemelk – breaks away to win the race with nearly a minute to spare.

Although riding in echelon formation is mostly seen in flat road events like the Tour of Flanders, the device is used in any race when a troublesome wind hinders progress. This set of photographs was taken in the 1976 Flèche Wallone classic in the Belgian Ardennes. The greater part of the 150 miles were over hilly, twisting roads where formation riding was not possible, but on the occasional stretches of straight, flat road, the strong men of the race soon got echelons working to fight the wind.

entering riders in a costly adventure like Bordeaux-Paris. In the old days a star rider took it for granted that his employers would expect him to contest Bordeaux-Paris – indeed he was eager to do so, and win. Today's counterpart is under no such obligation. To ride Bordeaux-Paris means not only the special training mentioned, but the setting aside of three or four days before the race and two or three afterwards, during which the competitor will not earn anything apart from his monthly team salary. In those seven days a top man could earn £1500 easy money for putting in an appearance in the short Criterium races – much more than he would get for winning Bordeaux-Paris! Small wonder, then, that nowadays it is the exception and not the rule to find big names on the starting list. Until now Eddy Merckx has not entered, but he promises to do so before retiring from racing. He acknowledges that although sacrificing about £5000 (Merckx gets £1000 an appearance in Criteriums!) victory in the 'Derby of the Road' would fill one of the few vacant places in his list of triumphs in the classics which – with the major Tours – are the only road races in which comparisons can be made down the ages.

Only a dozen riders set off into the night of 1 June 1975 and at the halfway stage only Hermann van Springel and his team mate Régis Delepine were in the running. When they were just over 100 miles from Paris, van Springel simply pulled away, without any fuss or commotion. The man in third place clocked in more than 34 minutes behind the winner, and the seventh and last man was more than an hour behind him. In 1955, 1971 and 1972 the organisers had to cancel the race altogether. What of the future, one wonders?

The history of the Bordeaux-Paris race is full of drama, of startling physical collapse followed by miraculous recovery. The man who wins through,

in spite of the distance, the exhaustion and his rivals, is rightly revered. The day after the 1907 race Van Hauwaert was accosted in Paris by a gentleman who offered him a high price for the shoes he had worn when winning the race, and also bought him 'a pair of luxury boots'. After choosing the boots the Belgian champion walked out of the shop, to find a crowd of bystanders round the shop window.

Balancing on a wide-necked cut-glass jar set on a crimson velvet cushion I recognised my racing shoes, with bits of them missing. A circle of thick pasteboard was inscribed with the words: 'The shoes in which the new champion Van Hauwaert completed the Bordeaux-Paris race. Note that the race was such tough going that the pedals have cut into the soles'!

So wrote the 'lion of Flanders' in his memoirs.

Once Maurice Martin, his beard growing whiter and fuller with the years, had lowered the starter's flag the competitors would leave the Quatre-Pavillons on the northern outskirts of Bordeaux, all warmly dressed for the long night ahead. It was unusual for a serious onslaught to be launched during this period in the dark, but it did give the top men a chance to leave the lesser lights behind. In the morning there would be an unspoken truce while competitors took off their leg-warmers, changed jerseys and generally put the night's exhaustions behind them. Soon the pacemakers, riding bicycles, would be grouped round their man and the annual ballet would build up to its usual rhythm.

A car would roar past, then stop 500 metres ahead of the pack. Two pacemakers would leap on to the road with their bicycles. They would pedal smartly away, but glancing back as they saw their cyclist approach and adjust their pace skilfully so that he was riding in their shelter.

The riders they had relieved would clamber into the vacant places in the car which would resume its place in the convoy. After a spell of rest and refreshment each pacing team would be back in action for another session

FACING PAGE: *Competitors in all Bordeaux-Paris races between 1938 and 1975 were paced by Derny motorised bicycles over the last 200 miles. They rode the first 160 miles steadily in a group. It is a busy scene in 1975 as riders pick up their pacemakers and the speed work really begins.*

ABOVE AND RIGHT: *A year later, Poitiers is once again the 'pick-up' town but there is an important difference. The Derny machines have been replaced by small motorcycles which provide better shelter from the wind. The field sets off at a cracking pace. Eating at speed is difficult, as Régis Ovion finds.*

RIGHT: *They used to say that a rider taking part in Bordeaux-Paris was knocked out for the rest of the season. Today's stars take the race in their stride. After covering the 360 miles at 27 mph and beating Van Springel by $4\frac{1}{4}$ minutes, Walter Godefroot was remarkably fresh and was racing again the next afternoon.*

on duty, forcing their man to new efforts. Each time he would respond with a burst of willpower, matching the pace his helpers were setting and overcoming exhaustion in a way that no animal could ever manage.*

The route included the narrow road along the river Loire, the endless journey across the Beaune region in heavy, thundery heat, the famous 'wall' just outside Dourdan, the Chevreuse Valley, where the race was really decided, Buc with its cobbles. Everywhere a surging mass of spectators, leaving little room for the competitors themselves, whose exhaustion was mingled with elation. At last one man, one happy man, would rocket towards the Parc des Princes.

Two men have won the race three times. Gaston Rivierre, he of the goatee beard and carefully prepared time-schedules, won in 1896 (when he shared first place with Arthur Linton of Wales), 1897 and 1898, while Georges Ronsse, a clever Belgian who was twice world professional road champion, came in first in 1927, 1929 and 1930. The most famous personality of all is still perhaps the great Francis Pelissier, who won the race in 1922 and 1924 and was second in 1923 and 1930. He somehow made Bordeaux-Paris 'his own thing'. When he had retired from racing you could see his tall frame perched on the platform of one of the formidable trucks that followed the race and watch him holding out food to his riders on the end of a special scoop. You might see him bending over one of his team who had collapsed into the ditch and see how he managed to plead, bully and even force the wretched fellow back on to his machine – and win. Francis Pelissier would think up all sorts of crazy bets on the likelihood of unknown protégés reaching the Parc des Princes ahead of the field – which they often did. His methods were not always orthodox – which explains why he became known as the 'wizard of Bordeaux-Paris'.

From 1931 pacing methods were modernised and ordinary road motorbikes appeared on the scene. In 1935 Edgard de Caluwé (Belgium) was paced throughout his record-breaking win at an average speed of 46·77 km/h (29.23 mph). In 1938 the race began to look as it was until 1975, because it was then that the special motorised bike known in France as a *Derny* (after the man who invented it) first put in an appearance. The sturdy Wim van Est (Holland), with his heavily lined forehead, caught up with Rivierre and Ronsse by winning the race three times (in 1950, 1952 and 1961). He also came in second three times (in 1951, 1953 and 1954), making an impressive total of pedal turns on a single road! Bernard Gauthier (France) reached even greater heights – he entered the race four times and won all of them (1951, 1954, 1956, 1957)!

Then the masterful manner in which Tom Simpson (Britain) pulled off his 1963 win must not be for-

gotten nor the example of courage set by Jacques Anquetil in 1965, when he showed that he was the best cyclist of his day by winning a difficult eight-stage race, the Dauphiné Libéré, in the afternoon of 29 May. He travelled first by car, then by plane from Avignon, where that race finished, to Bordeaux and was ready to set off, in his racing gear, at 2.30 a.m. on 30 May. After an uncomfortable night he managed to recover sufficiently to draw away up the Côte de Picardie half a long day later, and outdistance his last rivals.

What of the future of the Bordeaux-Paris race, that anachronistic but stirring relic of cycling as it used to be? The organisers are obviously anxious that it should not disappear from the calendar of classics. In 1976 they 'dropped' the Derny motorised bicycles which had given good service for nearly 40 years in favour of lightweight motor-bikes. The pacing experiment was a success and everybody happy – particularly Walter Godefroot (Belgium) who finished four minutes ahead of Hermann van Springel, the latter thus missing his fourth victory.

## One day winner – one year champion

Summer is drawing to a close. The major stage races have hogged the limelight from May to July. Then came the 'Criteriums', with a new one virtually every day. Then one fine day, competitors wearing their country's colours answer the 'roll call' of the entry list. Why do they wear this 'strip', which provides such a striking contrast to the usual outfit covered with advertising slogans that racers wear all season on behalf of their commercially-sponsored teams? Why do two men who've been team mates all year, though not of the same nationality, suddenly find themselves in rival camps? Why a rostrum and poles on which three flags will be hoisted in a few days' time? Because it is time for the world championships organised by the International Federation of Professional Cycling, under the aegis of the International Cycling Union (the Union Cycliste Internationale or UCI). The International Cycling Association, which is of British origin, was founded in 1893 but never managed to gain acceptance, although the track world championships started that same year, 1893. The representatives of Belgium, the United States, France, Italy and Switzerland signed the original articles of association of the UCI in Paris on 14 April 1900, and the Union has continued to develop since then. In 1921 it organised the amateur world championships for road racers and six years later launched the professional road-racing championships on the exacting Nürburgring, which is of course used for automobile grands prix. Professionals and amateurs competed together, but there were two separate sets of placings. Alfredo Binda came in well ahead of Girardengo and two other Italians, while Jean Aerts from Brussels, who finished fifth, twelve minutes behind the winner,

---

* André Reuze: *Coude à coude. Almanach du Miroir des Sports*, 1933 (p. 134).

There have been many 'specialists' of the Bordeaux-Paris road classic which dates back to 1891 when G P Mills of Britain was the winner. The most recent is Hermann van Springel of Belgium who is here 'dancing' (riding out of the saddle) during the 1975 event which he won comfortably with more than eight minutes in hand over the second man. This was the Belgian's third victory and his supporters were confident he would succeed again in 1976 and so join Bernard Gauthier at the top of the table with four wins. This was not to be. Van Springel rode well, but his compatriot Walter Godefroot was even stronger and scored an impressive win.

LEFT: *When will-power comes to the aid of pedal-power. After breaking away 15 miles from the end of the 150 miles 1975 French professional road championship, Régis Ovion is in danger of being overhauled, but sheer determination sees him through and he takes the title with half a minute to spare.*

*When the 1975 world road championships were contested in their country, Belgians were confident that 'home' riders would take both amateur and professional titles. In fact it was a double triumph for Holland. After Adri Gevers had taken the amateur title, Hennie Kuiper attacked 15 miles from the finish of the 160 miles professional race and is here crossing the all-important white line 17 seconds ahead of disappointed Belgian star Roger de Vlaeminck and Jean-Pierre Danguillaume (France).*

carried off the amateur championship. This combined experiment has never been repeated and there is now a separate contest for each category.

The decision to award the title of 'best road racer in the world' for a year as a result of a single race has long been a highly controversial one. It allows luck to play a part that bears no relationship to the competitors' athletic qualities, especially as the course is often extremely easy.

The world championships have often produced real surprises, as in 1946 (Hans Knecht, Switzerland), 1947 (Theo Middelkamp, Holland), 1952 (Heinz Müller, Germany), 1969 (Harm Ottenbros, Holland who beat Julien Stevens from Belgium) and even in 1964 (Benoni Beheyt, Belgium). In these cases the winner clearly was not the best road racer in the world, yet he could proudly bear the title for 364 days. Even if the basic formula is kept, a race divided into several different sections – a mass-start race, a hill climb and a time-trial – would be much fairer, as it would allow a true champion to emerge. Many advocate that the whole system be radically changed and the title awarded at the end of the season on a points basis. Placings in the major races would be added together according to a scale worked out in advance. That was the basic principle behind the Desgrange-Colombo Challenge Cup (1948–58), which in its day was remarkably successful in promoting international competition. This is still true of the French Super-Prestige Pernod, which was started in 1959 on a national basis. As early as 1961 it launched Jacques Anquetil, who had never managed to win the rainbow jersey in the one-day world championship race, but did get himself on to the honours list in the Pernod classification. The fact that Eddy Merckx has won the trophy seven times running since 1969 is an indication of how accurate that classification is. It happens too seldom – but it does happen – that the Super Prestige winner and the world champion are one and the same person.

Some people also claim that the 'rainbow race' is unrealistic. (It is so called because the jersey that the winner is entitled to wear for a whole year is white surrounded by five coloured bands in all the colours of the rainbow except violet.) In fact, instead of accepting the commercial teams among which the entrants are usually divided, the world championship recognises only national teams. This leads to illicit associations, because it is difficult for team mates who share the same commercial interests all year not to help each other, whatever their nationality. Even so, the formula used today is bound to survive for a long time to come, since the UCI gets most of its funds from royalties paid by the federation responsible for organising the championships, and the federation in its turn subcontracts to a local organiser. Also, from the sporting point of view, world championship day is awaited with great impatience, and the winners are usually of above-

Top professional road-racing cyclists change their colours every autumn, but only for world championship day when national jerseys are worn. For the rest of the season they race in trade-team dress. RIGHT: *The tightly packed bunch on the Montreal circuit during the 1974 championship.* ABOVE: *Italian jerseys dominate the finishing sprint of the 1972 race at Gap, France, with Mario Basso well ahead of Franco Bitossi and Cyrille Guimard (France).* ABOVE RIGHT: *But when, in 1976, the title race was contested in Italy, the home crowd were dismayed to see their favourite Francesco Moser outsprinted to the line by Freddy Maertens of Belgium. Here Maertens has donned the world champion's 'rainbow jersey' while Moser (left) and compatriot Tino Conti stand on the second and third levels of the podium.*

146

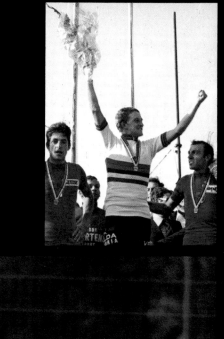

average quality. For instance Fausto Coppi won in Lugano in 1953, while Alfredo Binda was world champion 1927, 1930 and 1932; Van Steenbergen in 1949, 1956 and 1957; and Merckx in 1967, 1971 and 1974. Three Belgians have each been world champion twice – Georges Ronsse in 1928 and 1929, Albéric Schotte in 1948 and 1950 and Rik van Looy in 1960 and 1961.

Over and above the search for a road racer who is a better athlete than any of his contemporaries, the world championship is a very special kind of race. It is run over a closed circuit, which means that spectators can be charged an admission fee. Some athletes are temperamentally well suited to this type of race and reach peak form on the great day. We might call them 'championship men'. They concentrate hard, they feel at home on a route they have studied carefully in advance, and do not make mistakes in choosing gear ratios; they can thus give full rein to their intelligence and instinct for the race. It was no coincidence that Jean Aerts became professional champion in 1935 after being amateur champion in 1927, while Hans Knecht was the last amateur world champion before the Second World War, in 1938, and professional champion in 1946. Then Eddy Merckx first made his mark in the amateur rainbow race in 1964, held in Sallanches, and Paul Egli from Switzerland, amateur world champion in 1933, was third in the professional championships in 1937 and second in 1938.

This special ability to be 'turned on' by the idea of winning a jersey that is quite different from the ones worn by all the other roadmen emerges even more clearly if you combine the results of the various national championships. Here are just a few examples: Théo Middelkamp, who had such a surprise win on the Reims Gueux circuit in the heat of summer in 1947, and was labelled 'the Kermesse world champion', appears on the Dutch honours board in 1938, 1943 and 1947, and came third in the world championship as early as 1936 and second in 1950; Georges Speicher, world champion at Montlhéry in 1933, won the French championship over the same course in 1935, 1937 and 1939; Jean Stablinski, France's last world champion (Salo, 1962) was four times national champion (in 1960, 1962, 1963 and 1964). Nicolas Frantz is probably a unique case – he was Luxembourg's national champion from 1923 to 1934 and was only just beaten into second place in the world championships by Georges Ronsse. Similarly, Hennie Kuiper of Holland, who at the age of 26 shattered the hopes of the Belgian supporters when he beat the local favourites – led by Roger de Vlaeminck and Merckx – at Yvoir in 1975, had already won the Olympic title in Munich in 1972. A few weeks before his great feat he had set off in the Tour de France wearing the Dutch champion's red-white-and-blue jersey.

When a jersey and a championship title are at stake

the atmosphere at the outset of the race is quite different, though it is difficult to say exactly why. Even the most blasé professionals experience a feeling of excitement and seem surprised at not being able to overcome it completely. This means that in spite of the limits and the potential injustice inherit in the world-championship formula the sport can for once rise to a level it ought to attain all the year round. After all, a world championship is not 'just another race'.

## Pedalling 'greyhounds'

When September comes round the one-day road-racing season picks up again. The newspapers print stories about riders who have been out of the news during the long, hot summer stage races and discuss their chances of doing well in the 'autumn classics'. Soon the various cycle shows will be opening and the big teams starting to sign on new men for next year, renewing contracts for their best riders, sacking those who have not given satisfaction. Unemployment is high in the world of professional bike racing and all but the top men have an anxious time every autumn wondering what their lot will be. Some men may have had a poor season through accidents or illness and they will be determined to impress their employers with a good show in the remaining races of the year. Equally determined are the youngsters who have just secured their first professional contract after graduating from the amateur ranks – they will be all out to upset the applecart! Not only the cyclists themselves have the end-of-season feeling. The fans know that within a few weeks road-racing news will be confined to the odd paragraph tucked away amid columns and columns of football and (in France) rugby.

That sums up the prevailing atmosphere during the autumn races, which represent the third panel in the annual triptych, following on from the Spring period and then from the stage races. For a few Sundays the 'greyhounds', those fleet-footed beasts with a fondness of high gears and high average speeds, are all smiles again. Their appetites are whetted by two particular races.

The first two were in 1896 and 1901, but the Paris-Tours race can truly be said to have started in 1906, when Lucien Petit-Breton was the winner. Since then it has been organised every year except 1915, 1916 and 1940. In the 1920s the route was diverted via Chinon, which meant that the distance stretched to 342 km (214 miles), but subsequently it was cut back to approximately 250 km (156 miles). Francis Pelissier never managed to repeat his heroic feat in beating Louis Mottiat and Eugène Christophe in the snow in 1921. Paris-Tours became a speed race, featuring breakaways, pursuits, regroupments, fresh attacks and counter-attacks. Paris-Tours has always been dominated by 'punchers' such as Gus Danneels, whose 1936 win at an average speed of 41·455 km/h

(25·97 mph) earned him the 'yellow riband of the road' awarded by the daily sports newspaper *L'Auto* to the rider setting up a new speed record in a race more than 200 km (124·25 miles) in length. Danneels had already won the race in 1934, and would do so again in 1937 – the first man to score the 'treble'. Jules Rossi, an Italian living in Paris, took over the 'riband' from Danneels in winning the 1938 Paris-Tours at an average speed of 42·33 km/h (26·31 mph). It is interesting to note that this was in the early days of the racing derailleur and that Rossi had a single front chainwheel of 50 teeth, and a four-block freewheel of 15,16,17,18, giving a top gear of 7·12 m (90 in) which was considered huge at the time.

Cycling greyhounds can have a bit of the bull-dog in them – a bundle of muscles as well as a bundle of nerves. Among those answering this description were the two French winners, René Le Grèves (1935) and Paul Maye who scored three war-time firsts in 1941, 1942 and 1945, and the little Belgian sprinter Guido Reybroeck who also snatched victory three times (1964, 1966 and 1968). An ultra-fast race on good roads like Paris-Tours is an entirely different proposition from the 'steeplechase' variety such as Paris-Roubaix and some of the Belgian events. An unexpected breakaway can always happen, or even a suicidal attack by one man – who may even keep it up to the bitter end. Examples here are André Mahe (1950) and Albert Bouvet (1956) both from Brittany. Since Bouvet's win the French have rarely managed to be in front and have never won the race, although they had had so many successes in earlier years.

On other occasions the race may end with a mass sprint. Half an hour before the final show-down, some 32 km (20 miles) before the overhead banner proclaiming that *l'Arrivée* line is beneath it, the sprinter's team-mates start clearing the decks so as to jockey their man into the most favourable position. In the last ten kilometres breakaway attempts are non-stop, but the watchdogs are unflagging in their efforts to haul in the runaways. They shelter their leader so that he uses minimum energy. When the red banner indicates there are only 1000 metres to go, the team-riders pace their star man at such a speed that none of his rivals can dash ahead. Now the sprinter is on the launching pad. When the finishing line is only 250 metres away, either the pacer moves over to leave the coast clear for his captain to finish the job, or the star himself takes the initiative and rockets out of the mass of furiously pedalling riders. Before choosing his gear ratio he has taken into account the gradient of the last few hundred metres, and the strength and direction of the wind. Two different types of tactic can be adopted: athletes who are powerful rather than fast will go for a 'long sprint', while others will prefer a last-minute 'jump' that will enable them to break away in the final metres to outstrip by a

wheel's width, or even by a tyre's breadth, the man who was convinced he'd won.

If possible a sprinter will make sure that he launches into his sprint from the side of the road. That way no one can surprise him, because he can keep an eye on the rest of the road. I have seen sprinters start their final effort almost on the pavement, flinging up their arms, laughing triumphantly. But in laughing they were looking to the right – while on the left a fireball was flashing past down the narrow corridor that had been left open, thus snatching the victory 'on the line'. A properly executed sprint is a fitting reward for good team work, both for the sprinter himself and for the whole team. Team work is not easy in the general uproar as the pack races towards the finishing line. With all those competitors weaving dangerously all over the road as they approach the banner, many fine riders are thrown out of their stride. For instance even the great Eddy Merckx had to admit at the end of 1976 that the Paris-Tours race was still missing from his list of classic victories.

For the last two years Paris-Tours has become Tours-Paris! The point was that the journalists did not think much of this mass movement, because it gave them nothing to write about. The organisers had tried everything, even down to bringing back a fixed-wheel in 1965 and 1966. When, because of traffic problems, it was no longer possible to use the local finishing circuit that included the Alouette hill, they realized it promised to be a return to the same unsatisfactory formula of a mass sprint. So the competitors now set off from Tours towards Paris, or rather towards Versailles, which means that the hills in the Chevreuse Valley can be included at the end of the route. The last part of the race is now clear-cut once again, or at least it will be until the pack finds a way of parrying. In 1975 Dietrich Thurau (W. Germany) and André Dierickx (Belgium) nearly managed to stay away from the pack, but the two fugitives were caught and Freddy Maertens (Belgium) outstripped eleven competitors who were given the same official time.

There have been – and indeed there still are – other races for the 'greyhounds'. Examples are Zürich-Lausanne, Milan-Turin and Milan-Vignora, where Marino Basso (world champion in 1972, at Gap) sent the wheels flying. Paris-Tours is still the prototype. A fortnight before his win Freddy Maertens earned the 'yellow riband' in his turn, at a speed of 46·998 km/h (29·373 mph) between Paris and Brussels – a distance of 289·5 km (180 miles). If the wind is in the west Paris-Brussels has become a speed race as well. In the first hour 51 km (31·5 miles) were covered, which means that at times the field was moving at almost 60 km/h (37 mph).

Paris-Brussels was not run from 1967 to 1972. When it started up again in 1973 Eddy Merckx followed Felice Gimondi's 1966 win, outdoing the

*After 150 miles hard racing a pack of 75 riders is still together to contest the final sprint of the 1966 Paris-Tours race, and it is a clear victory for Guido Reybroeck (wearing his champion-of-Belgium jersey) from his compatriot Rik van Looy, on the extreme right. A closer look at their bicycles is interesting – they are not fitted with derailleur gears. Despite this restriction imposed by the organisers, the average speed was 27 mph (43·3 km/h).*

evergreen Frans Verbeeck (Belgium). The finishing line was only a stone's throw from Merckx's home. With the exception of the 1893 race, in which André J. Henry, a mason from Verviers, outstripped eight of the Belgians and a lone Frenchman, Francis Angenault, who came in third, and the 1906 race, which was restricted to amateurs, Paris-Brussels has been run 54 times, Belgians winning on 36 occasions – no further comment is needed! Yet their first professional success, by the indefatigable Louis Mottiat, did not come until 1914 – which shows how outstanding they have been since. The triple crown carried off by Octave Lapize (France, 1911, 1912, 1913) and the cheerful Félix Sellier (Belgium, 1922, 1923, 1924) has never been equalled.

## Time-trials

All the 'classic' races we have discussed are 'mass-start' one-day races; competitors all set off together when the starting signal is given, and the first to reach the finishing line is the winner. This is a per-fectly simple and natural way of doing things and it has given rise to a whole series of physical and tactical gambits. A mass-start race is a contest between rival teams, whose members can keep an eye on one another, talk among themselves and literally rub shoulders when riding in close formation. Each contestant will devise his own tactics by studying his opponents. If one of them attacks another will reply with a counter-attack. You can make a feint as in fencing, alter your rhythm or suddenly break an unspoken truce. Some cyclists are in their element at this sort of contest. They enjoy imposing their strength and intelligence on the opposition and seeing it crumble. They find this kind of hand-to-hand contest stimulating and manage to cover up a bad time by sheltering in their rivals' wheels. Then they suddenly come back to life, taking on all comers and attacking just once – but at exactly the right moment. They spring a surprise on the rival who thought he could not be beaten. A situation that looked hopeless ends with victory.

Time-trials, on the other hand, are more a matter of geometry. The contestants set off one at a time, at regular intervals, and the winner is not necessarily the one who reaches the finishing-line first. It all depends on who covers the course in the fastest time. In this type of race you are not swallowed up in a tight knot of riders and carried along by the overall movement of the pack; you are not sheltered from the wind or spurred on by a friendly word from a team mate. You are alone with your suffering, and with the constant need to keep on racing virtually all the time at the very limit of your strength. The general public would be amazed to find, if they studied the average speeds, that the lone cyclist often goes faster than the contestants in the usual type of race. This is because in a mass-start event the pace is by no means steady. The contestants weave about all over the road, slowing down, then suddenly rocketing off at incredible speed, whereas the lone cyclist riding unpaced can regulate his own speed, keeping his head down and his feet hard on the pedals with-out letting up for a second. He simply races ahead, mapping out his path as well as he can, unhampered in his movements by the fits and starts of the pack.

Time trials are almost abstract in that the contestant has no physical or visual contact with his rivals. It is difficult to judge progress in relation to the opposition. He worries, urges himself along, his brain spinning with questions and doubts: 'You're not going fast enough . . . what about the others? . . . I'm in agony . . . did I start fast enough? . . . wake up – you're going to sleep! . . . it's tough . . . I'm moving better now . . . only 10 miles to go . . . come on now, try really hard until that big tree on the brow of the hill . . . now continue the effort to that group of spectators . . . to that church . . .' It is an exhausting monologue. The effort demanded is quite merciless and some riders who do so well in conventional mass-start races go completely to pieces in time-trials, where 'class' really tells.

Above-average physical qualities are needed to be able to battle it out alone, and so is exceptional moral courage and the ability to use energy sensibly. The French star Jacques Anquetil gave a new impetus to this type of competition. Whereas time-trialists had always been advised not to push themselves too hard in the opening miles, Anquetil used to start very fast. His reasoning was twofold; firstly, if you already have the advantage you don't have to work for it; secondly, the rhythm established at the outset affects the rest of the trial. Instead of cutting corners and saving a few yards, Anquetil used to take them in the middle of the road and keep pedalling, whereas the 'cutters' were obliged to freewheel briefly and then 'get the gear rolling' again. Neither was it just good luck that Anquetil rarely punctured in a time-trial; little bits of gravel that are so fatal for light tubular tyres are more likely to be found on the edges than in the middle of the road. Anquetil introduced a slight lull towards the halfway mark to give himself a breather, then a sprint to the finishing line. He went on developing his technique throughout his career, and in the end he believed that a time-trial could be run as a single entity from the first mile to the last.

When we turn to the question of 'gears', Anquetil showed the way by using higher and higher ratios. This had always been considered a dangerous practice. Riders believed they would 'burn themselves out' and shorten their racing careers if they overgeared. Another important factor in Anquetil's success was his faith in strenuous training sessions behind the Derny motorised bicycle piloted by André Boucher who had coached him during his early days with the Sotteville club near Rouen. After turning professional Anquetil retained his confidence in M. Boucher and always sought his help when training for a big time-trial. Anquetil would even cover the complete distance at racing speed on the Friday, a bare two days before the actual event. The Normandy star was a law unto himself, and such a programme cannot be generally recommended.

The first big international time trial was held at the Olympic Games at Stockholm in 1912 and covered a staggering 320 km (198 miles). (Incidentally this category is still very common in Britain, for women as well as men, and in Scandinavia.) The South African cyclist Rudy Lewis took the gold medal in 10 hr 42 min 39 s, beating Fred Grubb from Britain and Carl Schutte from the United States by 10 minutes. This formula continued, though the distance covered was gradually shortened, down to the 1932 Games in Los Angeles, where it was raced over 100 km (62·25 miles). Armand Blanchonnet's 1924 win was remarkable; when he got off his machine at Colombes after covering 188 km (117 miles) in 6½ hr, he wasn't even sweating. Yet he was 9 min 39 s ahead of his nearest rival.

A special talent is needed to cope with the solo exertion demanded in this type of race. For instance when Blanchonnet turned professional he had little success in road racing, but was brilliant on the track. Yet this former leading light of the famous Vélo Club Levallois became French road-racing champion in 1931, because this time it was a time-trial run on the Montlhéry circuit. The same went for Ferdinand Le Drogo's win in the French championship in 1927 and 1928. Then in 1931 this brilliant athlete came second in the world championships at Copenhagen. This was the only professional world championship raced 'against the watch'. The winner, the Italian fireball Learco Guerra, had covered the 170 km (105·5 mile) course at 35·136 km/h (22 mph).

It was in 1932 that the journalist Gaston Benac launched the Grand Prix des Nations time-trial which finished on the track of the Buffalo stadium in Paris. It was soon to set a fashion. The pint-sized French cyclist Maurice Archambaud beat his Italian rival Alfredo Bovet by over 5 minutes. To be sure of Bovet's entry Benac had travelled as far as Castelgandolfo, where the Pope has his summer residence, because the Italian team were training there for that year's world championship. The Grand Prix des Nations started in Versailles, taking in the hills in the Chevreuse Valley. 'The midget', as Archambaud was known, covered the 142 km (88·5 miles) at an average speed of 37·129 km/h (23·20 mph). Antonin Magne, who won the race three times, broke this record with an average speed of 37·719 km/h (23·57 mph), but Fausto Coppi did even better in 1947, managing 38·456 km/h (24·03 mph) and beating Emile Idée by 8 min 15 s. René Berton from Bordeaux, with a fixed gear specified by Francis Pelissier, took the record to 39·152 km/h (24·48 mph) in 1948, then in 1951, his best year, Hugo Koblet outdid him with 39·738 km/h (24·7 mph).

It was two years after this that Jacques Anquetil's reign began. He took part in the Grand Prix des Nations nine times between 1953 and 1966 – and won it every time. Over this period the distance was steadily cut back, because the organisers found it increasingly difficult to find road racers willing to train for and take part in this testing race. At any rate Anquetil held the record for the 140 km (87 mile) distance with 40·226 km/h (25·14 mph) and for 100 km (62·25 miles) with 43·591 km/h (27·24 mph). He also took the record for 74 km (46 miles) to 46·843 km/h (29·27 mph).

In the immediate postwar period the finishing point for the Grand Prix des Nations had been in the Parc des Princes, but it was now transferred to the municipal track at Vincennes. In 1968 Felice Gimondi raised the record to an all-time high of 47·518 km/h (29·70 mph). Hermann van Springel won the famous trial twice, in 1969 and 1970. The race is now run in the Angers region and for the last two years it has covered a distance of 90 km (56 miles). Roy Schuiten from Holland, (6 ft 1 in and 11 st 11 lb) is the new 'governor' of the Grand Prix des Nations.

ABOVE: 'Place to Place' records are a feature of British road sport. In 1869 John Mayall jnr caused a sensation by pedalling a boneshaker from London to Brighton (52 miles) in 12 hours. Just 100 years later professional Les West made the same journey, and then back to London, in 4 hr 18 min! Record attempts are often made during the night before the coast roads are busy. On the tandem are John Patson and John Woodburn, collector of 'double machine' records. Their 1976 haul included Pembroke to London – 242 miles in 10 hours.

Unpaced riding on road and track is the speciality of the strongly-built Roy Schuiten (Holland), world champion pursuiter and Grand Prix des Nations winner.

Others were to follow the lead of the Grand Prix des Nations. There is the Belgian Grand Prix, for instance, which is competed for at irregular intervals; the Geneva Grand Prix, which is now defunct, and the Lugano Grand Prix, both of which were started at a time when the great Swiss roadmen were very much in the news. And lastly there is the Forli Grand Prix, a one-day 'regional' race which helped to make Ercole Baldini famous.

There is one continental time-trial that started before the Grand Prix des Nations itself, though in this case is contested by two-man teams. It is called the Trofeo Baracchi, a direct 'descendant' of the Milanese Tour first run in 1917 and won by Gaetano Belloni and Alfredo Sivocci, the 'human stopwatch'. But then, as the journalist Albert Baker d'Isy commented in an article written in January 1959,[*] whatever happened to Sivocci? The winning pair's average speed of 37.45 km/h (23.40 mph) was remarkably high for the period. It is important to note here that two great individual 'rouleurs' do not necessarily make a winning combination. The ideal team consists of a roadman-sprinter to step up the pace, and a time-trial star able to put in longer, steadier spells of pace-making. At the moment the record holder is Luis Ocana, the Spaniard from Mont-de-Marsan, partnered by Leif Mortensen from Denmark. Their average speed was 48.706 km/h (30.44 mph) over the 109 km (67.75 mile) course between Bergamo and Brescia.

The trajectory described by time-trial specialists is the ideal one for all racing cyclists, who must have a streamlined position and a fluent pedalling style. The man who rolls his shoulders and fidgets about in the saddle is wasting energy. It is noticeable that when a time-trialist breaks his rhythm on catching a slower rival and has a ding-dong battle with him before forging ahead, his average speed drops, his natural rhythm is broken and his pace is no longer steady. Elegance of style and high output must therefore go together, so that the rider's progress is a joy to watch and to study in depth. Yet what counts most of all is the athlete's will-power and his inherent abilities. This explains why Eddy Merckx – who has never looked as good on his machine as, say, Hugo Koblet – or Raymond Poulidor, who was compelled to improve his performance in this area to compete with his rival Anquetil, are among the winners of the Grand Prix des Nations and the Lugano Grand Prix.

## Hill climbs

Comparisons have often been made between the flexible and regular rhythm of the road racer travelling forwards with his high gear and the jerky pace and low gear of the hill climber. 'Rouleurs' are often tall and hefty chaps, while the best-known hill climbers are usually small in stature. There are

exceptions of course – some thin and gangling climbers, plus men like Merckx (him again!) who are strong enough to crush the opposition.

The word 'climber' is most frequently used in connection with the mountainous stages of the Tour de France, Giro d'Italia, etc. when competitors sometimes have to make as many as four punishing ascents – each 16 km (10 miles) long – during a day's racing. There are, however, shorter affairs over three or four miles, 'hill climbs' in their own right which can be as punishing to a rider as mountain tests. For these short climbs the rider need to be well 'warmed up' in advance, so that his body, lungs and heart are ready for action from the word 'Go'. The pace is fast. Your throat burns and you have to gulp in the air through wide-open mouth. Once again, it is necessary to try to keep at the head of the race, otherwise it will be difficult to counter your rivals' attacks, or bridge the gaps they open up.

The most famous hill climbs in France were the Mont-Agel and Mont-Faron races, which began in 1920. No less a man than Henri Pelissier was the first Mont-Agel winner, repeating this success the next two years. Then the future motor-pacer champion Charles Lacquehay took the trophy in 1923, when snow had transformed the last few miles into a dangerous running race. In the main these events were the province of the Mediterranean school of racers with a short and stocky build. Luigi Barral from Italy, the Minardi brothers, René Vietto, Francis Fricker and Jean Dotto swept the board in these events until two Spaniards – José Gil and Federico Bahamontes – took over. From 1952 to 1970 a second Mont-Faron race took place, 'against the clock' this time and starting with a flat stretch. In the last year of this second leg an unknown cyclist amazed everybody by overtaking famous names like Merckx (though admittedly he did have a fall), Felice Gimondi and Roger Pingeon. The newcomer was Bernard Thévenet and he was well and truly launched on his professional career. Other places in France that have featured on the hill-climb calendar are Puy-de-Dôme (on two or three occasions), La Turbie and the Mont Chauve, but the few remaining fixtures are a purely regional affair.

Spain, home of some outstanding hill climbers, has taken over from the French Riviera. There is the Urquiola race, and in particular the Arrate, and the Montjuich Park race in Barcelona. These promotions have set the fashion for calculating the winner by adding together the times taken in two successive matches. Sometimes both are mass-start races, on other occasions one is a time trial. This is a tough test of the contestants' powers of recovery. Yet the placings in the two legs are often very similar. I believe the French veteran Raymond Poulidor was the only non-Spaniard to win the Arrate race since the war, in 1966 and 1968, but turning to the Montjuich race we find that Bahamontes and Poulidor

*Albert Baker d'Isy: *Sport-Mondial* No. 35, January, 1959.

were joint winners in 1965, while Jesus Manzaneque took the title in 1973. Apart from these two Spaniards, only Poulidor, Gianni Motta from Italy and Merckx (with five wins under his belt) have added to the list of foreign winners.

Switzerland, with its classic 'Across Lausanne' race, run from 1940 to 1949 (with four wins for Kubler) and again from 1967, has also adopted the 'two-match' formula. It is great fun for the spectators, but not for the contestants – climbing up the town from the lake is hard work. In September 1975 the Swiss organised two other hill trials – Mendrisio and Grabs. The Grabs winner was the cyclo-cross specialist Albert Zweifel.

It is not surprising that a cyclo-cross specialist should prove to be a good climber since in the course of their tough sport the 'mud pluggers' are frequently called upon to scale rough paths as steep as the roof of a house. Thus we find successful cyclo-crossmen like Jean Robic and Camille Foucaux among the Mont-Faron winners. During the last war, by the way, track riders did well in cyclo-cross races contested in the steep streets of Montmartre in the heart of Paris.

There is another type of hill climb, quite different from these short and heated set-tos, and modelled on the famous 'Polymultipliée' which was run close to Paris, at Chanteloup-les-Vignes. It began in 1913, continued to 1962, then was revived for three years from 1967 to 1969. It was designed to show the differences between the various types of derailleur gear system and to encourage research and development in this field. It had an atmosphere all its own, because as well as the professional race, Cyclo-sportifs also competed in their own 'solo' and tandem trials on the well-known circuit. There was also an exhibition of cycles and this 'festival of cycling' attracted huge crowds. Since 1970 the 'Poly', as it is known, has been run further out of Paris between Sens and Paron. Then there used to be the 'Poly Lyonnaise', which did not continue as long as the parent race but was a pretty stiff test. The 'Poly' professional race was a gruelling test of about 150 km (93 miles) packed with uphill and downhill stretches. The same goes for the official Spanish Hill Climb Championship. In 1975 it was held over 215 km (130 miles) of mountainous terrain.

Once they have crossed the finishing line hill climbers are often 'all in' and breathing heavily. They tremble as they clamber wearily off their machines and spend a long time leaning on their bikes before recovering.

## Stage races

One last type of cycling trial brings all the other types together in a single event – the long-distance race divided into stages.

Jacques Marchand observed in his book *Le Cyclisme* ('Cycling'), which was published in 1963 but includes a very detailed analysis of the various facets of the machinery of cycling, that:

> Virtually all the major cycling events are run by newspapers. More often than not it's the journalists who are the leading lights behind the big races . . . The sporting press has always been full of ideas, perhaps because it is the only area in which journalists can make the news, whereas on the ordinary news desk they have to wait for things to happen.[*]

Incidentally this does not apply to cycling alone. For instance in football the European Cup was the direct result of an idea put forward by the great French journalist Gabriel Hanot. There are many other examples.

### The Tour de France, the Vuelta and the Giro

The idea of organising the Tour de France was the brain wave of Géo Lefèvre, the cycling editor of the French daily *L'Auto*. His boss Henri Desgrange gave him *carte blanche* to put his plan into action and he was backed up by the treasurer, Victor Goddet. According to Jacques Marchand it was a brilliant idea, because it offered the prospect of a show that could be extended by linking several races together. By setting up a series of separate stages it introduced the new factor of stopping the race and picking it up again the next day, thus creating a new surge of interest and suspense every day. It was like dividing a novel into a series of episodes.

Stage races vary considerably in length. A one-day race split into two 'half stages' could be termed a 'stage race', though this is unusual. The majority range from two days to a week. Then there are the major circuits, such as the Vuelta in Spain, the Giro in Italy and of course the grand-daddy of them all – the Tour de France. The long round-Portugal race has not achieved major international status – and this is in spite of the honourable niche that two of its leading lights, Alves Barbosa and Joaquim Agostinho, have carved out for themselves on the European professional circuit.

These major landmarks in the sport of cycling have three main features in common: firstly, because they are long-distance races the contestants have to be able to recover their form quickly; secondly, the mountainous roads play an important part; thirdly, they require very complex organisation.

Some top-class athletes are true thoroughbreds. Their nervous system is such that the stimulus provided by the excitement of one-day races brings out the best in them. All their senses are sharpened by the contest and they develop a sixth sense for any potential pitfalls. They have the precious ability to throw themselves heart and soul into the battle. After exerting himself on this scale a competitor must 'recharge his batteries' and this is difficult when a series of long stages follow immediately one after the other. Some racing cyclists have never managed to overcome this problem.

[*]Jacques Marchand: *Le cyclisme*. La Table Ronde, 1963.

155

Most big hill climb competitons are miles from anywhere. This famous event, the 'Across Lausanne', goes right through a city and is run in two sections : mass start road race and individual time-trial. In the first match, where mouths are wide open and there is no time to think of 'style', the winner will be No. 8, Joop Zoetemelk, with Eddy Merckx (who has his 'head down') only 6th. Although Bernard Thévenet beats Zoetemelk by 10 seconds in the time-trial, the Dutchman takes the combined classification by 16 seconds from Merckx.

The day's stage has ended, the riders are already at their hotels under the shower, perhaps even on the massage table. Soon there will be a big meal, a chat round the table – and bed. For the Press, however, work is only just beginning. There is a story to write and then to telephone to the office, then perhaps another article to prepare for tomorrow's first edition. Here are two well-known cycling specialists making for the Salle de Presse: Roger Bastide (Parisien Libére) right, and Noel Couedel (l'Equipe).

Diet plays an important part in this question of recovering strength. What you eat must be nourishing as well as suitable for getting rid of toxins, or otherwise strength gradually fades. You must, for instance, eat meat. Sleep is another important factor in success. A major Tour is won as much during the rest periods as when actually cycling, as you can only really rest when stretched out. Temperature must be taken into account – it is likely to be hot during the main stage-race season and some competitors can stand heat better than others – and also the problem of nerves. It is difficult to keep calm in the face of the crowd's excitement and all the other things you have to cope with, such as the media. You need to be exceptionally well balanced to take part in a long-distance stage race. Some champions find that techniques such as yoga help them relax and recover their composure.

The major circuits take an enormous amount of organising. It is almost as though a whole mobile town was being shunted about. First of all, before the actual race – normally about an hour – comes the publicity caravan. Waves of handbills, balloons and peaked caps come floating out of a whole lot of noisy vehicles. On arrival at the stage town they turn into a sort of travelling fairground, pouring out a terrific racket. All sorts of fun and games are organised by a series of fast-talking showmen. Each racing team has its group of technicians – masseurs, mechanics and a variety of other helpers without whom the team members and their machines would never be in a fit state to take to the road. Then there are all the fringe services – the mobile bank, telephonists, storemen, police motorcycle outriders, race stewards, doctors. And bringing up the rear, but most important of all, the Press. Without the Press it would be just another race – instead of which it is a real 'happening'. The journalists are always on the lookout for material to fill their screens, their airwaves and their columns and it is a remarkable sight to see these professional 'camp-followers' huddled frenziedly over their typewriters in the *salle de presse*.

A vast carpark is needed to cope with all this travelling circus and the uninitiated are sometimes amused and yet appalled by the contrast between the tiny number of cyclists and the army of vehicles in front of them, behind them, and sometimes hindering them. It could not be done any other way.

Yet there is no getting away from the fact that you would not have a race at all if it were not for the cyclists! The main problem they face is getting over the mountain passes – and not all of them manage it. The grandiose epic of the 'giants of the road' undoubtedly owes its splendour to the fact that the cyclists enter the 'kingdom of the eternal snows'. And that is not just rhetoric. It expresses the unalloyed admiration felt for these intrepid men who agreed to take on the mountain single handed,

nibbling away bit by bit at the most incredible climbs. After covering relatively flat roads in the first two years, the third Tour de France in 1905 included the Ballon d'Alsace climb in the Vosges mountains, and the minor Alpine *cols* of Laffrey and Bayard. In 1910 they tackled the Pyrenees, travelling via Peyresoude, Aspin, the Tourmalet and the Aubisque, and the following year Desgrange added a new giant – the Galibier. I have referred on several occasions to the state of the roads in those days – they were narrow and full of ruts, more like stony footpaths than made-up roads for civilised human beings:

> The path was getting worse and worse – it was full of ruts and pebbles and was constantly being interrupted by bubbling streams. It would twist and turn, reluctant to attack the fortress, doubling back to get a better run at it, creeping cunningly forward, climbing up towards the mountain tops which could now be seen in all their tragic barrenness.*

If it was raining it was pure torture.

> On the Galibier it was drama in the mud. As soon as they started climbing the leaders had to get off their bikes and push. The wheels spun uselessly in an appalling cesspit of mud. While the cars floundered and ground to a halt, obstructing the road, the cyclists ran through the puddles, their bare legs whipped by squalls of wind as they dragged or pushed their machines and eventually vanished into the low clouds, above which to the left, towered the terrifying white bulk of the Meije range.*

Those who took part in the Italian Giro soon had to come to grips with the Dolomites, where the road slithers between high banks of snow. The names Stelvio and Pordoï have a tragic ring.

Nowadays the crowds still thrill to the feats their heroes manage to perform and the humility with which they tackle them. There are no subterfuges or dodges here – each competitor labours away single-handed, dragging himself up the steepest gradient. Then, the summit reached, he has to pelt down the other side at 80 km/h (50 mph) risking his neck at every turn. Perhaps he will make up the ground lost on the way up; or increase his lead; or somehow manage to keep in the wake of a group of rivals for fear of seeing this lifebuoy vanish for ever. Whereas the best competitors are bursting their lungs to keep in front, their weaker brethren are struggling to avoid arriving at the finish after the time-limit has expired. They somehow keep themselves going in the midst of their sufferings in the hope that one day things will go better, because the terrain will be better suited to their talents. Apart from the overall classification, each separate stage gives the competitors a chance to shine. The sprinters do best on the flat stretches, while the unpaced specialists prefer the time trials and yet others come into their own in the mountainous stretches, which sometimes exceed 2800 m (9000 ft). A major Tour includes all these and is watched by huge

*André Reuze: *Le tour de souffrance*. Arthème Fayard et Cie, 1925.

157

*Every type of road racing has its place in the three weeks of a Tour de France. Before the start star riders are relaxed and obliging. Merckx signs autographs; Moser happily shows off his bright new yellow jersey; Poulidor is in good spirits.*

The human motor must not run out of fuel. Riders prepare pocket rations from bags and fill their bottles with drink – cold lemon tea is a favourite.

Just as the individual race leader is recognised by his yellow jersey, so are the team leaders by their yellow caps. Here Spanish members of the Fagor team are top of the table in that category.

The race director has dropped his flag. Another day's work for the tourmen has begun. There will be a good fat wage packet for the winner of the stage, and others will pick up useful cash bonuses on the way. For the rank and file it will be a hard day's labour for little pay.

crowds, who throng the roadside hours before the scheduled time of arrival.

The honours list of the Tour de France and the Giro d'Italia include the most brilliant names in this epic on two wheels. Nineteen Frenchmen, ranging from the bright-eyed Maurice Garin, with his pencil moustache and white linen jacket, to Bernard Thévenet in 1975, have won the Tour de France, along with ten Belgians and five Italians, while Luxembourg has produced three winners, Spain two and Holland one. The race has been run 63 times in all, with two of the champions heading the list with five wins each – Jacques Anquetil (1957, 1961, 1962, 1963 and 1964) and Eddy Merckx (1969, 1970, 1971, 1972 and 1974). Then come Philippe Thys (1913, 1914, 1920) and Louison Bobet (1953, 1954, 1955) with three wins each. But so many unforgettable champions deserve a mention, starting with Fausto Coppi (1949 and 1952), and so many famous or not-so-famous incidents have occurred. Then again a large number of riders have won great fame, and deservedly so, without ever coming first. One example is Eugène Christophe, who had the consolation of being the first man to wear the 'yellow jersey', the distinctive emblem of the man in the lead which was instituted in 1919. Then there is Raymond Poulidor, who came second three times (in 1964, 1965 and 1974) and third five times (in 1962, 1966, 1969, 1972 and 1976) but never managed to earn the right to wear the coveted jersey, not even for the odd stage here and there.

For a long time the Giro, which is also divided into about 20 stages, remained the preserve of the Italians. There have been 47 Italian wins between 1909, when Luigi Ganna beat Carlo Galetti and Giovanni Rossignoli into second and third places, and 1976, when Felice Gimondi won for the third time. Belgium has produced five winners; Switzerland, France and Luxembourg two each, and Sweden one (Gösta Petterson in 1971). Three champions have notched up five wins – Alfredo Binda (1925, 1927, 1928, 1929 and 1933); Fausto Coppi (1940, 1947, 1949, 1952 and 1953); and Eddy Merckx (1969 1970, 1972, 1973 and 1974). Then come Carlo Galetti, Giovanni Brunero, Gino Bartali, Fiorenzo Magni and Felice Gimondi with three each. This list underlines the overwhelming dominance of the Italian contestants.

In fact, it was not until 1950 that a *straniero* (foreigner), the handsome Hugo Koblet, scoring his first major international success, managed to keep the *maglia rosa* right to the end of the race. (A pink jersey was chosen to match the paper on which the *Gazetta dello Sport*, which organised the race, is printed, just as the yellow jersey worn in the Tour de France was chosen to match the newspaper *L'Auto*). When the Giro gets down to southern Italy the heat becomes overpowering and watercourses are very few and far between. The Giro is a unique

event and most roadmen think it is slightly less exacting than the Tour de France. Its international status has been on the up and up over the last 25 years. Italian sponsored teams recruit stars from all over the world and they normally enter their racers in the Giro, which starts in mid-May, before the Tour de France, which finishes in late July. These two factors have had an influence on the race. From 1930 to 1961, and again in 1967 and 1968, the Tour de France was organised on the basis of national and regional teams, which resulted in a special excitement that none of the other major Tours could match.

Financial considerations forced the organisers to change the formula and the Tour is now confined to sponsored groups which are the modern counterpart of the old teams financed by the cycle industry.

In line with the overall trend in cycling today, the stages are now shorter and faster. It seems like centuries ago that the contestants used to stay in the saddle for 20 hours at a stretch between Les Sables d'Olonne and Bayonne, a distance of 483 km (300 miles), the mountainous stages starting long before dawn, with car headlamps blazing. The French and Italian organisers vie with one another on their respective Tours, dreaming up new ideas all the time – an air lift, a sea passage and 'hops' in special trains or coaches to cut out unnecessary sections on the route and link the town where one stage ended with the starting-point of the next. The one really important element is always there – people still adore watching these long-running serials. Unless you have had the good fortune to follow a mountainous stage you will never realize that whole populations – tens of thousands of them – motor, pedal or walk up from the plain to perch precariously on the pebbly summits to spur on their favourites and to show all competitors how much they admire their strenuous efforts. Otherwise you will never realize how dangerous an 'all out' descent can be, or experience that spontaneous thrill that comes from watching the cyclists braving terrible agonies.

The ant that is man is an amazing creature, with the most extraordinary potential for courage and perseverance. The mountainous sections of stage races offer us an unforgettable picture of this fact.

## Track racing

Roughly speaking track cycling races can be divided into two separate types and two separate seasons. In the winter covered stadia with short wooden tracks – the maximum length is 250 m (273 yd) – and steeply banked corners come to the fore. Then, once the fine weather comes, the track specialists move to open-air grounds with cement tracks, which often run round a soccer or rugby pitch. This means that they are longer – up to 500 m (550 yd), though in some cases with more shallow bankings.

In fact, this picture is not entirely accurate.

Depending on the climate of the country concerned, open-air stadia, too, are often built round a fairly small wooden track, while on cement tracks the bends are sometimes very steeply banked, so that motor-paced races can be run on them.

This still means, however, that there are two different ways in which a young roadman can discover track racing. In the summer he may take part in road races with the finishing line in a cycle stadium, although this is not so common these days. If he is a professional he will find himself contracted to race on beaten-earth tracks, cinder tracks or more orthodox surfaces. If the town he lives in has a winter track he will overcome his frustration at not being able to indulge his passion for road racing by going to the stadium to soak up the atmosphere he loves so much. Either way the beginner will soon realize that track work will improve his performance in all types of racing. He may even decide that he was making a mistake in wanting to be a roadman, when his real talents lay in track racing. Some cyclists do not fancy racing round and round a track like lions in a cage until they are giddy – they prefer the change of scenery that is part of road racing. But others will decide to serve their apprenticeship on the track, either because they have taken a liking to this specialist branch of the sport, or because they

see the importance of adding another string to their bow.

If a young cyclist discovers track racing in the winter he will reach the track via the tunnel leading from the competitors' quarters. When he stands at the foot of a banking it will tower over him like a cliff and he will wonder how on earth he will ever be able to keep his balance on that steep slope. Someone hands him a cycle that has been hastily adjusted to his own 'position'. He sets off falteringly, and cautiously on the lower part of the track, getting used to the fixed gear, the streamlined posture – even more streamlined than for road racing – and the lack of brakes. Above him whole 'strings' of racers overtake him again and again. They make it look so easy! He gradually gets bolder. He moves up the banking a bit, notices that he isn't touching it because his pedals are narrow and his bottom bracket is raised further off the ground than it would be on a road-racing model – usually 27·5 cm (11 in) instead of 26·5 cm (10·5 in). He is still weaving about all over the place and the queue of cyclists catching up with him and roaring past like an express train let fly a volley of oaths and catcalls. He feels a fool and eventually takes his courage in both hands; he accelerates and moves higher up the track to the 'stayers line' about a third of the way up – this is

*Riding on the left – but not in Britain. It is a Tour de France incident featuring an important breakaway group on the second stage (Mulhouse-Strasbourg) of the 1970 race. A small col in the Vosges Mountains has split the field, and noticing that several of his main rivals are left behind, Eddy Merckx forces the pace to make sure that they stay there. Merckx can be seen at the front of the group in his yellow jersey of leadership. Despite this hard pace-making, Merckx will still have enough strength to outsprint Roger de Vlaeminck for first place at Strasbourg.*

162

LEFT: *Accident risk is high among road sprinters as they make their frenzied dash for the finishing line. Ironically this nasty crash involving Rik van Linden (Belgium) happened seconds after the race was over. He had been narrowly beaten in a Tour de France stage by Jacques Esclassan (France), who involuntarily made a 'switch' and caused the crash. Van Linden, bruised and cut, was back in action next day and finished the Tour as overall winner of the points competition.*

RIGHT: Sprint tumultueux! *The French expression perfectly describes the spectacular pile-up at the end of the 9th stage of the 1972 Tour de France. A leading group of 10 are pedalling furiously when Spruyt (Belgium) crashes 15 metres from the finishing line, bringing down with him Harings (Holland).*

*Houbrechts (Belgium) appears to be leapfrogging over them both, but he too came to grief. On the extreme left of the first picture is Michael Wright (Britain), at first declared winner of the stage, but photo evidence finish proved that he had been beaten by Huysmanns (Belgium) who, out of camera range, had sprinted safely to the line on the other side of the road.*

165

On the lower slopes of a
mountain pass, Eddy Merckx
in the yellow jersey is
already ahead. Is this the
start of another big attack
– or is the Belgian star
simply in a playful mood?

ABOVE: *The greatest free sporting show on earth. The crowd roars its encouragement to Bernard Thévenet during the 1975 Tour de France. He is wearing his Peugeot white-and-black 'colours', but tomorrow he will be in the coveted yellow jersey of leadership. The great Eddy Merckx, five times winner of the Tour, has been beaten at last!*

*Even the stars are occasional victims of the heat, the gradient, the altitude or the intensity of the competition. Such was the case when Eddy Merckx broke away on the 1970 Tour de France stage finishing at the summit of Mont Ventoux. Here he has two kilometres still to ride, and he was 'all in' at the end of the hardest winning ride of his career.*

In 1967 Felice Gimondi had an attack of stomach trouble during a hard Pyrenean stage of the 1967 Tour. Helped by strong-armed team colleagues and his own determination, the Italian ace saw the day through but lost valuable time. He finished 7th in the great race which he had won two years previously.

After 2500 miles the 1975 Tour reaches the most famous road in France, the Avenue des Champs-Elysées.

The racing world is full of riders of moderate ability who are convinced that their big day will come. On the other hand there are 'class' performers without confidence in themselves. In the latter category is the short, lightweight Belgian Lucien van Impe who in recent years several times won the Grand Prix de la Montagne competition in the Tour de France and twice finished third on overall classification. He was, however, convinced that he would never make the very top in the world's greatest road race. However in 1976 a new team manager, Cyrille Guimard, successfully 'talked' him into a remarkable victory. Here van Impe is leading a group of his chief rivals, 1975 winner Bernard Thévenet, Joop Zoetemelk and Francisco Galdos, during an Alpine stage.

ABOVE: *After finishing on a vélodrome in the Paris suburbs since its creation in 1903, the Tour de France came to town in spectacular fashion in 1975 when the final stage was fought out on a seven kilometre circuit up and down the Champs Elysées. The racing was watched by a huge crowd in holiday mood.*

the blue line above which a motor-paced rider must not ride if he is being attacked by another competitor.

Success! He actually manages to keep upright and not slither about. In fact he begins to feel better. He moves forward a little, then pressing his gloved hand against the front tubular, finally comes to a halt, feeling fairly pleased with himself. Next time he will go as fast as he can so that he can 'get up to the railings' separating the track from spectators' seats and from there he will be able to survey the whole track. Already forgetting that he was not so sure of himself a few days ago, he smiles rather scornfully as he notices a timid cyclist who cannot tear himself away from the 'Côte d'Azur', the flat inside of the track. Later still he will be able to ride up to the railings fairly slowly – the hardest trick of all. Then he'll be a real sprinter.

## Sprints

The sprint, representing as it does a contest between cycling thoroughbreds, was soon thrilling the cycling connoisseurs, having originally been a great crowd-puller in the heroic age of cycling. Nowadays it involves two very different types of competition – the traditional sprint involving two or more riders, and the individual kilometre time trial which is a comparatively newcomer to international racing.

## Speed

Speed events are usually raced over 1000 m (1100 yd) and are restricted to 'high voltage' specialists able to keep their legs spinning at lightning speed. They normally include a whole series of qualifying heats leading up to the final, in which only two or possibly three contestants take part. In the old days sprinters, like all other trackmen, used special 'inch pitch' chains and sprockets, such as 23 or 24 × 7. Nowadays they use the same sort of equipment as roadmen, as this allows the chain to work more effectively, as well as offering a wider range of gears. Gear ratios for the youngest competitors will be of the order of 44 × 14 (84·8 in), and otherwise 47 or 48 × 14 (90·6 or 92·6 in).

Any match with more than two contestants is very tricky, even for the fastest specialist, because a wide variety of situations can crop up. For instance the weakest of the three contestants (in theory, that is) may decide to go 'all out' from the starting pistol. If both his opponents hesitate before chasing after him, in case they become a cat's paw for the other one, it's all over. Then you may get a 'running wide' session, with one of the three racing off towards the line, while another forces the third man towards the outside, thus preventing him making a total effort. Or alternatively there may be a 'squeeze'; one of the three contestants is going 'all out' and following the inside line painted round the track; No. 2 sprints up alongside and leans on or 'squeezes' his adversary and puts him off his stride – allowing

No. 3 to come past them both to win. Of course if it is glaringly obvious what the schemers are up to, they will be disqualified. Disguising such moves as involuntary manoeuvres is one of the tricks of the sprinter's trade. A sprinter may also commit a tactical error. For instance No. 1 competitor is pedalling hard in the last lap and impeccably following the line painted round the inside of the track. If No. 2 is unwise enough to follow immediately behind – and also follow the same line – then up comes No. 3 half-way between the two contestants and close to them. Rider No. 2 is firmly 'boxed' in; the rules forbid him to pass inside the line, and he can only extricate himself from the mess by easing up . . . by which time his two opponents have crossed the finishing line.

This explains why a man such as Daniel Morelon is always nervous until he reaches the stage where there are only two contestants, which generally means the quarter-finals. 'Two up' contests are not as exciting or interesting, since there are fewer surprises, but at least they are clear cut fights and as such relatively uncontroversial. They may be less colourful, but they do make it easier to decide who's the better of the two – which is after all the object of the exercise.

A match between two top sprinters is a feast for the connoisseur, made up of intelligence and athleticism in equal proportions. The idea is not to allow your opponent to get into your slipstream and stay there until the last few yards, having what is known as an 'armchair ride', thanks to your own exertions. If such an error is made he will simply overtake you where and when he likes – probably about 50 yards from the finishing line. Spectators watching a 'two-up' speed race for the first time are amazed to find it more like a slow bike-race with the two contestants transfixed in a standing-still session. Yet it is perfectly logical, the idea being to avoid leading at all costs, and to drive your opponents submissively towards the beginning of the final 'straight'.

Nowadays the rules governing major sprint races have successfully cut down excessive 'standing still sessions' which were particularly rife in the first lap when nobody was willing to take the lead. In important races the riders now draw for starting positions, and the man who clicks the inside berth is obliged to lead for the whole of the first lap 'at not less than walking pace', after which the contestants are free, if they wish, to begin 'standing still' tactics. Some do so, but there are none of the notorious long drawn-out episodes that tried the patience of spectators in the old days.

In the following passage Gabriel Poulain, the ace French sprinter, describes the third leg of his challenge match with Henry Mayer in 1906. Mayer had courted publicity by issuing a challenge for a 'best of three' match for a 2000 francs stake (it transpired that he had no money in the bank!).

Poulain accepted, although he was not on his best form. Nevertheless, he managed to win the first race at Vincennes track by cunning tactics but was beaten in the second. The contest was a 'private' affair in that it was not part of any racing programme, but the public were at liberty to watch free of charge. So with the score 1–1 the two men strapped their feet to the pedals and prepared to take off (in a manner of speaking!) for the third and deciding match.

> When the starting signal was given I stood still. It lasted 20 minutes. Mayer punctured. We re-started – another session of 20 minutes without moving forward an inch, it ending only because my rival's tyre gave up the ghost again, worn down by his efforts to keep his balance. At the third attempt I decided to take the lead, but stopped at the first bend – for 25 minutes. Mayer led briefly into the back straight for a 20 minute spell of the mixture as before. Then another 42 minutes on the last banking – and 45 minutes in the home straight. The bell then rang to announce the last lap. Mayer was more nervous than I was and had greater difficulty keeping his balance, so he punctured a third time. So we started for the fourth time – 30 minutes standing still. The officials had had enough of these acrobatics and told us: 'We'll give you another five minutes. After that we're going home.' The five minutes went by. 'One last warning – three minutes more!' No change. 'This really is your last chance – another two minutes.' The good-natured fellows gave us two more reprieves of two minutes each, then decided to leave. There was nothing else for us to do but leave the track. Match drawn.*

This description of course caricatures the situation but before the rule I have mentioned came into force, the first lap of a sprint race was often a long-drawn-out affair and no doubt tedious to the spectator who did not fully understand the physical and psychological laws that govern this kind of match. Why did the contestants ride so slowly when one of them could be racing away at 35 mph and win by 100 yards?

There are two main types of sprinters. The most powerful will use an above-average gear and try to make an early attack, swooping from the top of a banking if possible to get their big 'engine' going fast. The speed specialists will hold back their sprint, waiting as long as possible so as to stake their all in the last few lengths. The main aim is surprise. The two ride a few bicycle-lengths apart in the preliminary stages since if you follow an opponent's wheel too closely you will have difficulty breaking free. The rider in the lead moves steadily up the banking to the railings, then swoops powerfully down. Once he's got that big gear revving he will be a hard man to catch. Or he may pretend to 'jump' whereupon his rival falls straight into the trap and promptly gives it all he's got, which means he will be an easy prey in the last 50 yards. There may be a whole series of feints. Both men have their heads turned slightly to watch one another, ready to stamp and pull on

*Lucien Michard et André Ravaud: *Le cyclisme sur piste – Vitesse.* S. Bornemann, 1933.

their pedals. The audience is curiously silent.

That's it! A series of sudden shouts, rising to a crescendo, and they shoot right up to top speed. They race forward, towards the finishing line, elbows out, breath coming in gasps, bodies arched like cats spitting with rage, racked by shudders like torpedo fish. The one on the outside seems to be gaining. They both fling themselves on to the finish-line. Who's the winner? It will be a photo-finish, to avoid any possible human error.

That is sprinting at its best. Men like Lucien Michard, when he was on peak form, Jeff Scherens or Reginald Harris were particularly exciting to watch. At the Munich Olympics in 1972 Daniel Morelon managed to fill nine-tenths of the cycle stadium single-handed with French supporters, who saw him repeat his success in Mexico in the individual event.

The world championships are still the major event in the sprinter's calendar. For many years the Paris Grand Prix enjoyed a renown unequalled elsewhere, but nowadays there are only a handful of sprint specialists. This means that Morelon has to chase all over Europe and even further afield to meet his amateur opponents – from London to Moscow, from Milan to Barbados.

A good match, on a covered track or in the open, always justifies the saying that 'the Sprint is the aristocrat of cycling sport', even if you admire road racers and their superhuman feats of courage.

## 1000 metres time-trials

Since the earliest days of cycle sport sprinters have been making or attacking short-distance records. Each track has its 'lap record' which is usually only of local interest, while there are national and world records at 500 and 1000 metres. The standing-start 1000 metres is one of the toughest of all and has been included in the Olympic Games since 1928 and has been part of the amateur world championships since 1966. Usually those who go in for it are out-and-out sprinters, though pursuit men have occasionally tried their luck in this very specialised field. (One example is Leandro Faggin from Italy, who became the Olympic champion in Melbourne in 1956.)

The first world title was contested in Frankfurt and was won by Pierre Trentin (France), who followed this up two years later in Mexico by winning the Olympic gold medal. All those who saw Trentin in Mexico feel that his was an athletic performance worthy to rank alongside the greatest in any sport. Trentin took a long time before he settled into the saddle, as he was busy beating hell out of his machine. He shot round the first lap like a cannon-ball. In the second lap contestants sometimes let up a bit, but Trentin never weakened for a second. The third lap was the deciding one. Trentin kept the pressure up right to the end, giving his all in the

Pierre Trentin (France) is a specialist at the tough, 1000 metres standing-start time-trial test. He won the 1966 world title, and nine years later was still good enough to fill fourth place. During that period Trentin also took the Olympic title in the 1968 Mexico Games with a world record ride of 1 min 3·91s.

Despite their great class, Daniel Morelon and Pierre Trentin (France) were often beaten by riders of less repute whose pedalling styles blended better on the double machine. Morelon-Trentin nevertheless won the world championship in 1966 and Olympic gold medals in 1968. Here they are attacking a Russian pair in a heat of the 1967 championships; they won, but were beaten in the final by Bruno Gonzato and Dino Verzini of Italy.

Latest in the long line of great Australian sprinters is John Nicholson, here fighting it out with his Danish rival Peder Pedersen. Pedersen beat Nicholson in the 1974 world professional sprint championship in Montreal, but the Australian turned the tables the following year to take the title. Third behind Nicholson and Pedersen in the 1975 championship was Ryoji Abe, the first Japanese to be placed in a world series.

174

This talented USA girl sprinter leading a Czech opponent is Sheila Young. In 1973 she was the first rider other than a Russian to win the sprint title since the series started in 1958. Miss Young is a fine all-round sportswoman, holder of world ice-skating records and winner of an Olympic gold medal in the 1976 winter games.

175

final 50 yards. His record time of 1 min 3·91 s has not been beaten at the time of writing. For a long time Neils Fredborg from Denmark thought he was the winner, but Trentin beat him by 0·7 of a second. When he finished his great ride Trentin dropped onto the grass track centre, gasping for breath. He had to be helped to his feet, as his tremendous effort had completely knocked him out. In using the last atom of explosive force Trentin reached the height of athletic achievement.

Since it does not appear to require complicated tactics the kilometre test has become the most internationally popular of all the world championship events, with every country represented. In Rocourt (Belgium) in 1975 there were 23 starters and the first 21 of them were covered by only four seconds, which is an indication of the overall improvement in performance.

This particular event involves a number of real specialists. In Rocourt Klaus Grünke (East Germany), who had been fifth the previous year, outstripped Eduard Rapp (USSR), who had beaten him in 1974 and had already won the title in 1971, with the 1973 champion Jan Kierzkovsky (Poland) third, followed by Pierre Trentin in fourth place. Fredborg would have been among the medals if he had not had a puncture on the last lap.

## Pursuit races – individual

When the starting pistol is fired the two contestants set off from opposite sides of the stadium, with exactly half the track between them. They stand on the pedals to 'get the gear rolling'. Then you see them racing forwards, absolutely straight, stretched out over their bikes. They give it all they have got. If they let up even for a second a few yards will be lost and, probably the match as well.

In the 1920s some pursuit matches were as long as 10 km (6·25 miles) and even as late as 1957 Albert Bouvet from Fougères in Brittany beat his Normandy rival Jacques Anquetil over that distance in a highly exciting race in the Vélodrome d'Hiver in Paris. Bouvet's time was 12 min 36·2 s, while Anquetil's was 12 min 36·8 s. In 1946, when this event became part of the world championships, the distance set was 5000 m for the professionals and 4000 m for the amateurs. (Since 1958 a women's championship has been contested over 3000 m.) Official events never take the form of a single duel between two contestants, but are made up of a series of heats. These distances have become standard and few pursuits nowadays exceed these distances.

For pursuit matches on well sheltered open-air cement tracks, gears of 51 or 52 × 15 (91·8 in and 93·6 in) are usual and on indoor tracks a lower gear has to be used, 54 × 16 (91 in); 50 × 15 (90·0 in) or 53 × 16 (89·4 in).

Every pursuiter has his own methods. Some make a very fast getaway. It is important to conserve your strength, but on the other hand things must not be taken too easily. You must not get obsessed by your opponent's position, but must be sufficiently aware of it to make sure that he does not catch you and put you out of the race by a 'knock out'. The important thing is to have enough reserve to allow you to react when only a mile of the contest remains to be

covered. Maybe you will have to use that energy regaining lost ground; maybe you will use it hanging on to the lead you have built up. Some pursuit riders who are as regular as clockwork find this difficult. Others are able to vary the pace and even launch into a frenzied sprint over the last lap and perhaps snatch victory in the final seconds of the contest.

Top pursuit men have to be in such good physical shape that they are among the aristocrats of cycle racing. Few entertainments excite the crowd as much as a match fought out by two stars. Just one example – the final match for the 1948 world championship title. It took place in Amsterdam, in appalling weather, and ended with the Dutch ace Gerrit Schulte beating Fausto Coppi by a bare 5 m (16·5 ft), to frenzied shouts of encouragement from his Dutch supporters.

## Pursuit races – team

Since 1962 the amateur world championships have included a very exciting event called the 'team pursuit' over 4000 metres. It had already been a part of the Olympic Games since 1920, but it is not generally known that a shorter version over 1810·473 m (to quote the official records) was part of the cycling programme at the 1908 London Olympiad at the White City Stadium, the United Kingdom winning, with Germany second and Canada third. Between 1920 and 1960 when the Games were held in Rome, Italy won the Olympic team pursuit seven times out of nine, the other two both going to France, in 1936 in Berlin and 1948 (London). The 1936 French team was outstanding, made up as it

was of four road men, all from the Vélo Club Levallois and under the direction of Paul Ruinart, who was a strong believer in making his men serve this sort of apprenticeship on the track.

Team pursuit racing is an exercise in precision. Each of the four cyclists leads for a lap, then swings up the banking and dives down on to the back wheel of the last of his team mates. (On a large track the riders often make these changes every half-lap.) It all has to be worked out to the last millimetre. The outstanding athletic qualities needed for this type of work are obvious. The winner is decided on the basis of the third man, not the first, which explains why it is essential to maintain the cohesion of the team up to the very last minute. For a long time the record set up by Ruinart's team appeared to be unbeatable at 4 min 41·4 s. But that once formidable time would not get 15th place today.

In 1962 the joint German team (in those days East and West Germany competed as a single unit in sporting events) won the first world crown in 4 min 30·6 s. Two years later, in Tokyo, they put an end to Italy's Olympic reign and a new page had been turned in the history of the sport, for the *squadra azzura* had far fewer wins from then on. It generally shares the honours with the USSR, the two Germanies and Britain. Team pursuit involves long and extremely painstaking training.

The final at the Munich Games was particularly fine. It was fought out between West Germany and East Germany and when the latter began to crumble the crowd nearly went mad. When their heroes had won they insisted that they do a lap of honour on

*Newcomers to the sport find it odd that the early stage of a sprint match is often a slow-bicycle race! The reason is that generally speaking, there is a psychological and physical advantage in riding behind one's opponent. When two minds have the same thought a 'standing still' session is inevitable. These three photographs were taken during a heat of the 1976 Grand Prix de Paris, the riders being Alex Pontet (France, nearer camera) and Benedikt Kocot (Poland). Pontet was the winner of this match and surprisingly won the final from Daniel Morelon and Giorgio Rossi (Italy). Track bicycles are fitted with 'fixed wheels' so that with controlled downward and backward pressure on the pedals skilled riders can balance for several minutes.*

177

The business end of a sprint. The go-slow tactics are over, the leading rider has sprinted by his opponent and pedals all-out for the line. The actors in this quarter-final match of the 1975 world amateur championship are grimly determined – Daniel Morelon (France) followed by Benedikt Kocot (Poland). Morelon was first and went on to win his seventh title.

Team pursuit riding is an exercise in speed, strength and technical skill. Had this photograph of a Polish team been taken a split second later, the fourth man would have been perfectly in line with the other three riders. After completing his spell of pacemaking at the front he had swung up the banking, then down on to the back of the group.

foot, which took a great deal longer than the winning time of 4 min 22·14 s they took to cover the 4000 m of the race.

## The cocktail

Track meetings can take many forms, sometimes with several different types of contest on the same day. Alternatively, the whole meeting may consist of a 'Madison', and of course almost a week is needed for a 'six-day' race.

### Handicaps, 'Devils' and 'Points'

One type of race, the handicap, has almost disappeared in Europe. This involved 'scratch men', 'limit men' and 'middle-markers' who were separated at the start by distances calculated on the known difference in their abilities. Handicaps could be very exciting, because the scratch man had to be outstanding if he was to make up the difference.

Among the handicap riders in the halcyon days of track racing, the Americans and Australians were strongest. Today 'Wheel Race Handicaps' are still top-of-the-bill items on Australian and New Zealand programmes. The quality of the top contestants is well known in Europe because, since the Second World War, star performers like Russell Mockridge and Sidney Patterson have won world and Olympic honours; indeed the 1975 and 1976 world professional sprint champion John Nicholson is another product of the fast and tough school of Australian handicap riders.

Handicaps are handicaps in any language, but many different names are used for another popular event which is something of a 'knock-out'. On the continent of Europe we call them Elimination races, in the USA they are Miss-and-outs, in Britain Devil-take-the-hindmosts. A race by any other name would be just as amusing. A field of, say, 20 riders start in a race, and at the end of every lap the last rider over the line is eliminated. Sounds simple enough, but many a star sprinter riding smugly in the middle of the bunch and without a care in the world, suddenly finds himself outflanked and completely 'boxed in' by wily opponents, and the next he knows is that his name is being called out over the public address system to get off the track. Although some 'devils' are deadly serious affairs, others are more free-and-easy and give the track clowns a chance to put on an act. They pretend not to hear their names called out by the judges and attempt to continue in the race. Eventually the field is whittled down to two riders who then put up a spectacular sprint for first prize.

Then there are points races. In 5 km events the first four men over the line at the end of each kilometre are awarded points (5, 3, 2 and 1 respectively, with double points for the last sprint). On large open-air tracks some races involve sprinting every lap. Sprinters in a points race are hopeful that the field

will remain compact so that they can do their stuff when the time comes. Of course the others are wise to this and try to break away from the sprinters, or failing this, to make the going so hard that their speed is blunted and ineffective.

'Devils', points races, sprints and pursuits may be grouped together to form a competition known as an 'omnium'. This may be organised on an individual or a team basis and is very popular with amateur clubs, particularly because it allows them to try out new competitors. The idea is that a first place earns one point and so on, the winner being the one who has the lowest points total at the end of the four events. A good all-round track rider obviously shines in a series of contrasting tests. Although there is no official world championship for omnium riders, the European indoor track promoters award a continental title annually, the events comprising: 5 km points race; 'devil-take-the-hindmost'; 1000 m flying-start time trial; 4000 m individual pursuit.

## The 'Madison'

A spectator having his first sight of a 'Madison' race is bewildered by a mass of 30 or 40 riders pedalling madly round a track. It is, however, organised chaos. Competitors are riding in pairs, one of them doing a brief spell 'on duty' at full speed while his partner slowly circles the outside edge of the track. Then with a well-timed 'relay' he relieves his partner who eases up – but does not dismount – and has a few minutes breather before taking over again.

Most popular distance for 'Madisons' is 100 km (62·25 miles) which professionals cover in about two hours – though this depends on the surface and size of the track – while amateur events are usually over half the distance. For many years they were the basis for weekly programmes on the winter tracks. If one team was a lap or more ahead of the field it carried the day. If several teams finished level on distance covered, the verdict went to the pair with the best total of points scored during the intermediate series of sprints.

The idea was to have the team's sprinter as well placed as possible when the bell rang to indicate the last lap of a sprint. The need for flexibility, the constant need to force the pace, the immediate use of reflexes, means that 'Madison' riders do not use gear ratios higher than 7 m (88 in). This type of race is almost like a ballet, thanks to the brilliant virtuosity with which the relays are performed – the first man racing up to his partner at top speed, grabbing the cotton wool pad sewn into the hip of his shorts and shoving him forward into the battle – the skill with which they avoid falling, the sudden acceleration of the sprints, the giddy whirl of silk jerseys.

The demolition of the Vélodrome d'Hiver in Paris and its equivalent in Brussels has prevented the faithful from practising a religion that was dear to their hearts.

*With a background of time-trial competition on the road and fast pedalling on the track, British riders have been well to the fore in world championship pursuit races which were instituted in 1946. After Norman Sheil had twice taken the amateur title, in 1955 and 1958, another tall, well-built specialist was even more successful in the professional series – Hugh Porter, seen here at speed in 1973 on the San Sebastian track where he won his fourth world title. There's quite a collection of gold medals in the Porter household, his wife* née *Anita Lonsbrough, was an Olympic swimming champion at Rome in 1960.*

181

## Six-day races

The most elaborate form of 'Madison' race was and still is the 'six-day' race.

> The scoreboard started to work overtime, with some numbers climbing up and others going down. The riders' quarters were concentrated at one end of the track. Each man had a little wooden cubicle with a camp bed sealed off by curtains. A floodlight shone into the furthest corners of the cubicles so that the crowd would not miss a single movement made by their heroes, even when they were resting. The attendants were constantly coming and going in their white hospital coats, surrounded by patches of petrol and grease, mixing embrocations from eggs and camphor.
> . . . Those who had just been relieved by their team mates would clamber off their machines to snatch a couple of hours' sleep.
> It was very late. The night sprints were over. The contestants pedalled on, palms upward to rest their wrists and enveloped in Balaclavas.*

In this extract Paul Morand has captured 'the night of a six-day event', thanks to his original and precise way of looking at things and his brilliant technique as a writer. In fact it really is the night that counts in a six-day race. It is a 'Madison' on a gigantic scale and based in the same way on the distance covered, and the number of points collected.

In the evening the pace quickens and the sprints follow in rapid succession. The race is at its height. On the track centre the restaurant tables are all taken. Elegantly dressed ladies and smartly turned-out men have come to see and be seen, now that the theatre shows are over. A well-known singer is at the microphone while an accordionist plays for all he's worth. Every now and then a loud 'klaxon' noise blares out from the loudspeakers, the signal that a 'prime' sprint is imminent (these are extra cash prizes put up by spectators and commercial firms; they add spice to the six-day race scene but have absolutely no influence on the final verdict). The riders flash by in a long line, in gaily coloured jerseys, their legs glistening with embrocation, black crash hats pulled down over their foreheads. The 'Mafia' goes into action, that is to say, the strongest riders who have ganged up together for tactical and financial reasons, and the lesser lights are soon struggling many laps behind the leaders. Tomorrow night they will be nominating a 'Queen of the Six' and the lady almost certain to be crowned is firing the gun for the start of yet another 'prime'. Catcalls and screwed-up balls of paper rain down from the crowd.

Six-day races were once very fashionable occasions and even nowadays, although so many permanent indoor cycle tracks have closed down, about 15 are organised annually. The series traditionally opens with the 'Six Day Bike Race' in London during September, but the 1976 event was not held owing

* Paul Morand: 'La nuit de six jours', in *Ouvert la nuit*. Gallimard, 1923.

to reconstruction work in Wembley Pool. The formula has changed. Endless laps in an empty stadium in the early hours of the morning are no longer considered necessary, and the trend is towards organising a series of evening sessions of varying length, which is a far cry from the original non-stop 144 hours. This means that the contestants have a chance to sleep, so the problem of combating tiredness is no longer the same. The problems of what to eat, the speed, the loss of weight every evening through sweating are nevertheless difficult to overcome.

## Motor-paced races

Although this type of race is now in decline, in its heyday those who specialised in it had to be real championship material. They needed to be able to put on very rapid spurts, to extend themselves to the limits at frequent intervals, to be supple, to have unlimited stamina and to be completely in step with their pacemaker. In the hurly-burly of the race the contestant does in fact communicate with his pacemaker, albeit briefly. A mere 'Go!' if he wants to move into the attack, or 'Oh! Oh!' if his pacemaker is going too fast.

Nowadays races are shorter and less colourful than they used to be. Contests behind huge motorbikes involve a large amount of technical work of a kind that few racing cyclists can put in, particularly since they have very few opportunities to gauge their progress, now that this type of event is becoming increasingly rare. Also, they hardly ever have access to the tracks for training, as it would be terribly dangerous for them to ride alongside ordinary racing cyclists.

The function of the motor-cycle is, of course, to shelter the cyclist from the rush of air that increases incredibly as the wheels move faster and faster. To get closer to his shelter, the cyclist uses a small front wheel of 60 cm (24 in) fitted in reversed forks. In the early days of the sport motor-pace followers went *too* fast and often ran out of control into the crowd. To reduce speed to safer proportions a 'roller' was fitted to the back of the motor-bike to force the cyclist to ride further back and therefore to get less shelter. Other rules designed to prevent excessive speed are: the peak of the cyclist's saddle must not be in front of a vertical line drawn up from the bottom bracket centre and the motor-cyclist's leather clothing is standard so that he cannot 'balloon' himself out to provide a greater area of wind-resistance.

Instead of a field of, for example, eight riders starting alongside one another as in a normal race, the motor-pace followers line up one behind the other in an order that has previously been decided by the luck of the draw. As the cyclists wait on their marks their pacemakers are circling the track in the correct order so that when the gun is fired for the race to start, the contestants are rapidly together in pairs and the battle is on. The order of start is important. The rider in the No. 1 spot is in a sort of no-man's land until he has caught and overtaken the man starting in last position. Tactics vary according to how the race is run and on a rider's make-up. One may decide to go into the attack immediately while, for the time being, another will be content merely to resist any attempt to overtake him.

Such decisions are, in fact, made by the pacemaker who 'does the thinking and leaves the pedalling to the cyclist'. Pacemakers are invariably former racing cyclists who know all the tricks of the trade. Provided other competitors are not impeded some pacemakers do not take the bends of a track in an arc, but move slightly upwards and then downwards in an egg-shaped trajectory so that they are able to go 'downhill' at great speed from the top of the steep banking. A pacemaker leading a highly-strung cyclist will go into action right away; others whose men are slow starters will give them time to warm up and play a waiting game. A thousand and one different factors enter this branch of the sport which is a world apart within the cycling universe, and a fascinating world at that.

The decisive moment has come. The supposed rival of the man in the lead has moved steadily up towards the railings. This time he rockets into an all-out effort. He comes close – and attacks. If there is no wind to speak of and it is a big, well-banked open-air track he will be using a gear of $70 \times 14$ (135 in); if it is a 250 metres lap, such as one of the larger indoor velodromes, the gear would be around $64 \times 14$ (123 in). The man in the lead has sensed his opponent's approach. He too accelerates, ready to respond. The onlookers may well be enthralled by the sight of two 'stayers' jostling one another, but in fact the one who comes up from behind will probably be the winner if he has managed to get on up level with his opponents. That means he has broken through the turbulence created by the motorbike pacing the man in front, which is at its worst at 5 or 6 metres behind it. Only on exceptional occasions will the first man have been able to keep enough strength in reserve to resist the attack. It can also happen that the duel goes on and on at such a pitch that both of them 'lose their motors' and a third man takes advantage of the situation to snatch and keep the lead.

A pace-follower's worst moments are when he fails to keep in the shelter of the motorbike's 'slipstream' – either because he has been forced to launch a second attack before recovering from the first, or because his pacemaker did not realise his cyclist was having a bad time.

Track cycling requires tremendous exertion and speed, plus a very pure style. It leaves you gasping for breath and it is essential that the trackman has an extensive warm-up before any type of race. In the big towns building development has speeded up the disappearance of some of the most famous tracks of all, and many outdoor velodromes in the provincial towns are scarcely ever used, so their concrete is cracking and their paint peeling.

Yet track work is still an essential form of training for anyone who wants to understand his sport and to improve his performance. It helps him to go faster, to improve his technique and become more alert. It is also a good apprenticeship for a roadman, helping him to cope with the dangerous mass sprints he will have to take part in from time to time.

The riders' quarters in the wings of a cycle stadium are a fascinating sight with rows of jerseys drying over a handrail and doors ajar to give a glimpse of a jumble of wheels, cycle frames and chainwheels. There is the massage table, oilcans and cartons of talc. 'Home trainers' on which to pedal if the track is not available. Endless spirited discussions. In the summer there is a game of *boules* under the trees contested by pacemakers who have temporarily lost their clients, a racer or two, plus one or two veterans. A mechanic trues up a wheel, or squeezes shellac on to a rim with reverent gestures, before sticking on a tubular tyre. The usual hangers-on are lounging about doing nothing, commenting on what everyone else is doing. A second-rate amateur has just been doing a spot of training. He loosens his crash helmet, slings the bike over his shoulder and sets off for his cabin to change, after perhaps lingering for a moment in the hope of picking up a useful tip. There will also be the autograph-hunter trying to dodge the door-keeper.

Track cycling is a pleasure that will never die, especially when you remember that the roads are becoming increasingly overcrowded. The track is a sort of museum of movement that will accept nothing but the best. It owes it to itself to keep its special place in the sport of cycling.

# Through woods and meadows
## Cyclo-cross

At the turn of the century only a handful of cyclists followed Daniel Gousseau, later secretary-general of the French Cycling Union, on his Sunday outings into the area round Paris every winter. They enjoyed them hugely, told others about them and soon there were 20 or 30 taking part. They were young and eager and proud to show that they could keep going even in the 'dead' season and that their bicycles would take them anywhere.

As the Sundays went by the idea of holding competitions emerged, on an impromptu basis at first, but later properly organised ones. In 1902 F de Baeder won the first French championship. The idea of awarding an official title for 'rough-stuff' racing did not catch on for a while, but it was a sign of things to come when the brilliant Octave Lapize

BELOW: *The pace quickens during a 'chase' in the Dortmund six-day race. The temporary 'off duty' riders pedal on the upper part of the track while the active participants are strung out on the line. Next move is for the relieving riders to drop down towards their partners. The inside rider grabs the pad sewn into his partner's shorts, and with a powerful heave, sends him flying off at full speed.*

A typical scene during a six-day race. This is an event in Brussels on a small track that can be dismantled and used in other cities. The car in the foreground is first prize in a series of sprint races held nightly, but which have no influence on the overall result.

Motor-paced racing. Fast, spectacular, noisy and still dangerous despite placing the 'roller' at a distance behind the motor-cycle to reduce the rider's speed. Although the pedaller obviously does the hard work, the pacemaker actually is the strategist who attacks or holds back according to how he reads the race.

became champion in 1907 – he was to start road racing two years later. 'Cyclo-cross', as it became known, really owed its existence in a permanent form to Eugène Christophe, who was unbeatable at 'mud plugging' between 1909 and 1914 and even staged a comeback to win the title again in 1921! The first Belgian champion, in 1910, was no less a person than Philippe Thys, whose three wins in the Tour de France were later to make him one of the big names in road racing.

Cyclo-cross has been called cycling's 'winter sport', and nowadays a number of riders specialise in it. This does perhaps show that this branch of the sport has made great strides, for it is no longer thought of as something to be taken up casually. On the other hand the top road racers now have such a heavy calendar of events that they only turn to cyclo-cross when assured a high 'personal appearance' fee irrespective of what sort of show they put up. Having their names on the programme means that the organisers are sure to make plenty of money. Then again it should not be forgotten that the raison d'être of cyclo-cross was to be a cycling event first and foremost, so the sections where natural obstacles are surmounted on foot should never be more than sub-plots in the drama.

Cyclo-cross is very demanding. You must be exceptionally dexterous in handling your machine, be in tiptop physical condition and have the right temperament. Each race normally lasts an hour or slightly more, though the rigours of the winter climate and of the course itself – with long stretches under snow, ankle-deep mud, and precipitous slopes – occasionally make the races last much longer.

Many people do not really understand what cyclo-cross is all about. From the point of view of the general public it is a sort of hybrid – they say that combining cycling and running is like putting chalk and cheese together. In fact, it deserves something more than an indulgent smile. You would revise your opinion if you stood at the top of a hill watching two cyclists battling for the title, cycles slung over their shoulders, gasping for breath, eyes streaming, leaping into the saddle when they get to the top of the hill and racing crazily down the steep descent, like a pair of tightrope walkers, increasing their lead over the long string of pursuers.

Special equipment is needed for this type of competition. The frame is basically the same as used for road racing, but with increased fork and stay clearance to stop (in theory!) the wheels becoming clogged with mud. Extra width is given to the brake arms for the same reason, while the bottom-bracket height is increased to 27·5 cm (11 in). Tyres have 'knobs' or studs to ensure a firm grip. Toe-clips are double-thickness to prevent them bending or breaking on hitting something hard. Cyclo-cross shoes have special spiked toe-plates fitted to the soles so that, as well as gripping the pedals, they also grip the ground when the rider temporarily becomes a runner; shoes also have an additional small strap fastening round the ankle to prevent them being pulled off by the mud.

Serious cyclo-cross riders reconnoitre a course several times before an important race and make sure that their whole system is well 'warmed up' before the word 'Go'. This aspect is most important because the heart, respiratory system and muscles are immediately hard at work and there is no possibility of taking the first few minutes quietly until they are functioning satisfactorily. The choice of gears is obviously important and often cannot be made until immediately before the race. A rider reconnoitres a course at 10 a.m. and finds it firm and fast. Then it begins to rain and by the start of the race at 2 p.m. the hard footpaths have turned into a quagmire. The cyclo-crossman therefore has several free-wheel 'blocks' in his tool bag and the equipment to make rapid changes before an event; for average conditions a suitable choice would be 50 and 42 front chainwheels, 15–17–20–22–24 teeth on the free-wheel. Ideally, the cyclist should remain a cyclist as long as he can – until he can go faster by turning into a runner.

Many cyclo-cross courses include an early stretch of reasonably good road, and it is important to use this to advantage as it will affect progress in the later 'rough stuff'. A man badly placed will have difficulty overtaking a string of rivals plodding single-file through a narrow gully. One of the few books on this branch of the sport, Cycle 100%, Série cyclo-cross by Robert Oubron and René Chesal, gives the advice that after running up a hill the competitor should not immediately leap into the saddle for the downhill dash while his legs are still trembling, but take a running jump on to the bike – a few yards can be gained that way, enough perhaps to gain the verdict in a closely-fought race. The book also stresses that the rider will have more control over his machine if he presses on the pedals even when going down the steepest hill.

The major annual cyclo-cross event is the world championship. The first 'International Criterium' was competed for in 1924 in Paris, the winner being Gaston Degy (France). In subsequent years the title was shared between France, Belgium and Luxembourg (Josy Mersch in 1935). The list includes some famous names, not all of whom were well-known at the time. There is Francis Pelissier (1926), whose brother Charles chalked up a total of three consecutive French titles in 1926, 1927, 1928; Sylvère Maes in 1933; and in particular specialists such as Camille Foucaux or Maurice Seynaeve from Belgium. Robert Oubron, who won in 1937, 1938, 1941 and 1942, deserves a place all to himself. He was unbeatable for several years and became known as the 'king of cyclo-cross', with his spotted jersey appearing first on countless occasions.

In the post-war period one of the international events became official, starting in 1950 in Paris. The 1947 Tour de France winner, little Jean Robic, was the first to don the 'rainbow jersey'. Down to 1958 the French school remained outstanding, but no one has come up since to take over from Roger Rondeaux (1951–3), André Dufraisse (1954–8) and their team-mates Pierre Jodet, Gilbert Bauvin and Georges Meunier. The two main contenders for the title between 1959 and 1967 were Renato Longo (Italy) and Rolf Wolfshohl (W. Germany), but Eric de Vlaeminck from Belgium, who won in 1966 and every year from 1968 to 1973, will long be remembered. His brother Roger, taking the place of their compatriot Albert van Damme, secured the title in 1975. The heyday of the Swiss may have started at Chazay d'Azergue in January 1976, with an outright win by Albert Zweifel from Zürich, at the age of 26. Peter Frischknecht was in second place, followed by two Frenchmen – André Wilhelm and Cyrille Guimard.

The amateur world championship was won, again at Chazay d'Azergues, by Klaus-Peter Thaler from West Germany, who had already won in this category in London in 1973 and was runner-up to Robert Vermeire from Belgium in 1974 and 1975. Whereas generally speaking cyclo-cross events are open, the decision to create a special amateur world title in 1967 has encouraged a wider range of countries to take part than the usual small group from Western Europe. Of the long line of 1976 contestants those from Belgium, Britain, France, Italy, Luxembourg, the Netherlands, Spain, Switzerland and West Germany found themselves competing with Austrians, Czechs, a lone Dane, Poles and even some North Americans.

A good cyclo-cross race held on a sunny day, or even in bad weather, is a crowd puller. If organised over a 'natural' cross-country course without artificial obstacles, cyclo-cross makes a valuable contribution to the sport of cycling, although it can become something of a circus. At the same time it can be a healthy introduction to an unusual type of tourism, which enables you

> . . . to discover hundreds of interesting things which you would have ridden straight past if you had not been tempted into hitching the bike over your shoulder, or simply pushing it along, and following a riverbed, or a footpath that may end in a spring or an unexpected view, or a lane that suddenly yields up some unexpected historical monument, or a lake you did not know existed.
> . . . Just try doing this on a bridle path in Savoy or in the Pyrenees and I'll be surprised if you don't find yourself singing for sheer joy. And when you're back down again, after clattering through streams and gulleys and stony paths, sometimes on the bike, sometimes on your feet, you will have enjoyed a wonderful experience.*

And so cyclo-cross, uniting as it does the delights of competition cycling and cycle touring, is yet another reminder that the bicycle is a wonderful invention, for quite apart from getting you about, it is an extra-special source of fun as well.

*Robert Oubron et René Chesal: *Cycliste 100%, série cyclo-cross*, Paris 1967.

Cyclo-cross was originally intended as a
winter diversion for road-racers who
were unable, or unwilling, to take part
in track competition during the close season.
It has developed into a serious sport
with its own world amateur and
professional championships. As well as
the ability to run and pedal well, the
cyclo-cross rider must be exceptionally
good at handling his machine. One
false move and he could be taking a
header into a muddy stream!

Cyclo-cross riders listen carefully to weather forecasts.
'Very cold and dry' means the course will probably be iron-hard
and fast for cycling. 'Heavy rain' that it will be muddy and slow.
Top riders will choose their equipment according to the conditions.
Others must be prepared for anything. Patterned tyre treads give
a good grip when cycling, spiked shoe-plates help when it is
necessary to run. The bottom bracket of a cyclo-cross machine is
high – and the bottom gear very low.

*For long periods top cyclo-cross riders have been 'specialists' who are only moderate performers in conventional road and track competition. This mud-covered star is Eric de Vlaeminck (Belgium), seven times world cyclo-cross champion, who had a good record of road race wins, including the Tour of Belgium.*

# IV
# THEY JUST KEEP ON RIDING

*To the purist some of these cyclists are 'not properly dressed', and don't know how to carry their belongings. But, by the look of them, they know how to enjoy themselves, and that is what pleasure cycling is all about.*

# What to wear

On being asked a few years ago about his life and early years, the French painter Gen Paul spoke of his passion for bicycles and recalled the days when he was too hard up to buy a machine but used to walk around Paris rigged out with cycle clips round the bottom of his trousers, to make people think he had one! Cycle clips do, in fact, make a good symbol for the wide range of cycling wear available.

Those who cycle every day – to school, to work, to the shops – can make do with ordinary clothes, although a pair of trousers in some tough and hard-wearing fabric is advisable. They should be cut in such a way so as not to touch the chain and get covered in grease, or catch in the chainwheel teeth. If you are going in for the various types of organised cycle-sport suitable clothing for the occasion and the weather is vital. As times have changed, there have been many ups-and-downs in cycling wear, and we can now smile at illustrations of 'outfits' that were once all the rage.

## Felt hats and divided skirts

In late 1886 a French tricycle champion called 'Baby,' writing in the *Revue du Sport Vélocipédique*, offered some 'practical tips' for travellers. He was very strict on the question of what was permissible and what was not:

> Any cyclist who has tried wearing woollen garments over his body and legs has no desire to travel any other way, indeed he could not – which only shows that it is the best possible solution. Woollen stockings should also be worn. If your calves are not sufficiently well-developed to hold the stockings up, try using a small knotted rubber band instead of garters. You can fasten it to the stocking and button it on to your knickerbockers. A shortish jacket, with a stand-up collar, also in jersey, is preferable to any other type of cloth or flannel jacket. A complete outfit for a roadman, simple yet practical, would consist of a collar or shirt-front, imitation-linen cuffs in rubber attached to the jacket, and a soft felt hat rather than a straw boater. If he is dressed in this way, a velocipedist will not be hampered in his movements during his runs. He can pedal in a jersey with bare knees and calves, when in the heart of the country and then do a quick change to make himself presentable, indeed stylish. If you feel the cold add a silk scarf, and a pair of anklets in the same pattern as the knickerbockers if you do not like the idea of displaying your calves to the envious glances of male and female alike, and all will be well.

The question of what to wear seems to have been an all-important topic in those early days. The first yearbook of the French Cycling Union, also published in late 1886, carried a long piece by 'Jean de l'Arieste' on how to prepare cycling kit for the road. He guarantees that if his instructions are followed 'there is no danger of inelegant creases appearing'. And we must not forget our headgear – that would be most improper!

> Hats are difficult to pack. If they are hard they take up too much space; if soft, liable to finish the journey creased. Yet you have to find some way of covering your head. I recommend as the most suitable head-covering a round knitted hat in the same shade as your outfit, which can also be worn in the street. The alternative is a felt hat, usually dark in colour and with a fairly low crown. You can fold it in two lengthwise and fill the concave part with handkerchiefs.

Indeed when the first golden age of bicycling dawned in 1892 Baudry de Saunier drew up a list for the tourist ready to set off on a three-day or four-day trip. It was designed to make packing as simple and easy an operation as possible.

> A spare flannel shirt – an extra detachable flannel collar – one or two detachable linen collars (rolled up), and a pair of linen cuffs, with cufflinks (also rolled up) – a spare tie – a pair of stockings – a pair of soft, light-weight flat slippers – a nightshirt – six or seven handkerchiefs – a clothes brush – a toothbrush – a razor and shaving brush (make sure you keep the razor firmly shut with a strong rubber band, as the vibrations could jolt it out of its case and result in a nasty accident when you unpack) – some soap, a towel, a few needles, some thick thread and a button or two, as all tourists must be able to sew! – and finally various odds-and-ends such as nail-scissors etc. Everything should be wrapped separately and wedged in place with sheets of paper and strips of linen.
>
> If you follow these instructions a mere five minutes in your hotel room will enable you to make yourself sufficiently presentable to go anywhere, since everybody is prepared to make allowances for tourists. Your luggage will weigh only a few pounds.

When we turn to the fair sex, we find that their apparel gave rise to violent arguments. A pamphlet containing the results of a survey carried out by the French journalist C de Loris* offers a helpful sum-

*C. de Loris: *La femme à bicyclette; ce qu'elles en pensent*. Paris, 1896.

195

mary of the various aspects of the controversy. The majority of women who were non-cyclists shared the view of Nellie Melba, the Australian singer whose lasting fame was assured by the invention of a peach and icecream confection. 'I loathe masculine clothes for women', said Dame Nellie.

Active women cyclists saw the matter very differently. One such was the music hall star Alice Bertin, who came second to Blanche Dupré in an Artiste's Bike Race. 'I personally believe that for someone like me who rides a bike regularly trousers are essential,' she declared. Alice agreed however, that for showing oneself off in the Bois de Boulogne 'a skirt, a very long skirt' was appropriate. Many 'veloci-pedestrians' solved the difficult choice facing them by plumping for a 'divided skirt', or culottes, as we should call them today.

French cycling fashions met with the same mixed reception when they found their way across the Channel. The correspondence pages of the British cycling press were filled with arguments for and against, often expressed in bitter terms. The 'rationalists' were all for women cyclists wearing a jacket and knickerbockers, or bloomers. 'Disgraceful' cried the opposition. A titled lady member of the CTC was refused admission to the coffee room of a Surrey hotel because she was wearing 'rational costume'.

In the subsequent legal action in which the hotel was indicted for 'wilfully and unlawfully neglecting and refusing to supply a traveller with victuals', a photograph of the plaintiff, Lady Haberton, was produced. It was described in court as a picture of 'an elderly lady, wearing a pair of exceedingly baggy knickerbockers reaching below the knee and a jacket which came well over the hips and opened sufficiently to reveal the silk blouse underneath'. Although judgement was given in favour of the hotel, the 'Haberton case' was an important early chapter in the story of Women's Lib.

This is only one example of the great part the bicycle played in the emancipation of women. It undoubtedly helped the movement along, before it was given a further impetus by the upsurge in winter sports, which tended to bring the clothing worn by both sexes together, or even to produce 'unisex' clothing, with the repercussions we all know.

So what is the most practical form of clothing for all those, male and female, who are planning seventy-five years later to cycle as often as possible and get the maximum enjoyment out of it?

## Road racing

As they have to face up to all sorts of conditions, training and racing when it is still freezing cold or pouring with rain or blazing hot, racing cyclists must combine efficiency with comfort. Serious attention has therefore been paid to the various items of clothing and cycle tourists are now starting to study the whole question themselves.

As training starts up again in the New Year, wool is an important factor. Wool has always been the cyclist's friend – as well as keeping the body warm it also soaks up perspiration, thus preventing it turning into freezing cold patches on the skin. What exactly should a racing cyclist wear?

First comes a vest – a woollen vest naturally, and a long-sleeved version if the weather is cold. A shirt may possibly be worn, but it should not be made from nylon or any other man-made fibre which cannot 'breathe'. It causes perspiration and does not allow it to evaporate. Next comes a racing jersey, with a high neck and handy pockets. On top, one or more woollen sweaters – one of them with a high polo neck. If the wind is cold an old cyclist's dodge is to tuck some newspaper between the jersey and the sweater.

On the whole it is better not to wear 'brief' underpants, which are liable to cut into you, but a pair of racing shorts with a chamois leather seat. A pair of woollen tights or leg warmers are essential if it is really cold weather. Some people favour a tracksuit, but a pair of cycling trousers, which end just below the knee, are excellent, especially if made from cavalry twill. They should be held up by braces – never ride with a belt as this restricts breathing and is uncomfortable across the stomach.

As for headgear, an Italian-type cap made in wool is the most suitable as you can pull it over your ears and prevent a biting wind turning them bright red. One or two pairs of socks are essential and should be made in wool. Woollen or lined gloves are also required. Special cycling shoes, which are traditionally black and have stiff soles and metal plates should be worn. The rear cage of a rat-trap pedal slots into a groove in the plates. This in itself makes pedalling much easier, as well as preventing the foot slipping, especially if the toe-clip on the pedal includes a strap. When the straps are tightened you and your machine form a single unit. As it is difficult to keep out the cold, some cyclists wear knee-length, fur-lined socks, even though they hinder pedalling to some extent. Some roadmen also wear silk stockings next to the skin, under their socks, as extra protection.

As the weather gets warmer the clothing for training can be lighter. Eventually you will be wearing just a short-sleeved vest, a jersey and thin sweater, tights, ankle socks and shoes.

So much for clothing proper. A racing cyclist's outfit will always include one vital item – a pair of cycling gloves with cut-off fingers. These give protection if the rider crashes, and he can rub his gloved hand over the tubular tyre from time to time when pedalling, to brush off small bits of gravel before they penetrate the thin rubber tread. For the first few events at the beginning of the season you will need one or two long-sleeved jerseys, tights and tracksuit bottoms or leg-warmers to protect your muscles.

*A February race in the south of France. The leader of this echelon, Michel Laurent, is stripped for action, but Raymond Poulidor – who seems to be enjoying himself – and Yves Hezard prefer long-sleeved vests under their racing jerseys.*

For track races silk jerseys without pockets are worn – you would not have time to pull food out of your pockets and anyway eating is difficult when going fast. For 'Madison' races a cottonwool pad is sewn into the hip of the shorts on the left side so that your team-mate can grab it and swing you forward with his right hand. If you go in for cyclo cross your shoe-plates will have spikes, so that when cycling is impossible you can run over slippery or steeply sloping ground.

Before plates are fitted to new shoes they should be ridden (using toeclips) until the pedals have made grooves in the soles. The plates are then tacked to the shoes so that the slots fall $\frac{1}{8}$ in behind the grooves. Unless the plates are fitted squarely, knee-ache may result. Shoe size decides the type of toeclip used – short, medium or long.

Caps are often useful, particularly when it is hot. The 'crash' helmet recommended by the Union Cycliste Internationale has not yet gained general acceptance, though it is compulsory for certain categories (very young competitors) and for specific types of race (especially races on hard tracks); and in some countries, Belgium for instance, it is compulsory for all races. It is an ugly piece of equipment and either heavy or so small as to be useless. The 'crash helmet' is not universally popular by any means, and is not always a safety factor.

When a young racing cyclist sees all the gear he's about to put on laid out on the bench beside him he is gripped by a growing feeling of jubilation – there are his shoes, his white ankle socks, his black shorts, his vest, his braces, cap, gloves and, best of all, his club jersey. The same emotion sweeps over every racer, even if an old hand, when, just before the first race of the new season, he opens his case and takes out the outfit in which he will 'see the new season in'.

## The touring and competition cyclist

The information gleaned from the 'élite' branch of the sport, true racing cyclists, has had some influence on the clothing worn by tourists and *cyclosportifs*. Of course, a special outfit is not absolutely necessary for pleasure cycling. This is plain when you see a motley throng of Sunday bikers riding merrily past wearing tennis shoes, baggy tracksuits, football shorts, ordinary jumpers, not to mention women in skin-tight trousers or dresses lifted above their knees by a mischievous breeze.

The basic points to remember are still: wool, braces not belts, simple and well-fitting clothes and cycling or touring shorts over a pair of racing shorts with a chamois leather seat. These basic items can be adapted in various ways, depending on how energetic you intend to be. For instance for long trips at night gloves coming well up over the wrist will be useful.

Unless the weather is really fine and the barometer is clearly set fair you should always take a light racing cape, rolled and fixed under the saddle. Avoid see-through nylon macs, which protect you from the rain all right but leave you drenched inside with condensation. A better choice is a long poncho-style cape which covers you completely, with a hood that should, in theory anyway, stop the rain running down your neck.

Things have been changing recently and cyclists who try for the major certificates like Paris-Brest-Paris do not look so very different from racing cyclists proper. However, the true cyclist is never flashily dressed, whether he goes in for racing or just for pleasant outings. Striking the right tone in this respect is not as difficult as finding the ideal gear ratio – but both matters require an intelligent approach.

197

ABOVE TOP: *An attacking group in the mid-March Paris-Nice stage race are well clothed against the cold on the Col de la Republique high above Saint-Etienne.*

ABOVE: *Unlike serious competition riders, club cyclists can enjoy an occasional spot of sport dressed as they please. This is a 'home trainer' race at the 1975 CTC York Rally. With the rollers reducing resistance even tourists can pedal at 50 mph!*

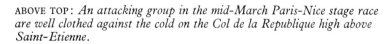

*Young lady on a lightweight.*

*Even at the height of summer temperatures can be low at the summit of a mountain pass.*

*The young man pumping up his tyre is guilty of a lapse that is more likely to lead to a chill than a soaking in a downpour : he is leaving his lumbar region exposed to the cold. A pair of braces would be a good investment!*

*Newcomers to cycling will hardly believe it, but there are actually people who enjoy a good pedal in the rain!*

When training is resumed after the winter break, the wise rider does not rush things. He dresses warmly and uses comparatively heavy tyres and wheels so that, when the racing season opens, he will feel the benefit of lighter clothing and equipment. Preparation for competition should be a building-up process so that a rider produces his best form in important races and not on training runs. Even when Paris-Roubaix comes round in April there is often still a touch of winter in the air. Here is Roger de Vlaeminck, the Belgian who has twice won the great classic, riding through the snow.

*The French have a word for this type of wheelman – Cyclo-sportif – mid-way between the serious racing cyclist and the leisurely tourist who is not concerned with speed at all. These hard-riding clubmen dress like* coureurs, *train like them, but their machines are fitted with mudguards, front carriers and (often) dynamo lighting sets.*

# Long live the bicycle!

Twenty years ago one of the bicycle's most ardent admirers pronounced the following 'funeral oration on the bike' – and he seemed to know what he was talking about.

> The few hundred touring cyclists who persist in pedalling on amid the torrential floods of cars and scooters may protest until they're blue in the face that the object of their anachronistic passion has fallen victim to a fad that will soon pass, but nothing will stop the bike being killed by laziness and vanity . . . Our great-grandchildren will never experience the joys of pedalling through the countryside. And moreover many of my contemporaries have already decided that they must move with the times and are abandoning the bicycle they used to love and that has given them so much. Personally, I shall take care not to follow their example, knowing how much I should lose if I did. I shall keep it up to the bitter end, even if mine's the only bike left . . .*

The old man did keep it up to the bitter end, in his own way. A quarter of a century had raced by since he embarked on his crusade to arouse enthusiasm for cycling and physical exercise, crying, 'Long live the bicycle!' He never lost his faith, but he was beginning to lose hope.

And yet now that we are riding on towards the year 2000, a new era is dawning. How delighted that staunch cycling enthusiast would have been if he could have stood by the road in Burgundy in September 1970 and seen 50-odd 'huffers and puffers' pedalling somewhat hesitantly past, very red in the face and headed by an intrepid gentleman of 70. They had come all the way from the USA to explore the fair land of France – by bicycle!

The cycling renaissance is remarkable. Planners are working out special cycle networks in the new boom towns, with lanes or tracks for cyclists only. There has been an impressive series of demonstrations in favour of two-wheeled traffic, linked to the most recent ecological preoccupations. The Mayor of New York rides to the centre of his vast city at the head of a long procession of cyclists. The outskirts of our largest towns and narrow country lanes are all ringing once again with jokes and laughter, with the swish of tyres and tinkling bells. Even the Catholic seminary in Saigon is starting to manufacture bike tyres! At the end of the 19th century an American reporter called Bishop stated that in a single year the consumption of cigars in the USA had dropped as a result of 'velocipeding' to the tune of a million a day. He went even further, writing:

> The tailors state that their industry is suffering an annual cutback of 25 per cent and the shoemakers are complaining even more bitterly. As for the hat-making trade, you will no doubt remember that it was a hatter who asked Congress to pass a bill compelling all bicyclists to buy at least two hats per year.

We do not need to take up quite such a militant stand, but we can state quite calmly that bicycles are in the process of winning a battle everyone thought they had lost. The 'enemy' forces in this battle are physical laziness, mechanisation and a general tendency to turn to less energetic and more sophisticated pastimes. Yet a bicycle is both a working tool and a leisure occupation, functional but fun, for people of both sexes and all ages. The hard grind of the uphill stretches is compensated for by the delights of skimming downhill and enjoying the fresh air. Then the whole vast and colourful pageant of competition cycling has grown up round the humble bike – races and riders, jerseys of every colour under the sun, and crowds of spectators thronging stadium and hillside.

The future may well lie in other directions. For instance new alloys and metals that are little known today may transform the mass production of cycles, leading to undreamt-of improvements, while the rapid strides being made in a country such as Japan are providing a new outlet for manufacturers who challenge the trading supremacy that some western European countries mistakenly thought was theirs for good. The USA may well make sweeping changes in the way the major competitions are run when the renaissance of the sport in North America has thrown up a large enough number of top-class champions. Remember that in February 1976 the Cubans made some major racing cyclists dance to their tune, in spite of the fact that they had come especially from Europe or South America to race round their national circuit.

> A bicycle allows a man to be proud of himself. You cannot be really happy unless you deserve to be, and we do deserve the pleasure of enjoying the scenery we've 'conquered' on our bicycles.

*Docteur Ruffier: In *Journal des Douze* by Maurice Goddet, December, edn., 1954.

*Away from the city the car is parked at the first open space. From the roof-rack and the boot the bicycles are made ready for a family spin.*

204

In the matter of clothing one racing cyclist looks much the same as another. The leisure rider has a free choice, but soon learns the right 'gear' to use!

Facilities for cyclists have become a priority for local authorities in all parts of the world since the resurgence of interest in pedal-power. The three youngsters are entering a cyclists-only track in the Bois de Boulogne, Paris, which was once the training ground of the world's greatest road and track racing men.

Most keenly contested are the events in which the 'gentleman' is paced by a current amateur or professional rider, with the result calculated on an a handicap basis. Although they were originally intended for over-40s who had never cycled competitively, former racing men now take part in Gran Prix de Gentlemen. When the hard pedalling is over everybody sits down to a full scale banquet!

A bicycle is constantly making you test your strength. You pay for each victory by the need to make a corresponding effort. With a bicycle you have to pay on the nail and adapt your expenditure to your capital!

That is how the humorist Paul Goth* sang the praises of *la Petite Reine*. Others have extolled the delights of the bicycle, and there will be even more tomorrow.

As for me, now that we have reached the end of our winding journey, now that we have covered together these few miles across the cycling world, I see in my mind's eye our stage towns – the history of the bicycle and cycling; the development and anatomy of that wondrous machine; cycle touring and racing. I also know all sorts of things we have

*Interview by Claude Jacquy in *Le cycliste*, No. 772, 1970.

not had time to talk about – how you should take a spoonful of glycerine before a hard competitive effort; the high-speed records and the strain they may involve; the dangerous illusion of drugs and the moral abuse of your body it implies; and so on.

If I have been successful in making you share my admiration for this amazing machine and my conviction that it can bring you happiness; if we have felt the wind in our faces and experienced together the burning heat of the sun; if we have hauled ourselves over a mountain pass and raced through a forest, flying from bend to bend; if we have ridden slowly in the quiet of the late afternoon, at the time of day when nature grows still before settling down to sleep – then writing this book was worth it, as well as being fun.

The rider 'out of the saddle' is tackling a hill in an unusual (for him) direction. He is Jean-Claude Killy, who, like many other top skiers, includes cycling in his training programme. The other photographs are typical of those found in any tourist's album – riding alone, in company, high up on a snow-flanked col, lazing in the sun. Cyclists for all seasons.

Cyclists all. One is a 92-year-
old priest from a little village
in the Creuse; another a
six-day star, Albert van
Lancker. The three energetic
young roadmen in a road-race
'break' are Roland Smet,
Joel Hauvieux and Bernard
Bourreau. The group of
cyclosportifs on mudguarded
machines are anonymous.
Cyclists all, so different yet
so much alike.

There was a time when spectators used to pedal hundreds of miles to see a Tour or classic one-day race. Then came the motor-car and a change of habits. Enthusiasm for cycle racing was greater than ever, but petrol took the man and his family to see the show, not the pedal. Nowadays more and more weekday motorists are becoming Sunday cyclists – and not all of them content to ride at a leisurely pace. Some white-headed enthusiasts train more seriously than their grandsons!

*This book is nearly closed, but the road is always open.
Some readers perhaps will be inspired by the stories and
photographs of the champions and seek to emulate them.
Others will be content to regard cycling as a pastime rather
than a sport. Some will ride to work to save the fare. It
takes all sorts to make up the world of wheels.*

# Useful information

## Addresses

There are three main national bodies administering the sport and pastime of cycling:

**The Cyclists Touring Club:** Cotterell House, 69 Meadrow, Godalming, Surrey GU7 3HS.
The CTC confines its activities exclusively to touring but members are free to take part in competitive events organised by other clubs and associations.

**The British Cycling Federation:** 70, Brompton Road, London SW3 1EN.
The national governing body for road and track racing. The BCF also offers a touring service to members, most of whom are affiliated through clubs.

**The Road Time Trials Council:** *Secretary,* D. Roberts, Dallacre, Mill Road, Yarwell, Peterborough PE8 6PS.
The Council supervises the organisation of a big programme of club and 'open' time trials, from 10-mile speed tests to 24-hour marathons.

The CTC has kindly provided the following list of other useful addresses:

### Organisations concerned wholly or partly with cycles or cycling

**Association of Cycle and Lightweight Campers:** The founder section (in 1901) of the Camping Club. *Secretary,* Mrs J Abram, Sinnott House, Birch Street, Southport, Merseyside.

**British Cycling Bureau** *(cycle industry publicity consultants)* : Greater London House, Hampstead Road, London NW1.

**Bicycle Association of Great Britain** *(representing manufacturers)* : Starley House, Eaton Road, Coventry.

**Duke of Edinburgh's Award Scheme:** 5 Prince of Wales Terrace, Kensington, London W8.

**English Schools Cycling Association:** *Secretary,* G G Mayne, 22 Quaves Lane, Bungay, Suffolk.

**Fell Club:** *(pedestrian and cycle campers)* : *Secretary,* Miss C Bladon, Sicklebrook Lane, nr. Coal Aston, Derbys.

**Friends of the Earth:** 9 Poland Street, London W1.

**National Association of Veteran-Cycle Clubs** *(historical cycles)* : Mrs B Ellis, Cheylesmore, Garnsgate Road, Long Sutton, Spalding, Lincs.

**Rough Stuff Fellowship:** Formed in 1955, for cyclists who enjoy exploring cross-country tracks. *Details:* H G Robson, 23 Spring Terrace, North Shields, Tyne/Wear.

**RoSPA** *(Cycling Proficiency Scheme)* : Cannon House, The Priory Queensway, Birmingham.

**Tandem Club:** Formed in 1971. *Secretary:* R Allen, 8 Coachways, Mapperley, Derbys.

**Tricycle Association:** Formed in 1928. *Secretary,* J H Mills, 58 Townsend Avenue, West Derby, Liverpool 11.

**Youth Hostels Association:** Formed in 1930, Trevelyan House, 8 St Stephens Hill, St Albans, Herts. **Scottish YHA:** 7 Glebe Crescent, Stirling.

**Sports Council:** 70 Brompton Road, London SW3.
**Central Council of Physical Recreation:** 70 Brompton Road, London SW3.

### Organisations dealing with touring and the countryside

**Alliance Internationale de Tourisme:** Links touring clubs of all kinds throughout the world. CTC members going abroad may obtain an Introduction Card entitling them to advice and assistance from other AIT associations.

**British Tourist Authority** *(coming events and tourist information including addresses of regional offices)* : 64 St James's Street, London SW1. **Tourist Boards (English):** 4 Grosvenor Gardens, London SW1; **(Wales):** 3 Castle Street, Cardiff; **(Scottish):** 2 Rutland Place, West End, Edinburgh.

**Commons, Open Spaces and Footpaths Preservation Society:** Suite 4, 166 Shaftesbury Avenue, London WC2.

**Council for Nature:** Zoological Gardens, Regents Park, London NW1.

**Council for Protection of Rural England:** 4 Hobart Place, London SW1; **Council for Protection of Rural Wales:** 14 Broad Street, Welshpool, Powys; **Association for Preservation of Rural Scotland:** *Secretary,* 20 Falkland Avenue, Newton Mearns, Renfrewshire.

**Countryside Commission** *(National Parks, Long-Distance Paths, Country Code, etc.)* : John Dower House, Crescent Place, Cheltenham, Glos.

**Department of the Environment** *(admission to Historic Monuments)* : Room G1, 25 Saville Row, London W1; Argyle House, Lady Lawson St, Edinburgh 3; Central Office for Wales, Galbalfa, Cardiff.

**Forestry Commission:** 25 Savile Row, London W1.

**National Trust:** 42 Queen Anne's Gate, London SW1; **NT for Scotland:** 5 Charlotte Square, Edinburgh 2.

### Organisations concerned with competitive cycling

**British Cyclo-Cross Association:** *Secretary,* R Richards, 5 Copstone Drive, Dorridge, Solihull, West Midlands.

**British Professional Cycle Racing Association:** *Secretary,* M Cumberworth, Hebden Hall Park, Hebden, nr. Skipton, North Yorks.

**Women's Cycle Racing Association:** Formed 1956. *President:* Mrs E Gray, 129 Grand Avenue, Surbiton, Surrey.

**Women's Road Records Association:** Formed in 1934. *President,* Mrs C M Watts, 45 Juniper Road, Langley Green, Crawley, Sussex.

**Veterans' Time Trials Association:** Formed in 1943, the national authority for time-trial records by cyclists aged 40 or over. *Secretary,* S E Hayward, 137 Glenwood Avenue, Westcliff-on-Sea, Essex.

**Road Records Association:** Formed in 1888, to verify and certify the genuineness of claims to best performances by cyclists on the road. *Secretary,* W H Townsend, 100 Betham Road, Greenford, Middx.

**Irish Cycling Federation:** J McQuaid, 2 Fitzmaurice Road, Glasnevin, Dublin 11, Eire.

**Northern Ireland Cycling Federation:** J Henry, 10 Fairfield Park, Bangor, Co. Down, Northern Ireland.

**Scottish Cycling Union:** R Londragan, 293 Rosemour Place, Aberdeen AB2 4YB.

## Metric conversions

| | | | | | |
|---|---|---|---|---|---|
| 1 centimetre (cm) | = 0·393 in | 1 inch (in) | = 2·54 cm | 1 gramme (g) | = 0·0353 oz |
| 1 metre (m) | = 1·093 yd | 1 foot (ft) | = 30·48 cm | 1 kilogramme (kg) | = 2·205 lb |
| 1 kilometre (km) | = 0·621 mile | 1 yard (yd) | = 0·914 m | 1 ounce (oz) | = 28·35 g |
| | | 1 mile | = 1·609 km | 1 pound (lb) | = 0·454 kg |
| 1 kg/sq cm | = 14·22 lb/sq in | | | | |
| 1 lb/sq in | = 0·07 kg/sq cm | | | | |

## Metric Gear Table

| Number of teeth on chainwheel | | | | | | | | | | | | | | | |
|---|---|---|---|---|---|---|---|---|---|---|---|---|---|---|---|

| Number of teeth on chainwheel | 12 | 13 | 14 | 15 | 16 | 17 | 18 | 19 | 20 | 21 | 22 | 23 | 24 | 25 | 26 |
|---|---|---|---|---|---|---|---|---|---|---|---|---|---|---|---|
| 40 | 7·12 | 6·57 | 6·10 | 5·69 | 5·34 | 5·02 | 4·74 | 4·50 | 4·27 | 4·07 | 3·88 | 3·71 | 3·56 | 3·42 | 3·28 |
| 41 | 7·30 | 6·73 | 6·25 | 5·84 | 5·47 | 5·15 | 4·86 | 4·60 | 4·37 | 4·17 | 3·98 | 3·80 | 3·64 | 3·50 | 3·36 |
| 42 | 7·47 | 6·90 | 6·40 | 5·98 | 5·60 | 5·27 | 4·98 | 4·72 | 4·48 | 4·27 | 4·07 | 3·90 | 3·73 | 3·58 | 3·45 |
| 43 | 7·65 | 7·06 | 6·56 | 6·12 | 5·74 | 5·40 | 5·10 | 4·83 | 4·59 | 4·37 | 4·17 | 3·99 | 3·82 | 3·67 | 3·53 |
| 44 | 7·83 | 7·23 | 6·71 | 6·26 | 5·87 | 5·52 | 5·22 | 4·94 | 4·70 | 4·47 | 4·27 | 4·08 | 3·91 | 3·76 | 3·61 |
| 45 | 8·01 | 7·39 | 6·86 | 6·40 | 6·00 | 5·65 | 5·34 | 5·05 | 4·80 | 4·57 | 4·37 | 4·18 | 4·00 | 3·84 | 3·69 |
| 46 | 8·18 | 7·55 | 7·01 | 6·55 | 6·14 | 5·78 | 5·45 | 5·17 | 4·91 | 4·67 | 4·46 | 4·27 | 4·09 | 3·93 | 3·78 |
| 47 | 8·36 | 7·72 | 7·17 | 6·69 | 6·27 | 5·90 | 5·57 | 5·28 | 5·02 | 4·78 | 4·56 | 4·36 | 4·18 | 4·01 | 3·86 |
| 48 | 8·54 | 7·88 | 7·32 | 6·83 | 6·40 | 6·03 | 5·69 | 5·39 | 5·12 | 4·88 | 4·66 | 4·45 | 4·27 | 4·10 | 3·94 |
| 49 | 8·72 | 8·05 | 7·47 | 6·97 | 6·54 | 6·15 | 5·81 | 5·50 | 5·23 | 4·98 | 4·75 | 4·55 | 4·36 | 4·18 | 4·02 |
| 50 | 8·90 | 8·21 | 7·63 | 7·12 | 6·67 | 6·28 | 5·93 | 5·62 | 5·34 | 5·08 | 4·85 | 4·64 | 4·45 | 4·27 | 4·10 |
| 51 | 9·07 | 8·38 | 7·78 | 7·26 | 6·81 | 6·40 | 6·05 | 5·73 | 5·44 | 5·18 | 4·95 | 4·73 | 4·54 | 4·35 | 4·19 |
| 52 | 9·25 | 8·54 | 7·93 | 7·40 | 6·94 | 6·53 | 6·17 | 5·84 | 5·55 | 5·29 | 5·04 | 4·83 | 4·62 | 4·44 | 4·27 |
| 53 | 9·43 | 8·70 | 8·08 | 7·54 | 7·07 | 6·66 | 6·29 | 5·95 | 5·66 | 5·39 | 5·14 | 4·92 | 4·71 | 4·52 | 4·35 |
| 54 | 9·61 | 8·87 | 8·23 | 7·69 | 7·20 | 6·78 | 6·40 | 6·07 | 5·76 | 5·49 | 5·24 | 5·01 | 4·80 | 4·61 | 4·43 |
| 56 | 9·97 | 9·20 | 8·54 | 7·97 | 7·47 | 7·03 | 6·64 | 6·29 | 5·98 | 5·69 | 5·43 | 5·20 | 4·98 | 4·78 | 4·60 |

The continental way of expressing the développment (gear) of a bicycle is more logical than the archaic British system, printed on page 76, which dates from the days when the Safety Bicycle was taking over from the Penny Farthing. A gear of 7·12 m is the distance covered by the road wheels with one complete revolution of the cranks. The formula is similar to that employed in Britain, except that the circumference of the road wheel and not the diameter, is used. Although the circumference of a heavy cyclo-cross tyre is greater than that of a 5 oz featherweight used by track sprinters, a standard of 2·136 m is usually used.

A bicycle fitted with a 50 tooth front chainwheel and a rear sprocket of 15 therefore has a gear of 7·12 m:

$$\frac{2\cdot136 \times 50}{15} = 7\cdot12$$

# Maps and 'Profiles' for Cyclists

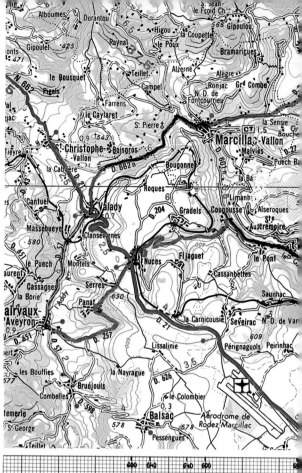

Avid readers often say of a book that 'they can't put it down'. Cyclists find the same fascination in maps which can always be depended upon to tell a good story. The tourist plans out the general lines of a trip with their aid and afterwards—perhaps years afterwards—will find the smallest details coming back to life as the itinerary is retraced on the well-worn map.

Road racing cyclists, too, find maps useful. When it is not possible to look over a new course in advance reference to a large-scale map will be a great help. Many races have been won that way by a good tactician who has a mental picture of the road ahead, its ups and downs, twists and turns, sheltered stretches through a forest or wind-swept coastal miles.

Of great value to the competitor in the Tour de France, Milk Race Tour of Britain and other big stage races, is the 'profile' issued by the organisers. This gives a good general idea of the rise and fall of the day's racing. Preparing such plans for a 22-day race is obviously a major undertaking, but with the aid of the right kind of map anybody can make a profile of a touring or racing route.

The map used must clearly show 'contours', which are lines following land of the same height above sea level. They vary between compact and almost circular to irregular and wide. Roads follow contours as much as possible, but when they cross them a 'gradient' is the result. If the contour lines are widely spaced the rise or fall of a road crossing them is only gradual; if the lines are close together it is abrupt.

The illustrations given here are based on the Institut Geographique National map of the scale 1 : 100 000, or 1 centimetre to every kilometre. The most popular British map to this scale is the Bartholomew new series which, coloured according to height above sea level, give an excellent idea of topography, but are not contoured in detail and are therefore not suitable for profile work.

Ideal for the purpose is the recently revised Ordnance Survey series known for generations as 'Inch to the Mile' but now scaled to 1 : 50 000, or 2 centimetres to the kilometre. The contours are drawn at 50 feet intervals, but in a future issue they will be every 10 metres.

First step in the making of a profile is to take a piece of squared paper and place the top edge along the chosen road. Each time the road crosses a contour line a mark is made on the paper and its height noted underneath.

The choice of a vertical scale depends on the type of country. In France where 'cols' are as high as 9000 feet (2800 metres) a scale of 1 centimetre to represent 500 metres is recommended. Since few British roads reach 500 metres (1625 feet), the scale needs adjusting for home use. In very high areas—such as the Scottish Highlands—a scale of 1 centimetre to 100 metres would be suitable, and 1 centimetre to 50 metres for most other parts of the country.

When the vertical scale is decided, the height details on the edge of the paper can be marked in their correct positions, then linked by a continuous line to make the profile. Because of the wide difference in horizontal and vertical scales the severity of hills is greatly exaggerated—some will look like unclimbable and undescendable church steeples!—but the overall impression of the race or tour route is usefully conveyed.

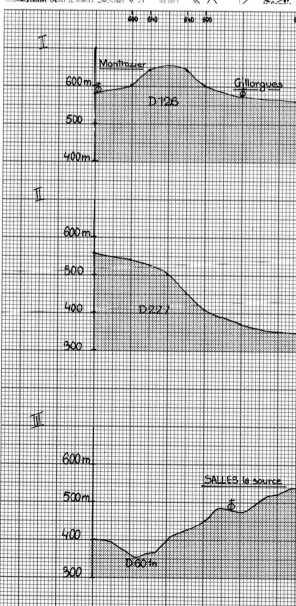

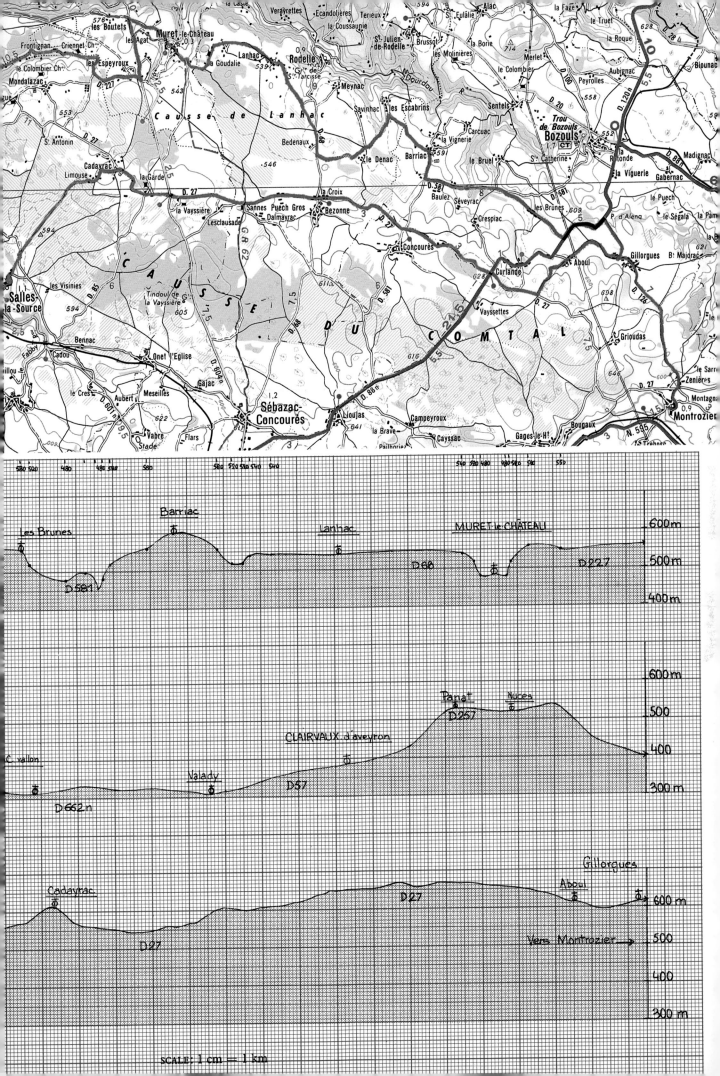

SCALE: 1 cm = 1 km

# ACKNOWLEDGEMENTS

**Original Translation:**

Vivienne Menkes

**Editorial co-ordination**

Beatrice Frei
Sue Gullen

**Layout:**

Jean Desaleux

**Drawings:**

Arlette Boudier

**Picture editor:**

Hocine Khélil.

**Illustrations supplied by:**

Presse-Sports, except for: G. Asaria, pp. 208, 210,
211; Batavus, pp. 64, 65; Bianchi, pp. 54, 57, 58,
59, 64; J. Boon, p. 107; C.N.C., p. 60; *Cycling*,
p. 127; G. Davies, p. 104; Excelsior, p. 209;
Gavilet-Diapress, p. 156; Gitane, pp. 55, 57, 58, 61,
62; Tim Hughes, p. 107; I.G.N., p. 219; Keystone,
pp. 49, 212; P. Knottley, p. 104; M. Langrognet,
p. 206; *Le Cycliste*, p. 91; Lejeune, pp. 54, 59, 60,
62, 63; B. Mace, p. 198; G. Marineau, pp. 40, 204;
H. Maylin, p. 191; Mercier, pp. 54, 55, 57, 58, 60,
62, 64, 65; Motobécane, pp. 8, 42, 54, 55, 56, 59,
60, 63; Musée du Sport, pp. 16, 19, 25, 26, 27;
J. Otway, p. 153; E. Pagnoud, pp. 68, 69; Pav-
lowsky-Rapho, p. 132; J. Perey, p. 153; M. Pernot,
pp. 68, 106; R. Perrin, pp. 20, 21, 23, 26, 28,
83, 99, 209, 220; Peugeot pp. 46, 55, 57, 58, 61,
63, 64; Press Library, British Embassy, p. 36;
A. Pronier, p. 83; Raleigh, pp. 55, 57, 59, 61, 62, 65;
J-N. Reichel, pp. 41, 211; G. de Panafieu, pp. 37,
77, 95, 118, 194, 199; Snark International, p. 12;
Socquet (Megère), p. 209; Sven Simon, pp. 190, 191;
*The Guardian*, p. 87; Touring Club, p. 14; A. Valtat,
pp. 93, 223; J. Way, p. 87. Copyright for Jean
Béraud's painting, p. 12: Spadem. Page 219: map
58 'Rodez-Mende', série verte; copyright I.G.N.;
No. 993274, 1 September 1976.

# OTHER GUINNESS SUPERLATIVES TITLES

## Facts and Feats Series:

**Air Facts and Feats,** *2nd ed.*
John W R Taylor, Michael
J H Taylor and David Mondey

**Rail Facts and Feats,** *2nd ed.*
John Marshall

**Tank Facts and Feats,** *2nd ed*
Kenneth Macksey

**Yachting Facts and Feats**
Peter Johnson

**Plant Facts and Feats**
William G Duncalf

**Structures—Bridges, Towers,
Tunnels, Dams . . .**
John H Stephens

**Car Facts and Feats,** *2nd ed.*
edited by Anthony Harding

**Business World**
Henry Button and Andrew Lampert

**Music Facts and Feats**
Bob and Celia Dearling

**Animal Facts and Feats,** *2nd ed.*
Gerald L Wood

## Guide Series:

**Guide to Freshwater Angling**
Brian Harris and Paul Boyer

**Guide to Mountain Animals**
R P Bille

**Guide to Underwater Life**
C Petron and J B Lozet

**Guide to Formula 1 Motor Racing**
José Rosinski

**Guide to Motorcycling,** *2nd ed.*
Christian Lacombe

**Guide to French Country
Cooking**
Christian Roland Délu

**Guide to Saltwater Angling**
Bryan Harris

## Other titles:

**English furniture 1550–1760**
Geoffrey Wills

**The Guinness Guide to Feminine
Achievements·**
Joan and Kenneth Macksey

**The Guinness Book of Names**
Leslie Dunkling

**Battle Dress**
Frederick Wilkinson

**Universal Soldier**
edited by Martin Windrow and
Frederick Wilkinson

**History of Land Warfare**
Kenneth Macksey

**History of Sea Warfare**
Lt.-Cmdr. Gervis Frere-Cook and
Kenneth Macksey

**History of Air Warfare**
David Brown, Christopher Shores
and Kenneth Macksey

**The Guinness Book of Answers**
edited by Norris D McWhirter

**The Guinness Book of Records,**
*23rd ed.*
edited by Norris D McWhirter

**The Guinness Book of 1952**
Kenneth Macksey